Professional Radio Advertising Sales

Professional Radio Advertising Sales

*The Complete Course for a Professional Career
in Radio Advertising Sales*

Spike Santee

FolioAvenue Publishing Service
2031 Union Street, Suite 6
San Francisco CA 94123
415-869-8834 (866-365-4628)
www.folioavenue.com

About the Author

Spike Santee is an author, public speaker, small business owner, and entrepreneur. He started his Radio career at 16 years of age at the local Radio station in his hometown of Lawrence, Kansas. Since then, Spike has been a disk jockey, program director, salesperson, sales manager, general manager, regional vice president, senior vice president, president, and company owner.

For the past 25 years, Spike has devoted his energy and talents to improving the relevance and profitability of Radio advertising for the advertiser, the salesperson, and the Radio station, **in that order**. He has personally trained over three thousand salespeople, presented to over 30,000 local companies and helped local Radio salespeople sell over $500 million in Radio advertising.

Spike's first book, *The Four Keys to Advertising Success, A 1-Hour Guide for Local Small Businesses*, is the result of thousands of interviews with local business owners to discover what works and what doesn't in local advertising. Spike has launched a complete local Radio sales system registered under the trademark, The Four Keys to Advertising Success®.

In this new book, *The Profession of Radio Advertising Sales*, Spike brings the skills and knowledge he has assimilated in his career, into one comprehensive textbook for the salesperson who wants to become a **professional** advertising salesperson.

From the first day on the job in Radio advertising sales to the first annual advertising contract, *The Profession of Radio Advertising Sales* details every step the new salesperson needs to master to ensure professional success. Using *skill-stacking*, Spike teaches how to master each skill in his successful sales process in the proper sequence. You can find Spike's online training resources at *www.myradioschool.com*.

For more information, contact Spike directly.

www.spikesantee.com

www.myradioschool.com

spike@spikesantee.com

Table of Contents

"Our greatest weakness lies in giving up. The most certain way to succeed is always to try just one more time." – *Thomas Edison*, American inventor. (1847 – 1931)

1

Welcome to Radio Advertising Sales

Thank you for taking the time to pick up this book, *Professional Radio Advertising Sales*.

If you are a newcomer to Radio advertising, welcome! You could not have picked a better time to enter the Radio advertising business. Radio plays a more significant role in our daily lives than ever before.

As of this publication, **AM & FM Radio now has more listeners than at any time in the history of the medium**. According to the Nielsen Company, 249,111,000[1], people listen to either an AM or an FM Radio station every week.

As of March 31, 2019, Sirius XM, the satellite Radio company reported to their shareholders in the 10-Q Quarterly Report that the company has approximately 34.2 million subscribers. **AM & FM Radio, terrestrial Radio, has nearly ten times more listeners than Satellite Radio.**

According to the Infinite Dial Report issued in March 2019, **approximately 172 million Americans use Facebook**[2]. That number was down from the all-time high in 2017. On the other hand, the number of people who regularly tune into AM & FM Radio is growing every year.

Today, nine out of ten Americans listen to AM & FM Radio every week, and the average listener spends about two hours every day listening to their favorite Radio stations. Radio has been a resilient and evolving medium from the very beginning. When television was first introduced, people said that was the end of Radio. When MTV came on the air, people said that

---

[1] RADAR 141, June 2019 Copyright Nielsen Audio Persons 12+
[2] The Infinite Dial, March 6, 2019 Edison Research and Triton Digital

was the end of Radio. When satellite Radio was launched, people said that was the end of Radio. When Internet Radio started streaming, people said that was the end of Radio. When Facebook and social media came along, people said that was the end of Radio. But today Radio is stronger and more relevant than ever before.

Whether this is your first job in Radio advertising sales, or you have been in the business for several years, the opportunity for professional and financial growth in Radio advertising sales has never been better.

Before 1996, the year of deregulation, most Radio salespeople had only two or three Radio stations to offer to their advertisers. Their product offering might also include some marketing promotions like a coupon book, calendar, or a monthly newsletter.

But today, the modern Radio advertising salespeople can sell advertising on five or six different Radio stations with many different formats and audience groups. You have a Radio station and an audience for almost any company.

Radio has embraced the Internet Age in a big way with advertising on station websites, mobile apps, streaming audio, email marketing, and podcasting. Some Radio stations even offer a full suite of digital marketing tools like search engine marketing, OTT Video, geofencing, and geotargeting.

Not only does the modern Radio advertising salesperson have more products to sell, but there are also many more companies who need to buy advertising than ever before.

Finally, there is one more thing in your favor in Radio sales today. There are fewer Radio advertising salespeople in the business. That's good for you because you have fewer competitors in your building and fewer competitors at the Radio station across town. In no time at all, you could be the top billing salesperson in your organization, making way more money than you ever imagined.

While this is good for the individual salesperson, it's not necessarily a good thing for most Radio stations. They have so much product to sell but not enough salespeople to sell it. That's why there is a big push to hire more salespeople at most Radio stations. Perhaps that is why the Radio station hired you.

The Telecommunications Act of 1996 was the first significant overhaul of the Radio business since 1934. Before deregulation, a Radio company could only own two Radio stations in seven different cities, two Radio stations multiplied by seven cities is 14 total Radio stations. Even the big companies like ABC, CBS, and NBC could only own a total of 14 Radio stations across the entire country.

At one time, Clear Channel Communications, now iHeart Radio owned over 1,100 different Radio stations! Companies thought they could consolidate smaller companies, reduce the staff, and reap big profits. It hasn't worked out that way. Today, the big consolidators, iHeart, and Cumulus Media have both declared bankruptcy as they try to sort out their business plans.

Other smaller consolidators have come and gone for many of the same reasons.

There isn't anything wrong with AM & FM Radio! Two hundred and forty-nine million people listen to AM and FM Radio, more than at any time in the history of Radio! That's more people than watch TV or cable, use Facebook, visited YouTube, watched Netflix, read a newspaper, listened to Internet Radio, or listened to Pandora or Spotify. AM and FM Radio reach more people for less money than any other advertising option available! There's nothing wrong with the product; the problem was the way the early consolidators tried to run the Radio companies.

Radio companies have figured that out, and sweeping changes are happening. Radio companies are trying to hire Radio salespeople wherever they can. That's one of the reasons I decided to write this book.

I started working in Radio when I was 16 years old. The Boy Scouts were trying to launch an Explorer Scout group at the local Radio station, KLWN AM & FM in Lawrence, Kansas. I went to the first organizational meeting, but the group never mustered enough interest to continue. But at least I had my foot in the door at the Radio station.

My story is a lot like other young people fascinated with Radio back then. I hung around the Radio station all the time, taking out the trash, helping organize the records and setting up equipment at the county fair. One day, they decided they should pay me! I was in! I was a paid Radio person!

Since then, I've been a disk jockey, a salesperson, sales manager, general manager, owner, Regional Vice President, Senior Vice President, and even the President of a Radio company. It has been an incredible career so far, and I'm not done.

The most rewarding work I've done in Radio is the work I've done with the advertisers and the salespeople. It has been rewarding work because when I help a business owner or a Radio salesperson grow and become more successful, not only am I helping someone else achieve their dreams; I'm making a nice living at the same time. Getting paid to help people is the perfect job for me.

I decided to write this book about Professional Radio Advertising Sales to help the new Radio salesperson AND the experienced Radio salesperson recognize and capitalize on the incredible opportunity for professional and financial growth they have before them.

If you are reading the material in this course, you have *chosen* to take a job in sales. However, are you just taking a *job* in sales, or are you deciding to join the *profession of sales*?

The difference this book offers is the emphasis on *professional*. The world of selling has changed dramatically. Regardless of the industry, whether Radio advertising, retail, insurance, automotive or pharmaceuticals, the old ways of selling don't work anymore. Buyers today are more sophisticated and busier than ever before. They have developed super-powered BS detectors that will tune you out in nanoseconds if you don't up your game through ongoing professional development.

In selling, resourcefulness and perseverance are the two most highly valued attributes you need to earn more money and have more free time. There is no other profession where your success is more dependent on your initiative than selling. Selling is the most crucial component of economic growth. Nothing happens in the economy until someone sells something.

Regardless of your upbringing or environment, scientists are learning that people have more capacity for lifelong learning and brain development than they ever thought. It doesn't matter if you are rich or poor, whether you graduated from college or not, you can make a profound change in your life if you only decide to do the work.

Of course, everyone is different, and some are more fortunate than others. But with experience, training, and personal effort, you can go much further in life than you ever dreamed.

The inventor of the IQ test, Alfred Binet, was a big champion of this view. He developed the IQ test to help identify children who were not benefiting from public schools so that new educational programs could be designed to get them back on track. Binet believed that education and practice could bring about fundamental changes in intelligence.

Binet wrote in his book, *Modern Ideas About Children*,

A few modern philosophers assert that an individual's intelligence is a fixed quantity, a quantity which cannot be increased. We must protest and react against this brutal pessimism. With practice, training, and above all, method, we manage to increase our attention, our memory, our judgment, and literally to become more intelligent than we were before.[3]

Robert J. Sternberg is an American psychologist and psychometrician. He is Professor of Human Development at Cornell University and an expert on human intelligence. In his book, *Wisdom, Intelligence, and Creativity Synthesized*, he writes, "The main constraint in achieving expertise is not some fixed prior level of capacity, but purposeful engagement involving direct instruction, active participation, role modeling, and reward."[4]

Carol S. Dweck is the Lewis and Virginia Eaton Professor of Psychology at Stanford University. Dweck is known for her work on the *mindset* psychological trait. After more than 20 years of research, Dweck concludes in her book, *Mindset: The New Psychology of Success,* "[t]he view you adopt for yourself affects profoundly the way you lead your life. It can determine whether you become the person you want to be and whether you accomplish the

---

[3] Binet, Alfred. *Modern Ideas About Children* (Presses De l'Atelier Graphique Saint-Jean 1909/1984) 105-106

[4] Sternberg, Robert J. *Wisdom, Intelligence, and Creative Synthesized* (Cambridge University Press 2007) 71

things you value."[5] She writes that people are either one of two mindsets, the *fixed mindset*, or the *growth mindset*.

A person who believes their personality and intelligence are predetermined, and there is nothing they can do about it have a fixed mindset. People who suffer from a fixed mindset often feel pressure or urgency to prove themselves over and over, look smart, don't look dumb. A person with a fixed mindset believes they are as smart as they're ever going to be. Consequently, they need to appear smart. This need to look intelligent leads to:

- Avoiding challenges
- Giving up too easily
- Viewing effort as fruitless
- Ignoring useful negative feedback
- Feeling threatened by the success of others

As a result, people with a fixed mindset may plateau early in life and achieve less than their full potential. Their viewpoint, and subsequently, their life confirms their perception that there's nothing they can do about their life. It is what it is.

The growth mindset depends on the belief that your essential qualities are things that you can cultivate and improve upon through your efforts. Even though people may differ in education, personality, aptitude, and talent, people with a growth mindset believe that everyone can change and grow through application and experience.

A person with a growth mindset believes that they can improve their intelligence. This mindset leads to a desire to learn and therefore, a tendency to:

- Embrace challenges
- Persist in the face of setbacks
- View effort as the path to mastery
- Learn from criticism
- Find lessons and inspiration in the success of others

As a result, people with a growth mindset reach ever-higher levels of achievement. They enjoy a greater sense of free will.

Does that mean by having a growth mindset, you can become the next Steve Jobs or Bill Gates? It's difficult to see that far into the future. What it does mean is that your true potential is unknown until you make the decision and devote yourself to a life of growth mindset activities.

This course is for those who have decided to become a professional salesperson, to make their living through the profession of selling. A profession is an occupation, practice, or vocation

---

[5] Dweck, Carol S. *Mindset: The New Psychology of Success* (Random House 2006, 2016) 6

requiring mastery of a complex set of knowledge and skills through formal education and practical experience.

A profession is something more than a job; it is a career for someone **who wants to become competent in their chosen sector through training; maintains their skills through continuing professional development (CPD).**

Whether you are just starting in your professional life or, if you are in a mid-life career change, becoming a professional salesperson can dramatically improve your personal life, your family life, and your business life, but, only if you make the right decisions.

The great sales trainer Zig Ziglar says that your commitment to professional development is what differentiates you from everyone else in the pack. He asks, "Are you going to be a **random generality** or a **meaningful specific**?" That is a foundational decision you need to make before you proceed with the training in this course.

There are many reasons to avoid becoming a *random generality* and strive to be a *meaningful specific*. A lot is riding on your choice. Your financial situation depends on your decision. If you have a family, their future security depends on your decision.

Deciding to become a meaningful specific involves a personal commitment to an ongoing routine of personal and professional development. Always say to yourself, "I can't learn less, I can't learn less." The idea that you can't learn less will guide you to better physical, emotional, and professional decisions, and you will live a better, more fulfilling life.

You could go back to school and get a graduate degree. That new degree could open doors to you for career advancement and a higher paycheck. However, that would require a decision to go back to school. It would take time and money, too.

First, there is the cost of tuition, books, and supplies. Second, there is the cost of your time. Chances are you would need to attend night classes in addition to holding down your regular job. You might be working eight hours at that job and another three to four hours at night going to school and doing your homework. That's in addition to helping with the kids and taking care of the house. In two years, you could take that new degree and go forward and see what the world has to offer.

Starting your new job in the profession of sales is much like going to graduate school to get a degree. First, there is the cost of tuition. You don't pay tuition in your new job, but you might be making a little bit less than you'd like because you're just getting started in this new profession. Second, there is the cost of your time. Remember, *"I can't learn less."* Your new profession will require after-hours study. There is a lot to learn. There is a lot to read. People like Bill Gates, Warren Buffet, and Oprah Winfrey read at least one book a week and sometimes more!

In the profession of sales, you will need to attend after-hours, and sometimes for the early-birds, before hours networking functions and community mixers to meet possible leads. Weekends also provide abundant networking opportunities for the professional salesperson.

The great thing about becoming a professional salesperson is that you won't have to wait for two years to see what that new diploma will do for you. In the profession of selling, your advancement depends on the effort you put forth.

Consider this, in the profession of selling, **at first you learn, then you earn**. That is especially true in advertising sales because of the annual cycle of things and your efforts to get in sync with that cycle. In year one, you might miss out on a transaction based on timing, but afterward, you'll know to put that on your calendar for next year a bit earlier.

The profession of selling is the profession of helping people. **You're not selling the product; you are selling what the product does for the buyer**. You must believe in what your product does for your customer if you want to be successful in selling your product.

Radio advertising is a wonderful product to sell because you are helping local business owners achieve the American dream of building a company into something special. You can call on every company in your region, city or town. Unlike other sales jobs, your product line does not limit your selling opportunities. Plus, the amount of money spent on advertising grows year after year.

In multi-level selling, you are often required to buy a starter inventory of the product to use for yourself. Some people say that "You can't sell the product if you're not on the product." When you are a user of the product, you know firsthand the benefits of owning the product. When you encounter a stall or an objection, you'll be able to answer the prospect's concerns with firsthand knowledge.

In the profession of Radio advertising sales, the Radio station is not going to make you buy a monthly advertising schedule before you can sell Radio advertising. However, if you were required to purchase advertising for yourself on the Radio station, you would be better prepared for stalls and objections. When your prospect says they don't feel like they can afford it, you can say, "That's what I thought at first, but I have had so many leads call me, I've closed more sales with the advertising than I ever did without it." That's a compelling reason for the prospect to say yes to your proposal.

Yes, you will encounter stalls and objections. Some people will even lie to you. However, if you choose to become a meaningful specific, you can overcome those experiences with training, study, and preparation. It's a choice, and the choice is yours. It is an excellent choice.

I love the Radio advertising business, and I want to teach you how to be successful in Radio advertising so you will love it as much as I do. Get your **growth mindset** on and let's get started. Remember, the first year you learn, the second year you earn. Don't drop out before that.

Summary

In this chapter, we discussed the following topics:

- Regardless of why you decided to take this job in selling, now is the time to make a new decision to begin your career as a professional salesperson.
- Selling offers an unlimited earning potential based solely on your resourcefulness and perseverance.
- Psychologists believe that people see themselves through one of two possible mindsets, either the fixed mindset or the growth mindset, and the mindset you choose will profoundly affect how you live your life.
- *"First you learn, then you earn"* should be your mantra for your first year in professional selling.
- You can't learn less!

"All I wanted to do when I was a teenager was get dropped off at a radio station - one of the ones I listened to - and watch how the shows worked. After a point it was about showing up and driving people crazy, driving the van to promotions and sneaking on the air." - *Ryan Seacrest*, radio personality, television host, and producer. (1974 –

2

Radio Station Organization

This chapter is designed to introduce you to the basic organizational structure of a Radio station. Most Radio companies operate in much the same manner. Your company's organization might be slightly different in some cases but much the same in others.

The goal of this chapter is to help you understand the functions of the different departments and the role they play in the overall performance of your group of Radio stations. Your understanding of the various roles people play will help you operate more effectively within your organization.

The Market Manager

At the top of the organizational chart in a Radio station is the Market Manager. The term Market Manager is a relatively new term for the top job that came about since the year of deregulation, 1996. That is the year the Federal Communications Commission deregulated the ownership limits imposed on broadcasting companies. Before deregulation, a Radio company could only own one AM Radio station and one FM Radio station in the same market.

With deregulation, a company can now own many more Radio stations. In a market with more than 45 different Radio stations, one company can own up to eight Radio stations, with a limit of five in any one broadcast band. That means, in a big market, one company can own five FM Radio stations and three AM Radio stations.

With the increase in the number of Radio stations a company could own, came increased responsibility for the **General Manager**. Over time, the title for the top job evolved into the **Market Manager**. General Manager and Market Manager are synonymous.

Another new term that evolved from deregulation is a **market cluster.** When a company could only own two Radio stations, it was common to call that a **"combo of Radio stations."**

The Market Manager is responsible for everything that goes on in your market cluster. At the highest level, the Market Manager is responsible for delivering a profit for the company. Therefore, the Market Manager has **P&L Authority;** they are accountable for the **profit** (P) and **loss** (L) of the operation. Consequently, the Market Manager works with the various **Department Heads** to make decisions that affect the sale of advertising and the expenses required to do so.

The primary source of revenue in a Radio station is the sale of advertising and promotional services. Radio stations don't receive any money from the Government to stay on the air, and in virtually every case, a Radio station doesn't have paying subscribers. Some Radio companies may earn money by leasing tower space to other Radio stations or telecommunications companies. Rather than build a tower of their own, these companies rent space on your company's tower.

The following is the basic organization of a Radio station:

- Sales Department – Director of Sales or General Sales Manager
  - National Sales Manager
  - Local Sales Manager
  - Digital Sales Manager
- The Business Office – Business Manager
  - Traffic and Billing Department - Traffic Manager
  - Continuity Department – Continuity Director
- Programming Department – Operations Manager
  - Program Director
    - Music Director
    - Promotions Director
  - News Department - News Director
  - Sports Department – Sports Director
- Digital Department – Digital Director
- Production Department – Production Director
- Promotion Department – Promotions Director
- Engineering Department - Chief Engineer
  - IT Department – IT Director

Depending on the size of your market cluster, your company may have other positions. Perhaps some people in your organization have multiple titles and responsibilities.

The Sales Department

Before deregulation and consolidation in 1996, a company with just one AM Radio station and one FM Radio station would typically have one General Sales Manager to lead the entire sales department. Now, a market cluster with eight Radio stations may have multiple sales managers, each responsible for one or two Radio stations. With so many Radio stations, a new role evolved in the sales department, the **Director of Sales**.

The Director of Sales

The Director of Sales is responsible for coordinating the various advertising sales activities among all the Radio stations in your cluster. It is the Director of Sales' responsibility to generate the advertising and promotional revenue goals set by the company. All the individual **Sales Managers** report to the Director of Sales.

Your market cluster may have a **National Sales Manager** that reports to the Director of Sales. This person works with the **national rep firm** and **national advertisers**. A national rep firm is a company that your Radio station hires to sell advertising time on your station to national advertisers. A national advertiser is a company with such a large advertising plan that they don't work with individual Radio stations. They work with the national rep firms who represent hundreds of Radio stations to place the advertising.

There might be a **Regional Sales Manager** to work with **regional accounts** if there is enough market demand. Otherwise, those responsibilities fall on either the National Sales Manager or a Sales Manager. A regional account is a company with locations across an area of a few states or more.

General Sales Manager

Another scenario might have a **General Sales Manager** at the top of the sales department with individual **Local Sales Managers** working with the various Radio stations. The structure is much the same but with different titles. However, the title Local Sales Manager signifies that the manager's primary responsibility is **local advertising,** not regional or national advertising.

Some market clusters with active digital advertising sales initiatives have a **Digital Sales Manager** and possibly some digital-only salespeople.

Regardless of the titles, the sales managers are responsible for staffing and talent development within the sales department.

Regardless of how your sales department is organized, your company has made these organizational decisions to focus the sales energy and resources on the most lucrative opportunities. You may sell for only one or two Radio stations out of your market cluster. Perhaps you get the chance to sell all the Radio stations. Regardless, there is an excellent opportunity awaiting you when you have a growth mindset. Devote your energy to become the best salesperson you can be with the products you have.

The Business Office

In a Radio station, the **Business Manager** is responsible for the regulatory and business paperwork, accounting, HR, traffic, and billing. Depending on the size of your market cluster, some employees may have multiple titles.

Traffic and Billing

Traffic is the practice of scheduling the commercials that broadcast on your Radio stations. You don't want to use the word *traffic* or *traffic department* in front of your customers; they might think you mean the Radio station has a helicopter and a reporter following the traffic on area roads. A much better term to use with your customers is the term *Scheduling and Billing Department*.

The **Traffic Director** schedules all the commercials on the Radio station. With the help of computer software, they ensure that the commercials are on the air on the date and time that the customer ordered. Even with built-in computer tools like priority codes and product separation codes, the Traffic Director oversees the placement of the commercials to ensure all contract requirements are fulfilled, and no scheduling conflicts occur.

When the Traffic Director has finished scheduling all the commercials correctly, they create the **commercial log**, the official schedule of commercials for that day. The commercial log can be printed out and manually followed by the DJs, or it can be computer generated and loaded into a broadcast computer system. In either case, the Traffic Director sends the commercial log to the Programming Department to follow throughout the day. They must follow the commercial log precisely to ensure that the Radio station can accurately charge the customers for what they ordered.

The Traffic Director is responsible for the generation, reconciliation, and production of all necessary financial reports and billing paperwork. They design and produce all required daily and weekly reports for sales and management, including inventory, pacing, receivables, and projections.

Excellent communication between the Sales Department, the Traffic Department, and the Programming Department is essential to maintaining a correct accounting of commercial inventory and providing timely and accurate billing information.

As the salesperson, you are expected to turn in your paperwork promptly and accurately. Pay close attention when you receive your training on submitting your sales orders. Do your very best to submit error-free paperwork. Mistakes made on your sales order will reverberate throughout the system, causing lost productivity to correct the error.

The Programming Department

As you have learned, companies today can have up to eight different Radio stations in one building. Additional Radio stations complicate and compound the work of the Programming Department. In the past 20 years, many Programming Departments have experienced a five or six-fold increase in work activity. There are more announcers, more promotions, and more commercials. The **Operations Manager** is the person responsible for coordinating all the activities to properly program and promote multiple Radio stations in a market cluster today.

The Operations Manager

The **Operations Manager** (OM) participates in the establishment, organization, and implementation of short- and long-range goals, objectives, policies, and operating procedures; monitors and evaluates program effectiveness; and effects changes required for improvement.

The Operations Manager oversees and coordinates the continuous, daily operations of the radio station, ensuring compliance with broadcast standards, company policies, and relevant federal and state laws and regulations.

The Operations Manager maintains accurate schedules, records, discrepancy reports, and follow-through communications, and ensures that all on-air broadcast programming complies with FCC rules and regulations. They perform recruitment, training, scheduling, retention, problem resolution, and performance management.

The Operations Manager may provide services as an on-air host, produce commercials and other job-related duties as necessary.

The Program Director

The **Program Director** (PD) is responsible for all content on a Radio station. They oversee the overall *sound* of the radio station. They manage the station's programming, music, promotions, and staff. The Program Director ensures that the station always sounds its best and suits the needs of its listeners. They are responsible for attracting, keeping, and increasing your station's audience. They make the general format decisions at the station, subject to the approval of the company management. Many Program Directors use some form of audience research to help them develop the most effective programming strategy.

At music-intensive stations, the Program Director oversees the music selection, frequency of airplay, news, and public affairs programming, and maintains the guidelines for the broadcasting of commercials and programs sold by the station. For example, the PD supervises the number of commercials broadcast in any given hour, as well as the lengths of the commercial breaks in those hours.

The Music Director

Radio stations in large markets or within a large cluster of Radio stations may employ a **Music Director**. The Music Director often serves as the primary assistant to the Program Director and is generally responsible for selecting what music will be presented on the station and in what order or *rotation* it will broadcast.

Large market clusters are more apt to fund this as a full-time position. Today, automation has taken over in this area and maintaining the station's music library is a function of knowing how to manage the computerized database. In a smaller market, the responsibilities of a Music Director are often handled by the Program Director.

The News Director

The **News Director** is responsible for gathering and reporting the news. A Radio station with an all-talk or news format will place greater emphasis on this position than a Radio station with a music format. The News Director at a news/talk station sets the journalistic standards for the station and manages the reporting staff.

Sometimes the News Director is a member of the on-air team, giving news reports at scheduled news breaks within a show.

The Sports Director

The **Sports Director** is responsible for sports programming on your Radio station. They are responsible for play-by-play broadcasts and daily sports reports. Not every Radio station employs a Sports Director.

Sometimes the Sports Director is a member of the on-air team, giving sports reports at scheduled sports breaks within a show.

The Digital Department

The Internet has opened up many new opportunities for a Radio station to market access to the audience. Most Radio stations now offer their listeners the opportunity to listen to the Radio station over the Internet when they are beyond the signal of the Radio station or if the listener is in a building with poor reception. The Radio station has a website with Radio station information the listeners can access. Some Radio stations now have "an app for that."

Many Radio stations now have a Digital Department to curate the content listeners can access over the Internet. Depending on the size of your Radio station and the amount of digital content produced, your digital department could have many employees.

In addition to creating unique digital content for your listeners, your Radio station and your digital department may also be creating additional digital advertising opportunities for your advertisers such as Internet display advertising, paid search advertising, and even social media management.

The Promotions Department

In addition to selling commercials, Radio stations create and sell promotional advertising events and activities to generate revenue. Radio stations are exceptionally good at creating promotional events that engage many people because the audience listens to the Radio station because **they like what they hear**. They listen because they enjoy your Radio station. Listeners feel personally involved with their favorite Radio station, and **they respond to what they hear**.

This relationship between your Radio station and the listeners is a powerful marketing tool for your advertisers, and your Radio station capitalizes on it by creating and selling promotional sponsorships.

The **Promotions Director** is responsible for developing and implementing advertising promotional events at your Radio station. They work closely with both the Programming Department and the Sales Department to ensure a successful promotion. A successful promotion is one that attracts and retains listeners while at the same time offers the advertiser access to the audience to tell their story. A good promotion is balanced between the interests of both the Programming Department and the Sales Department.

The Promotions Director will participate in both sales meetings and programming meetings to be entirely up to date on the activities of both departments.

The Production / Continuity Department

The **Production Director** is responsible for the creative process involved in recording the commercials you hear on your Radio station. In a large market company, the position of Production Director is often a full-time dedicated position. In smaller markets, the Production Director might also serve as a Program Director or an announcer.

The Production Director takes your written instructions and creates your commercial. They will assign the task of recording the commercial to themselves or one of the various announcers at your Radio station. They will supervise the use of music or sound effects according to your instructions. It is their responsibility to ensure the recording is completed on time for the customer's approval and broadcast on the air.

The **Continuity Director** checks your commercial script for legality and policy compliance. The Continuity Director works closely with the Production Director and the Traffic Manager to see that commercials are correctly prepared and broadcast. Some Continuity Directors will also write scripts.

Depending on your Radio station organization, you might find the Production Director working in the Programming Department and the Continuity Director working in the Business

Office. In either case, that highlights the level of coordination that is required between departments to run an effective operation.

In this training, you will learn how to write emotionally engaging Radio scripts. Your skill at scriptwriting will become one of the most compelling competitive advantages in your Radio advertising sales career. We can't stress this enough. There is an axiom in advertising that states, **"Whoever controls the creative process, controls the account."** When a national company like McDonalds or Budweiser changes advertising agencies, they don't change because the new agency will do the job for less money. They change agencies because **the new agency can make a better commercial**. You will surely experience a competitive situation where all things are equal, but it will be your commercial scriptwriting skills that will make the sale.

The Engineering Department

No job within a Radio station has seen as much change as that of the **Chief Engineer**.

Radio transmitters today are more reliable than earlier models. They don't require as much maintenance or monitoring. In the studio, computers replaced the turntables and tape machines. The modern Radio station is a system of computers networked together to create the final on-air product.

In addition to traditional Radio technology skills, the Chief Engineer in a Radio station needs to be well versed in computer and digital technology. Your Radio station may have an **IT Director** working in the Engineering Department.

If you work for a smaller company, perhaps your Radio station employs a **Contract Engineer** to fulfill the company's technical and legal requirements and a computer technician to maintain the Radio station's digital infrastructure.

Summary

In this chapter on Radio Station Organization, we covered the following topics:

- The **Market Manager** is responsible for everything that goes on in your market cluster and is responsible for delivering a profit for the company.
- The Market Manager works with the various **Department Heads** to make decisions that affect the sale of advertising and the expenses required to do so.
- The **Director of Sales** or **General Sales Manager** is responsible for coordinating the various advertising sales activities among all the Radio stations in your cluster with individual **Local Sales Managers** working with the different Radio stations.
- The **Promotions Director** is responsible for the development and implementation of advertising promotional events at your Radio station.
- The **Business Manager** is responsible for the regulatory and financial paperwork, accounting, HR, traffic, and billing.

- The **Traffic Director** schedules all the commercials on the Radio station.
- The **Operations Manager** is the person responsible for coordinating all the activities in the Programming Department.
- The **Program Director** (PD) is responsible for all content on a Radio station. They oversee the overall **sound** of the radio station.
- The **News Director** and the **Sports Director** are responsible for gathering and reporting the news and sports.
- The **Digital Department** is responsible for the creation and delivery of digital marketing products.
- The **Production Director** is responsible for the creative process involved in recording the commercials you hear on your Radio station.
- The **Continuity Director** checks your commercial script for legality and policy compliance.
- The **Chief Engineer** is responsible for the maintenance and repair of the equipment in the Radio station and the timely preparation for regulatory paperwork required by the Federal Communications Commission.

"Tell me, and I forget. Teach me, and I remember. Involve me, and I learn." – *Benjamin Franklin*, Founding Father, and diplomat. (1706 – 1790)

3

The Four Keys to Advertising Success®

The Definition of Advertising

Dictonary.com defines advertising as **the act or practice of calling public attention to one's product, service, need, etc., especially by paid announcements in newspapers and magazines, over Radio or television, on billboards, etc.**

The Definition of Branding

Entrepreneur.com defines branding as **the marketing practice of creating a name, symbol, or design that identifies and differentiates a product from other products.**

The Definition of Marketing

The American Marketing Association defines marketing as **the activity, set of institutions, and processes for creating, communicating, delivering and exchanging offerings that have value for customers, clients, partners, and society at large.**

The understanding that advertising and branding are not the same is fundamental to successful marketing. Branding is all about creating the message about a company, and advertising is all about spreading that message around. Advertising and branding are part of marketing. Marketing includes a wide range of activities from inventory decisions, hours of operation, staff training, and so much more.

The first criterion of marketing is a sound company that offers fair value to the customer. **No amount of good advertising will fix a bad restaurant**. The food will still be cold, the service will still be slow, and the prices will still be high. Good advertising will tell thousands of people about the restaurant, and they will discover for themselves; it is not for them.

Successful advertising requires a well-crafted branding message. A company can buy lots of advertising but **if the message isn't emotionally engaging**, people will be exposed to the message, but **they won't feel compelled to store the message in long-term memory**.

As a Radio advertising salesperson, you can only influence branding and advertising. There isn't much you can do about how the company operates.

For the first 20 years of my advertising and marketing career, I met hundreds, if not thousands, of business owners who struggled with this question regarding their advertising: "What works and what doesn't work?" I also heard comments about their past advertising experiences: "I tried advertising once, it didn't work." Better yet, "I tried *radio,* or I tried *newspaper,* or I tried *cable* advertising once, and it didn't work." Insert any form of advertising, and the refrain was often the same: "I tried it *once,* and it didn't work."

Advertiser frustration is a familiar feeling among business owners. They've tried to advertise, but they've been disappointed with the results. Many business owners who place an advertising plan and are then disappointed with the results will say that the *advertising didn't work.* The business owner is quick to blame the **medium**. We find out, though, that the medium did its part. We know that consumers see and hear the advertising message from the circulation figures, traffic counts, viewer, and listener estimates. Indeed, consumers see and hear the commercial. However, the consumers said, "No" to the offer. Chances are, the real reason for the disappointing response to the advertising may have been **the message didn't resonate with the consumers**; or perhaps the ad **didn't reach the target audience**—two key elements may have been missing.

I found that the root cause of a business owner's disappointment is that they don't have a grasp of how advertising works—how certain vital elements need to come together.

The Research

In 1992, I had the perfect opportunity to find the answer to the question: "What works and what doesn't work?" That year, I joined a large broadcasting company with over 1,000 small businesses that advertised with the Radio station each year. With 1,000 firms to talk to, I could conduct some comparative research between business owners who said their advertising *worked* and business owners who said their advertising *didn't work.* With such a large pool of businesses, I had plenty of both kinds of research subjects.

When the research began, I divided the subject business owners into two groups: satisfied business owners/advertisers, "advertising worked" and dissatisfied business owners/advertisers, "advertising didn't work." Most business owners in the research groups had no formal training or education in advertising and marketing. The only criterion for separating the business owners into the two control groups was their *opinion* about their advertising.

The goal of the research was to identify the key factors of success that the satisfied advertisers used. The study found a common thread of four key elements that were always present in the successful campaigns: a commitment to a **consistent** plan, the proper mix of **reach** and **frequency** for the advertising budget, and an **emotional, engaging message** about the business. Thus, emerged my book *The Four Keys to Advertising Success®*.

The successful campaigns **included all four key elements**, while those considered not successful were missing one or more of these critical variables.

As the research evolved, we started to show the dissatisfied advertisers these four key elements and encouraged them to include them in their advertising plans. Once they agreed to do so, it took about **four to six months** for the formerly dissatisfied advertisers to report that they were **feeling better about their advertising efforts**. They also said that they began to **understand** how to make advertising work for their business.

Four Keys = Satisfaction

The research, having taken place over several years among thousands of business owners, showed a real correlation between the **presence of the four key factors** in the business owners' advertising and marketing efforts, and the **level of satisfaction** expressed by the business owners. At the same time, the research uncovered even more fascinating information, specifically, the conditions or actions that cause a business owner to become dissatisfied in the first place.

BADvertising = Dissatisfaction

My good friend Jason Skaggs first shared with me the word *BADvertising*. I'm borrowing this term from Jason to describe the pitfalls that lead to dissatisfaction among advertisers.

Dissatisfied advertisers—including those who started to implement the Four Keys but later ignored them—succumbed to *The Four Pitfalls of BADvertising*:

- The lack of a written business plan and **poor business practices**; no amount of good advertising will overcome lousy business decisions.
- Succumbing to the desire for instant gratification; in other words, **becoming impatient** and **inconsistent**.
- Letting your **reach** and **frequency** get **out of balance**; again, becoming impatient.
- Trying to advertise your business from the inside out; **not listening to the customer**.

It has become clear to me in hundreds of meetings with business owners/research subjects that you must fully understand the pitfalls of BADvertising at the same time we learn about *The Four Keys to Advertising Success®*. You must fully understand the negative consequences of BADvertising to realize why you need to stick with *The Four Keys to Advertising Success®*. Consequently, the training includes knowledge and skills to help you teach your advertisers how to identify and how to avoid the pitfalls that will get in the way of their advertising success. Better yet, this training is designed to help you understand how to prevent poor selling skills that are responsible for the unsatisfied advertiser buying the *BADvertising* in the first place. Don't sell the BADvertising!

The training begins with a thorough examination of the *Four Keys to Advertising Success®*: **consistency**, **reach**, **frequency**, and **engaging message**.

Next, you will learn about the essential **psychological fundamentals** that drive consumer behavior. You will learn about two incredibly important concepts, the *Triggering Event,* and the *Path to Purchase*. Without a firm understanding of the triggering event and the path to purchase, you will find it difficult to become a professional advertising salesperson. When you learn about the triggering event and the path to purchase, you will be able to explain to your customers why consumers respond to some advertising messages and why they don't respond to others.

Begin your selling career with a fundamental understanding of **the psychology of consumer behavior**. You will encounter customers who are in a hurry. They will be eager to buy advertising from you, on their terms, with unrealistic expectations. They don't want to wait for the Four Keys to Advertising Success® to work for them. They want to do it their way. After all, who are you to argue with the customer. When the advertising doesn't deliver as they want, they will be quick to blame you and your Radio station when they were practicing BADvertising. You will deserve part of the blame because you agreed to omit one of the Four Keys and sold them the BADvertising.

Consistency – The First Key to Advertising Success

The First Key to Advertising Success is **consistency**. It is also the most difficult of the Four Keys to practice because we live in a world of instant gratification. We have grown accustomed to getting what we want when we want it. In today's high-speed, on-line world, a consumer can go on to the Internet and order what they want, and have it delivered within hours. We hate to wait. Just like everything else, it's natural to want instant results from your advertising efforts.

Persuading your customers to commit to a consistent advertising plan is the fundamental building block of success in everything, including advertising your business. However, don't confuse consistency with spending large sums of money. Consistency is not about how much money your customer spends on advertising every year. Consistency is all about establishing an advertising budget that your customer can spend *consistently* on advertising, year after year after year.

Consumer perception studies often show the company with the higher awareness scores in the market is not the company that spends the most money but the company that has been **consistently** advertising the longest.

The Temptation of Instant Gratification

The biggest mistake a business owner can make in advertising is to expect instant gratification from their advertising efforts. Successful advertising depends on gaining an understanding of what consumers go through before they decide to do business with your customer. The *Decision Journey* later in this guide explains this in more detail.

We have all heard the idiom "Haste makes waste," acting too quickly (haste), and making mistakes, and then ending up with poor results (waste). "Haste makes waste" teaches us that **it is better to do things carefully than to do them quickly and carelessly**. The idiom is exceptionally true when it comes to teaching your customers about how advertising can work for them.

In pursuit of instant gratification from an advertising investment, a business owner or manager will often hastily move their advertising from one medium to the next when they don't feel as if they are getting the results they want as quickly as they want. If that business owner or manager understood the natural laws that govern consumer behavior, they would realize that about the time they hastily move their advertising to a new medium, the consumers using the previous medium were starting to become aware of the business. In other words, the consumers' awareness of that business was finally reaching the level where consumers would begin to respond. However, when the advertising drops from view, and the company loses that foothold in the consumer's mind called **awareness**.

As a professional advertising salesperson, no matter what kind of advertising your customer decides to use, encourage them to make the commitment to stick with it for the long haul. Business goes where business is invited. Your customer's advertising is their invitation to your audience. When they're not advertising, they're not asking your audience to come do business. The most satisfied advertisers keep inviting customers to do business with them over and over, consistently.

Consistency is the hallmark of virtually every advertising campaign that was considered to be effective by the business owners themselves. Whether they set out to be consistent or not is hard to determine. What is clear is the consistent long-term advertiser was more satisfied with their efforts than the business owner who followed a less-consistent strategy.

Consistency Takes Long-Term Commitment

Advertising is a lot like exercise. If you are out of shape and overweight, we all know that going to the gym **one time** isn't going to fix the problem. You will need to make a commitment to go to the gym on a regular basis a few times a week, week after week, to make a difference.

Your brain is not a muscle, but it responds to mental exercises just like a muscle does. Mental **exercise** helps the brain grow stronger, faster, and better able to function. Advertising **exercises** the hippocampus, the part of the brain where memories are formed and then indexed for later recall. Just like going to the gym to stay in shape, consistent advertising creates a lasting memory in the brain.

Setting an advertising budget is like weightlifting. You should always recommend that your customers start with a budget that is challenging but something they can maintain. They can add on more advertising as their business strength improves. Don't start them out with such a big advertising commitment that they **pull a financial muscle** and injure their business. They will have to stop advertising and sit out until they can recuperate. Even worse, they may quit advertising altogether.

As you learn more about consumer psychology and human behavior, you will see why consistency is the First Key to Advertising Success. You want to teach your customers that their advertising must be consistent to create awareness before the consumers find themselves in need of what your customer has to offer your audience.

The buying process is more about human behavior, and the thought process consumers go through than about what your customer is advertising because advertising doesn't cause people to buy things. Advertising doesn't make people come into your customer's store. Advertising doesn't make people pick up the phone to call your customer or to go on-line to their web site. Those are the intended consequences of your advertising efforts. It is essential to your customer's success to understand this basic premise: **people buy when they have a need or a desire for a product or a service**, not because your customer is advertising a sale or a discount.

Reach – The Second Key to Advertising Success

Reach is the term used to describe how many people will see or hear an advertisement. Many business owners are already familiar with the term reach. We know this because one of the first questions a business owner will ask the advertising salesperson is "How many people will drive by my billboard?" or "How many homes will get my direct mail piece?" or "How many people will hear my commercial?"

When analyzing reach, it is essential not to confuse the medium's audience size with the reach of the business owner's advertising message. Many media salespeople lead their presentation with a description of their subscriber base or viewing or listening audience. The **size of the medium's audience is _not_ the reach of the advertising message**.

The newspaper salesperson may say the newspaper has 100,000 subscribers. That is the **circulation** of the newspaper, not the **reach** of a display ad in the paper. For example, if the display ad is in the sports section of the newspaper, only those readers who read the sports section have a chance of seeing that display advertisement. If the ad is small, there is a chance that not all the sports section readers will see it. Depending on many factors, there is an excellent chance that the reach of the display advertisement could be much smaller than the newspaper's total circulation.

If you want to reach the total circulation of the newspaper, you would have to buy many display ads in all the sections of the newspaper over all the days of the week. Even then, you wouldn't reach all the newspaper's paid circulation. Some of their subscribers might be on vacation that week and not read the newspaper at all.

The TV salesperson may claim that the TV station has 100,000 viewers. That is the **viewership** of the television station, not the **reach** of a TV commercial. Maybe the salesperson narrows down the audience estimate to just the viewers of the 6:00 news. One commercial in that 30-minute time slot won't reach all the viewers. Maybe some of them tune in late. Perhaps others want to watch only the weather. Some tune in only for the top stories.

To reach all the viewers of the 6:00 news, you would need to buy several commercials within the newscast.

Now with new technology like DVR, experts estimate that when viewers are watching on a delayed basis, anywhere from 50 to 70% of the commercials are passed over so the viewer can skip ahead to the next scene in the show.

The radio station salesperson may claim that the radio station has 100,000 listeners. That is the **listenership** of the radio station, not the **reach** of the radio campaign. If your customer runs their radio commercials only in **drive time**, the listeners who work overnight won't hear your customer's commercial.

Don't confuse a medium's total audience with advertiser reach. It takes a well thought out advertising schedule to create reach. You will learn how to build effective advertising schedules later in our training.

Frequency – The Third Key to Advertising Success

Reach has a cousin, **frequency**, the Third Key to Advertising Success. The most satisfied advertisers in our research study were those business owners who had achieved a **balance between both reach and frequency**. That balance is dictated by the advertising budget you help your customers establish.

The dissatisfied advertisers often had an imbalance between reach and frequency. The two most common causes of this imbalance were the business owner's ego and the advertising salesperson's media hype. These two often steer the small business owner in the wrong direction.

Since advertising the business owner's company is often a direct reflection on the business owner, their ego can easily get involved in their advertising. A crafty commission-driven media salesperson will often exploit the small business owner's ego to make an *easy* sale.

The salesperson will talk all about the features of their medium, building it up in importance while never really addressing the real issue of the balance between reach and frequency.

In other words, when ego and salesmanship drive the decision-making process, the balance between reach and frequency is often the casualty because the business owner has been seduced by the **sizzle** of the advertising salesperson's sales pitch.

It's Not About Ego

For example, many small business owners want to advertise in the media that they themselves consume. If they watch the number one TV news show, they often want to advertise on the show they watch. They watch that show; they perceive that all their friends watch that show, so that's where they feel they need to advertise. Their ego wants to advertise in that TV show because they are focused solely on the reach. They will tell their friends, "Yep, I'm advertising on WXYZ TV, the biggest TV station in town."

However, if their ego exceeds their advertising budget, they may not be able to buy enough commercials to achieve enough **frequency**. So, they have the potential to reach many people with their message, but they don't have enough budget to buy **enough** commercials to achieve a level of effective frequency. Lots of people may see the business owner's television ad, but most people won't see it enough times, **frequently enough**, for the message to **sink in and be effective**. Many people won't see the small business owner's commercial at all.

Bigger isn't always better. Advertising on a medium with a big audience is naturally going to cost more than a similar medium with a smaller audience. Research indicates a company can achieve advertising effectiveness on a smaller Radio station with lower prices. The company can buy more frequency than they can achieve on a bigger Radio station with the same advertising budget.

The Balancing Act

Reaching the broadest audience sounds reasonable to many small business owners. However, without adequate frequency, that advertising budget will be wasted. If the business owner can take their ego out of the mix and consider advertising on a medium with a smaller audience where **they can buy more commercials** and achieve more frequency, they have a much better balance between reach and frequency. This can be a challenge because the small business owner must come to grips with the limitations of their advertising budget. They may have to face the reality that they cannot afford to be on the *big* station.

In the science of reach and frequency as it relates to advertising success, reaching a smaller audience frequently is more desirable that reaching a larger audience infrequently.

Don't Forget Consistency!

When balancing reach and frequency, remember to use the First Key to Advertising Success, consistency. For most business owners, branding or image advertising is the first order of business. If done correctly, branding/image advertising can be beneficial and affordable. However, the business owner must practice consistency.

Consistency isn't about how much money the business owner spends. Consistency is about how long they spend the money they have budgeted on the same medium. The overwhelming body of evidence indicates that to be effective, an **advertisement must reach the consumer a minimum of three different times within seven days** from the first exposure to the advertisement.

Beware of media salespeople who use the term **average frequency of three**. The average frequency of three means some consumers will be exposed to the advertising message only once; some will be exposed to the message more than that. You need to explain how many people will **hear** your advertiser's commercial three or more times. That is the **effective reach**.

Spread Too Thin

If a business owner is trying to have a special sale or a big promotion, they will need to do **Call to Action** advertising. Call to Action advertising is very expensive. It requires a lot more money in a very short time. Many business owners try to do Call to Action with an image-building budget. They don't have enough money to buy enough commercials across a wide range of media. Consequently, they won't achieve the levels of **reach** and **frequency** required for a successful sale or promotion.

Another pitfall of BADvertising is **trying to implement a media mix on a small budget**. The business owner ends up spending small amounts of money with lots of different media. Because the budget is spread so thin, none of the media involved have enough budget to reach any meaningful levels of reach and frequency.

The proper way to implement a media mix is to build a schedule on **one medium that reaches a level of effective reach and frequency** before moving on to the next media choice.

A Word of Caution

It's easy for a business owner to mistakenly assume that good advertising is **all about the frequency** of the message, that is, flooding the market with their message will assure success. However, without a compelling creative message that speaks to the heart of the consumer, a business risks advertising their business into the *Zone of Irritation*.

The Emotionally Engaging Commercial

The Fourth Key to Advertising Success is an **emotionally engaging creative message**. You must learn how to write commercials that will help your customer's advertising differentiate them in the market, **clearly articulating the unique value of their product or service**. For the message to resonate with prospective customers, it must evoke **emotion** or feeling. Engagement is the route to all successful advertising, and engagement is driven by **emotion**.

Engaging messages need an **easy on-ramp**, that is, accessible, quick, and immediate for the listener. Consumers will allow approximately 3 seconds for any single detail or part of the script to register an emotional response that they can relate to; otherwise, they will tune out the commercial.

Two approaches to the 3-second rule

It's essential, then, to always keep in mind the 3-second rule, ensuring everything in the script can be absorbed, reflected, and responded to quickly. It is vital to keep the message as simple as possible with a single core idea to bring the commercial to life and make things happen around it. There are two ways to address this.

First, the commercial itself is simple, giving the consumer easy onboard access. At the same time, there are novel ideas in the script and execution.

Second, there's some degree of complexity, but the ingredients are familiar enough so that, once again, people have an easy on-ramp.

Four Creative Elements Every Ad Must Have

To be effective, every advertisement should include these four creative elements:

1. The single most important word to the consumer: *You.* The most important word **isn't** a *sale* or *discount* or even *free*. The most important word to the consumer is the word **you**.

2. The *felt need* of the consumer. The felt need is something that the consumer feels: **emotion**. They feel it or think about it whenever the subject comes up. It is something that they want or need but haven't yet decided to act.

A good advertisement combines the first two creative elements early. For example:

"You love your home. But you hate your bathroom. It's small, it's cold, and it's old- fashioned. You want a new bathroom."

This first part of the advertisement has the most important word, *you,* in it three times. And many of us can **identify with the felt need for a larger, warmer, more modern bathroom.**

3. The *Call to Action*. This critical element describes what the consumer needs to do to address their felt need.

"Call the bathroom remodeling experts, ABC Bathrooms. They can make your bathroom dreams come true right before your very eyes."

4. Return on Investment. This element tells the consumer what they'll get when they call or, more importantly, how their life will be better after calling ABC Bathrooms.

"Before you know it, you will be relaxing in your larger, warmer, more modern bathroom."

Marketing slogans like "We're family-owned," "We're local," and "We have good prices," on their own, without articulating a direct consumer benefit, don't do much to motivate the savvy consumer in this competitive age.

Instead, slogans like "The next time you have a backed-up drain, call ABC Plumbing where there is never an extra charge for service on nights or weekends" will have better results. This slogan differentiates one plumber from the competition with the feature of no charge extra for nights or weekends. If you're like me, it seems like it's always at night or on a weekend when I have a plumbing problem. Some might ask how ABC can afford not to charge extra on nights and weekends. With that kind of a positioning statement, ABC could charge a little bit more all the time.

Once a compelling creative message is crafted to your customer's liking, put it on the air, and just let it run and run. Encourage your new customer to be patient and don't forget the First Key: consistency! Frequent changes in their message can sharply reduce campaign effectiveness. About the time they are tired of hearing their message is when consumers are just starting to take notice.

The Psychology of Consumer Behavior

To become a professional advertising salesperson and use the Four Keys to Advertising Success® effectively, you must know some basic principles about the **psychology of consumer behavior**.

Needs drive consumer behavior. *Maslow's Hierarchy of Needs* can be used as a basis for understanding why a consumer decides to buy a product or a service.

In his 1943 paper *A Theory of Human Motivation*, Abraham Maslow proposed that the motivation for action is an unfulfilled need. Maslow's research suggests that humans seek to satisfy their needs and desires in a specific hierarchy. Maslow contends that people must fulfill their most basic needs first before they can go forward and meet the more sophisticated needs.

Professional copywriters begin their training by learning about *Maslow's Hierarchy of Needs*. They learn how to use just the right words to trigger the emotional response center in the brain; the area focused on needs and desires.

Companies spend billions of dollars in advertising to target consumer needs and desires using scripts that begin with an understanding of *Maslow's Hierarchy of Needs*.

You will learn more about *Maslow's Hierarchy of Needs* later in your training when we cover how to write emotionally engaging commercials in a later section.

Needs and Emotions: The Core of Consumer Behavior

When you understand the psychology of consumer behavior, you begin to realize that you are not just selling a product, you are selling the **idea** of the product, the **image** of the product, and the **result** of the product. We are essentially promising to fulfill one or more of the needs in the hierarchy.

At the core of any purchase is an **emotional** reason that is driving consumer behavior. Harvard Economics Professor Theodor Levitt (1925-2006) said, "People don't want to buy a quarter-inch drill, they want a quarter-inch hole." However, people don't want a hole in their wall, do they? They need a hole in the wall to mount a hook that will hold that beautiful new family portrait.

Many things affect consumer behavior, but the most important element of a successful advertising script addresses the consumer's **needs** and the **emotions** related to your products and services. Advertising and branding are most effective when the message establishes an emotional connection with the audience while telling the story of why your business is the right one for their needs and desires.

To become a professional advertising salesperson, you must first learn what triggers consumer awareness and their decision-making process. People don't just rush out and buy something when they hear or see an advertisement. **They go through a process that usually takes longer than you or your customer would like.** If your customer is in a hurry to sell their products or services, **having a sale or a special promotion usually doesn't speed up the process**. All they do is give away their hard-earned profit margin to someone who was probably already going to buy from them.

Advertising Creates Awareness

Small business owners are often surprised when they learn that advertising alone doesn't make people buy things. It doesn't cause people to come into their store or call them on the phone.

Those are the intended consequences of good advertising. **Advertising can do only one thing for an advertiser: create awareness about a company**. Advertising can let people know who the company is, where the company is, and what the company can do for them. People enter the market to buy a product or a service **when they have a need or a desire**, not because they are exposed to advertising. Your customer should use advertising to raise awareness of their company's products and services. Consumers must know about your customer's company before their need or desire arises.

Awareness Is Mindshare

Consumers must know you before they need you. This awareness of your customer's company within the marketplace is called mindshare. Mindshare is the percentage of the population that recalls your customer's company name when asked to name a company within their product category.

Growing mindshare is one of the primary objectives of effective advertising and promotion. When people are prompted to think of examples of a product or a service, they usually have a few brand names that come to mind. For example, a prospective buyer of toothpaste has many different brand names to choose from. However, they may be able to only think of a few, the brands with mindshare.

Mindshare Is Market Share

Mindshare can be measured. When a small business owner advertises, over time, the mindshare increases. Likewise, when a small business owner stops advertising or cuts back, the number of people in the market that can recall that business name first begins to decline.

Mindshare equals market share. Eighty-six percent of respondents say **they are likely or very likely to shop with the first name they think of when the need or desire surfaces**. That's why you must always stress to your consumers that **they must be known before they are needed**.

However, the same research discovered that across many popular product categories, the number of consumers who couldn't think of a name was remarkably high. In some cases, as much as 80% of the respondents couldn't think of the name of a company when prompted by a random business category.

This is fantastic news for a company looking to grow its market share. There are many consumers out there without a clear-cut preference in a wide range of standard business categories. This is the upside potential for a company that embarks on a consistent branding campaign.

Most purchases are consumer-driven, meaning, the need or desire comes from within them. Advertising to build mindshare ensures that when those needs and desires bubble up for products or services a company offers, the consumer thinks about that company first.

Companies try to maximize the popularity of their product so that the brand name defines the category. Kleenex is a type of tissue. However, because it has gained popularity among consumers, it is frequently used as a term to identify any tissue, even if it is from a competing brand. Google has become a verb describing the act of searching for information on the Internet.

Other examples of how the brand name has come to describe the category include *Escalator*, *Chapstick*, *Tupperware*, and *Band-Aid*.

Although these are extreme examples of mindshare, the premise remains the same for businesses large and small: to increase short- or long-term sales, and market share, a company must first focus on building their mindshare.

The Decision Journey

The customer's **decision journey** can be short or long, depending on the type of product or service being considered. For example, a car purchase usually involves a long decision journey, while grocery shopping involves a short decision journey. Whether quick or well thought out, **virtually every buying decision is driven by some event that triggers the need or a desire for a product or service**.

When the consumer begins the process of selecting a product or service to satisfy a **triggering event**, they have a pool of options from which to choose. During this evaluation phase of the decision journey, the consumer will **add and subtract different brands** as they learn more about their choices. As the consumer learns more, their selection criteria can change too. This change in search criteria is more a function of the consumer's search for more information rather than advertising and marketing.

The Triggering Event: The First Stop on the Decision Journey

The decision journey begins when a consumer has a **triggering event.** A triggering event is something that happens in the consumer's life; it occurs on the consumer's timetable, and no amount of advertising can change that. It is the triggering event that changes the status quo for the consumer. It is the triggering event that triggers the need or the desire for a product or a service.

When a consumer has a triggering event, they begin to evaluate the brand names that are top-of-mind, the brands that the consumer thinks of first. They think of these brands first because they have been exposed to advertising, in-store displays, or an encounter with the product through a friend or acquaintance.

For example, a plumber could advertise all day long, discount here, discount there, savings this, savings that. Most people won't call regardless of the offer because they don't have a leaking pipe or a plumbing project on the horizon. They don't have the need or the desire no matter how much the plumber advertises or discounts the price.

Another example could be a body shop that repairs cars after a collision. It doesn't matter how much the body shop advertises or what kind of a discount or special they offer if the consumer doesn't have any damage to their car, they won't respond.

Did the advertising work? Yes, it did. People saw or heard the message. They said "No" to the offer because they didn't have the need or desire.

This is a good example why, in most cases, offering a discount or a special price does nothing to further a business owner's efforts to establish their company on the *Ladder of Importance* (more about that later). The plumber who advertises a discount price may be seen or heard by the consumer, but because there is no need or desire, the consumer says no to the offer.

And since the offer is time-sensitive and discount-based, the brain quickly forgets the message and moves on to other tasks.

The plumber and the body shop are examples of immediate triggering events in product categories that are not frequently used. Other **triggering events take more time to develop.**

The mother of all triggering events is a couple getting married. Not only does the couple spend money, but so do the parents, brothers, sisters, grandparents, aunts, uncles, cousins, and friends on both sides of the family. This new couple needs everything to start a household.

Starting a family is a triggering event. It triggers the need for medical services, perhaps a new home or a remodeling project, baby clothes, baby furniture, car seat, insurance, daycare, toys, and the list goes on and on.

A kid growing up is a triggering event to buy new clothes that fit. A change in season may trigger the need for warmer clothes. Getting tired of the lime green paint in the kitchen is a triggering event to repaint with a new color. Renewal time is a triggering event for insurance, especially if the premiums go up.

Virtually every purchase decision is preceded by some form of a recognizable triggering event. Without the triggering event, there is little need or desire for the product, regardless of the offer. Except for businesses that experience high-frequency purchasing, like food, fuel, and other consumables, **having a sale is not a triggering event**. By offering a sale price, the company is giving away their hard-earned profit margin to someone who was probably going to shop with them anyway.

Roadblocks on the Journey

We live in **the over-communicated society**. Research from Yankelovich Partners and other marketing experts estimate that most Americans are exposed to around 4,000 to 10,000 ads each day. With the proliferation of new technology, the flow of information will only increase. Studies on the human brain have determined that it can process only so much information before reaching **sensory overload**. At some point, the brain can't keep up with the flow of information and stops processing. Much like a sponge can only hold so much water, the brain can only process so much information. There are some **physical roadblocks** in the brain that prevent most advertising from leaving a lasting impression.

The human brain has some built-in features that help it manage the massive amounts of information we are exposed to every day. These are the roadblocks to your customer's advertising. The **reticular cortex** is the part of the brain that controls awareness or alertness. It is the reticular cortex that is continuously scanning our surroundings for the vital information we need for survival. All sensory information flows through the reticular cortex first on the way to other parts of the brain for processing. The reticular cortex acts as the dispatch system in the brain and **determines the priority** of sensory data and routes that data on for further processing **or discards the information** as nonessential and sets it aside. The reticular cortex checks all sensory data against **our mental database of needs and desires**, and if there is no match for this new information, it is disregarded and quickly forgotten.

Professor Hermann Ebbinghaus was a German psychologist who pioneered the experimental study of memory. Ebbinghaus was the first person to describe **the learning curve**. But Ebbinghaus also discovered **the forgetting curve**. The forgetting curve represents the exponential speed at which we tend to forget new information. The sharpest decline occurs in the first 20 minutes, then in the first hour, and then the curve evens off after about one day.

Ebbinghaus' research was done over 120 years ago, long before the information age, long before the onslaught of mass media and information technology. It is hard to imagine that the information overload of today doesn't speed up the forgetting curve in the mind of the present-day consumer.

Unfortunately, for many local business owners trying to advertise their business, the brain rejects much of what it sees and hears on a daily basis. The brain tends to accept information that fits into previously established perceptions and is **relevant to the individual's needs and desires**.

The Ladder of Importance

Once **accepted information** enters our brain, we tend to organize our thoughts in order of preference, putting the things we like most at the top of our list. List-building is a crucial organizational characteristic of the human brain because of the vast amount of information we are exposed to and our natural limitations.

In their book, *Positioning, the battle for your mind*, Jack Trout and Al Ries first introduced the metaphor of a mental ladder to help explain how the brain classifies information. The product or service you like the most within a given product category will be on the top rung of the ladder. Your second preference will be on the second rung, your third preference on rung number three and so on. Imagine a different ladder in your mind for each different product category.

When a consumer places a business name on their ladder, they have put a name into their memory. But how many rungs can there be on a ladder? How many names can people remember?

Harvard psychologist Dr. George A. Miller is the author of *The Magical Number Seven, Plus or Minus Two*. In this highly respected work, Miller presents his findings on the study of memory performance. Miller observed that working memory has limitations; we can keep track of only so many things at one time. His work suggests that our memory span is around seven elements at a time, but the limits of memory span vary by the type of information. Subjects recall numbers (seven items) better than letters (six) and letters better than words (five). Memory span is also influenced by the length of time, and how familiar we are, with the elements.

With so many factors influencing working memory, Miller proposed that the memory span in young adults was four to seven items, less with children and older adults. Nonetheless, as Jack Trout and Al Ries suggest, each product category has a different ladder. But some ladders will be longer than others depending on the importance of, and the consumer's interest level in, that category.

The value of a position on the Ladder of Importance is significant. History suggests that the company that **ranks at the top very often has twice as much market share** as the company on the next rung and that company has twice as much market share as the company on the third rung. If your company isn't in the top few positions, there isn't much market share remaining.

The **goal of any advertising plan should be to rank in the top position** on the Ladder of Importance within your product category. However, merely flooding the market with an advertising message won't elevate a business to the top rung of the Ladder of Importance. Without an **emotional** message that speaks to the heart of the consumer, the advertiser risks advertising into the *Zone of Irritation*. Remember, it takes **all** four of the *Four Keys to Advertising Success*® to reach the top of the Ladder. You must propose a **consistent** plan that has the proper balance of both **reach** and **frequency** for your customer's budget, and their **message must be relevant to the consumer's needs and desires.**

The Buyer's Awareness Cycle: The Middle of the Decision Journey

The time between the actual triggering event and the eventual purchase is called the Buyer's Awareness Cycle. The consumer passes through **four distinct phases of cognitive thought** as they move from being 1) just an **ordinary person** with no need or desire for the product, then they become 2) a **prospect**, then they become 3) a **researcher** and then eventually 4) a **buyer**.

The length of time a consumer spends in the Buyer's Awareness Cycle will vary from a few days, weeks, months, and even years, depending on the product category and the amount of money required. It is during the Buyer's Awareness Cycle that real preferences are formed. But it's hard to recognize the process is underway because people in the Buyer's Awareness Cycle are not walking around with a large sign advertising that they are a potential customer. These **prospects** and **researchers** are mostly **invisible to the business owner**, but they are seriously in the market.

The Dangers of Discounting

When a local business owner sets out to learn about advertising, they often imitate or mimic what they perceive to be successful advertising. They usually try to do **Call to Action advertising**. That's when you see or hear an advertisement for a product or service with a significant discount. The advertisement says that the offer is only available for a short period so "You must act now," "You must call before midnight tonight," "Sale ends Saturday."

Most companies use Call to Action advertising as a matter of last resort. The company is usually in an overstocked condition, and they need to move a lot of inventory quickly. Not only do they increase their overhead with massive spending on advertising, but they also lower their profit margins by reducing the sale price.

Unfortunately, **the desire for instant gratification** drives most advertising you see and hear today. Consequently, many business owners **focus their marketing** efforts on the **buyers** and not the prospects or the researchers. Their advertising messages are focused mainly on those consumers in the final stage of the Buyer's Awareness Cycle when the prospect is ready to make a purchase. The business advertises price and item information to get the buyer to shop with them. This strategy ignores the critical **research** phases the consumer goes through in the Buyer's Awareness Cycle when real preferences and buying decisions are formed, **based on value**, not on a low price or a special offer.

Business owners believe that a discount price or a special offer moves a prospect into the market for what they have to offer when all it does is give away their hard-earned profit margin to someone who already was likely to shop with them anyway. Price and item advertising gives a business owner a false sense of their ability to track their advertising effectiveness because the customers will either mention they heard or saw the ad. Perhaps the customer will bring the ad in when they come to shop.

Too many marketing plans **advertise only to the buyers** and not the prospects and researchers. Little thought is given to attracting the prospects and researchers while they are in the Buyer's Awareness Cycle. This strategy is unfortunate because it is **not** the most useful strategy for long-term business success. The consumers start to think of the business as a discounter and will come to expect nothing more than just a low price. Discounting **erodes the hard-earned profit margins** and puts the future of the company at risk as it tries to compete on **price** and not on **value**.

Consumers move into the market for a product or a service **because of the triggering event, not because of the discount price**. Once the consumer recognizes this need or desire, they enter the Buyer's Awareness Cycle and begin their search for the product or service that will satisfy their triggering event. By the time a consumer reaches the buying phase of the Buyer's Awareness Cycle, **two-thirds have already formed an opinion**[6] on how to satisfy their triggering event **before price ever becomes an issue**.

Successful marketing and advertising recognize that the buying process originates with the **triggering event**. The consumer moves from being a **prospect** to a **researcher** before they become a **buyer**. Two-thirds of the decision-making process is accomplished during the research phases of the Buyer's Awareness Cycle; only about one-third arrive at the buying phase without a clear preference. Strategies that focus simply on the buyers are missing the real opportunity to influence the decision-making process. Getting your customer's message out consistently during

---

[6] David C. Edelman. *Branding in the Digital Age: You're Spending Your Money in All the Wrong Places.* (Harvard Business Review, December 2010)

all phases of the Buyer's Awareness Cycle helps the **researchers** include your customer in the purchase decision.

The AIDA (awareness/interest/desire/action) Funnel

E. St. Elmo Lewis (1872-1948) was an American businessman who spent his life promoting and teaching other businesspeople about the benefits of advertising. Lewis was a co-founder of the Association of National Advertisers in 1910. Today, the ANA's membership includes over 400 companies with 9,000 brands. These companies collectively spend over $100 billion a year in advertising and marketing. It is the Association of National Advertisers who is responsible for many of the standards that drive the advertising industry today.

Back in 1898, Lewis was trying to explain the effects of advertising and the influence advertising has on the buying process. Lewis determined that consumers pass through four cognitive phases in their decision-making process. He described the process as the AIDA Funnel.

The first cognitive phase of thought is the **Awareness Stage**. If you have a car wreck, you are immediately **aware that you need repairs**. If there is water in the basement, you are very **aware that you need a plumber**.

But within many product categories, the process of becoming aware of a need or desire can be more gradual and take more time. Waking up one morning and finally deciding you can't take that lumpy old mattress is an awareness that you want a new mattress.

Once a consumer is aware of their need or desire, they must move through the second phase, the **Interest Stage**. This stage is the logic stage of the process where the consumer is **analytical, rational, and objective**. They may start to ask around to members of their family or their friends for advice. They might go on the Internet and do some research. The consumer must work up the interest to do something about the need or desire.

If someone has an accident in their old pickup truck and it was their fault, and they don't have enough money to fix it, they may not make it past the Interest Stage of the AIDA Funnel.

For whatever reason, it's going to take too much time, it's going to cost too much money, or they don't know where to go, many triggering events don't result in a sale.

When a company advertises, the message informs the consumer how the company can reduce the time required, can make the solution affordable, and how the company is the one the consumer can trust. These are essential elements to move the prospect past the Interest Stage.

Once a consumer has made it through the Interest Stage, the **Desire Stage** takes over. During this stage, the consumer works up to their **desire to spend the money**. They've done all the relevant research, and everything seems in order. Now the **emotions** start to come out. The consumer wants to get the product or service. Both the **Interest** and the **Desire** Stages work together at this point.

Once the consumer has worked their way through the Awareness, Interest, and Desire Stages, they are ready to act. They are prepared to spend. The **Action Stage is very short**, usually 24-48 hours. It is short because the consumer has done almost all the work necessary to be **ready to spend**. Because the Action Stage is so quick and the prospect is ready to buy, a business owner will often mistake this eagerness as a result of a sale price and not the result of the time spent in the decision journey. In other words, this eagerness to buy sends a false signal to the business owner that can cause them to stray from the first key to advertising success, *consistency*.

The Changing Shapes of the Decision Journey

Marketing scholars now believe that instead of a funnel-shaped process, a decision journey can look more like a bowling pin. Rather than systematically narrowing their choices, the consumer is likely to add and subtract brands from a group under consideration during an extended evaluation phase. A good example would be prospective car buyers who begin their research a year or more before they plan to replace their current vehicles.

When the consumer begins the process of selecting a product or service to satisfy a triggering event, they have a pool of options from which to choose. But as they explore those options, it is now clear that the pool of possibilities expands instead of growing smaller, especially with the search power of the Internet. As the consumer researches their choices, the process pulls in information and opinions from various sources: advertising, research, and other people.

For many product categories, the first stop on the Internet **is not Google**, Yahoo, or Bing; it is Amazon Dot Com or Consumer Reports Dot Com. Consumers want to know how other people feel about the product or service they need or desire.

The opinions of other people are called **consumer advocacy**, a powerful influence in the decision journey. Consumer advocacy has been around forever. A couple of friends are having a cup of coffee, one complains about their transmission acting upon their car. The other friend suggests a local repair shop that took great care of them when they had a problem.

Consumer advocacy is compelling; it can often override price concerns because the opinion is coming from an existing customer or someone the prospect trusts.

Consumer advocacy goes back to a crucial point: a business brand is what the customers say about the company when they are describing their consumer experience with that company.

The bowling pin model also applies to short decision journeys, especially in today's fast-paced society with constant information. The proliferation of mobile devices is causing a seismic shift in consumer behavior. When you get hungry, for example, you may spend all of 15 minutes on that decision journey. You can conduct product research while you are standing in the aisle of the store. Smartphones can scan a bar code and link to a web page with information. The consumer can even watch a short video about the product. **But this only reinforces the need to be known before you are needed**.

Voice-activated search gives the company that is known before they are needed a competitive advantage. Instead of saying, "Find a hardware store near me," consumers can say "Call Cottons Hardware."

Either a funnel or a blowing pin shape illustrates the decision journey. Regardless of the diagram depicting a decision journey, remember that good advertising builds mindshare. Good advertising communicates a positive message about a company and how that company can satisfy needs and desires. Eighty-six percent of the consumers surveyed said they were **likely** or **very likely** to shop with the first name they think of when they have the triggering event.

Don't let your potential customers get lost along their decision journey and end up at your competitor's company. Commit to being consistent with your advertising; it is the First Key to Advertising Success.

Summary

In this chapter on The Four Keys to Advertising Success®, we covered the following topics:

- There are Four Keys to Advertising Success®. Based on research with thousands of local business owners, an understanding of the Four Keys will help you explain why some advertising works and why some advertising doesn't.
- Advertising is **the act or practice of calling public attention to one's product, service, need, etc., especially by paid announcements in newspapers and magazines, over Radio or television, on billboards, etc.**
- Branding is **the marketing practice of creating a name, symbol, or design that identifies and differentiates a product from other products.**
- People don't buy things because they are on sale; the psychology of consumer behavior drives the purchase decision. People buy things because they have a need or a desire to own the product or service.
- Consumers follow a **path-to-purchase** or a **decision journey** that begins with a triggering event. The duration of the path-to-purchase varies by category.
- Discounting or having a sale is costly for a local business owner. They lower their profit margins and increase their advertising expenditures. Discounting is a measure of last resort designed to generate cash-flow, not profit margins.
- The **sales funnel** for describing the decision journey is no longer a uniform shaped funnel with a big opening at the top and a small opening at the bottom. Today, the sales funnel is more like a bowling pin shape, because consumers are exposed to more information, and their initial **known-set** of options will grow and contract as they consider their options.
- Advertising builds **mindshare**. Mindshare equals market share. Tell your prospects, **"They gotta know ya before they need ya."**

"I don't focus on what I'm up against. I focus on my goals, and I try to ignore the rest." – *Venus Williams*, professional tennis player. (1980 -

4

Goal Setting

Before you can become a ***successful*** professional salesperson, you must know what your goals are. You should establish your personal goals that guide you in your own life, your family life, and in your professional life. These personal goals are your personal road map for how you plan to conduct yourself in all aspects of your life.

When it comes to setting your personal life goals, we recommend you read Stephen R. Covey's *Seven Habits of Highly Effective People*. Dr. Covey presents an approach useful in attaining goals by aligning oneself to what he calls **true north principles** such as fairness, kindness, dignity, charity, integrity, quality, and service. True north principals are objective and external as opposed to values which are subjective and internal. We must have an inner compass that always points to true north because events and people can send us off course. The internal compass will help us get back on track. In short, your professional life can't be successful if your personal and family lives are in turmoil. Likewise, your personal and family life can't be fulfilling if your professional life is unfulfilling.

This chapter on goal setting will focus on how to set professional goals that will ultimately help you with your personal and family life goals.

Setting Sales Goals

Professional goals are a collaboration between you and your company. You must know what your company expects from you in terms of the amount of advertising sold, number of customers, average order, and other considerations.

When you know your goals, you can make better planning decisions. You will be able to focus more on what you know is essential. In this module, you will learn how to break down your goals into the number of customers you need to sell, the number of presentation and client interaction calls you must make, and, ultimately, the number of prospecting telephone calls you need to make every day.

During your orientation, your sales manager should have assigned you some sales goals. Sales goals at a Radio station are often monthly, quarterly, and annually. Ask your sales manager if there is a corresponding bonus plan for reaching your monthly, quarterly, and annual sales goals.

Using the Goal Setting Worksheet (represented in Figure 1 and found in Appendix A), write down the goals assigned to you by your sales manager.

In this example, we assume you are an entry-level salesperson building a new customer list from the ground up. Even if you are an experienced Radio sales professional and already have a list of active customers, you too should fill out the sheet to ensure that your sites are correctly set on your target goal.

Goals Worksheet

	Month	Goal		Avg Order		No of Customers
1)	April	$ $1,500	÷	$	=	
2)	May	$ $2,500	÷	$	=	
3)	June	$ $3,500	÷	$	=	
4)	July	$ $4,500	÷	$	=	
5)	August	$ $6,000	÷	$	=	
6)	September	$ $8,000	÷	$	=	
7)	October	$ $10,000	÷	$	=	
8)	November	$ $12,000	÷	$	=	
9)	December	$ $14,000	÷	$	=	
10)	January	$ $14,000	÷	$	=	
11)	Februray	$ $14,000	÷	$	=	
12)	March	$ $16,000	÷	$	=	

FIGURE 1

The worksheet has twelve places representing the twelve months of the year. Fill in the name of the upcoming month on your calendar in the spot labeled 1) on the worksheet to serve as the first month of this goal-setting process. Then fill in the rest of the month names for the next 11 months.

Next, you want to understand the nature of the average order currently running on your

Radio station. You need this information to begin to formulate an idea of how many average customers you need to sell each month to reach your sales goals. Ask your manager for the average order size in dollars on your Radio station.

The average order size on your Radio station is probably going to be lower than what you want to aspire. The average order on your Radio station is an average of good long-term branding campaigns and not-so-good, short-term advertising, usually consisting of sales packages.

There is nothing inherently wrong with short-term sales packages if you build them correctly. Your station may have sales packages for the County Fair, or Back to School, or for Valentine's Day. And you may need to sell a lot of these packages. But in our training, you want to learn how to sell long-term branding campaigns. That is the backbone of a profitable profession in Radio advertising sales.

You need to know what the average order size is because you're just getting started and **you certainly don't want your average to be below average**. As you gain more knowledge and skill, you will know what you need to sell to be above average.

Goals Worksheet

	Month		Goal		Avg Order		No of Customers
1)	April	: $	$1,500	÷ $	$1,000	=	2
2)	May	: $	$2,500	÷ $	$1,000	=	3
3)	June	: $	$3,500	÷ $	$1,000	=	4
4)	July	: $	$4,500	÷ $	$1,000	=	5
5)	August	: $	$6,000	÷ $	$1,000	=	6
6)	September	: $	$8,000	÷ $	$1,000	=	8
7)	October	: $	$10,000	÷ $	$1,000	=	10
8)	November	: $	$12,000	÷ $	$1,000	=	12
9)	December	: $	$14,000	÷ $	$1,000	=	14
10)	January	: $	$14,000	÷ $	$1,000	=	14
11)	Februray	: $	$14,000	÷ $	$1,000	=	14
12)	March	: $	$16,000	÷ $	$1,000	=	16

FIGURE 2

Once your sales manager tells you what the average order size is, return to your Goal Setting Worksheet and enter that number in the formula. If you divide your sales goal by the average order size, now you have a rough estimate of how many customers you need to sell to reach your sales goal.

This example (Figure 2) of a goal sheet demonstrates a gradually growing goal of a few accounts each month. Your goal sheet may look quite different, especially if you have previous Radio advertising sales experience and if you are inheriting some billing accounts. Regardless, you must convert your goal from dollars to accounts to organize your selling activities.

This worksheet is just the beginning of your goals setting process. From this information, you will be able to make many decisions that will affect the quality of your work and the level of your income.

Short Term Sales versus Long Term Sales

We can see from this example that in your first month, you need to sell at least two advertising orders at the average order size to reach your sales goal. A year from now, in March, you will need to sell sixteen orders at the average order size to reach your sales goal.

So, if you must sell two orders in April, three in May, four in June and so on, if you add that all up, that comes to 108 advertising orders. That's a lot of advertising orders. That's a lot of customers. That is if you sell only short-term advertising packages.

In advertising sales, **consistency** is the foundational building block of a successful advertising campaign. You want to teach your customers why they should pick something and stick with it. Starting and stopping, going from month to month is not good advertising advice. According to the company's training manual, McDonalds sells 75 hamburger every second of every hour of every day. But McDonalds doesn't advertise month-to-month. They follow a consistent advertising plan, week after week, month after month, **and** year after year.

You have chosen the path of the professional advertising salesperson. You are going to recommend sound advertising strategies based on The Four Keys to Advertising Success® of consistency, reach, frequency, and an emotionally engaging, creative message.

When you recommend a consistent adverting strategy, you don't need to make 108 different advertising sales to reach your goal. You need to make 16 sales with consistent annual branding campaigns or advertising plans to reach your sales goals.

In our example, (Figure 3) your April goal is two sales. Then in May, your goal is three sales. If you sold your first two orders in April as an annual advertising plan, in May, you already have two contracts on the books, you need three, so you only need one more annual sale. The same is true for June. As you begin the month, you already have three advertising orders on the books; your goal is four, you need one more.

The consistent annual advertising plan is the best advertising recommendation you can present. A regular strategy is more effective than start-and-stop advertising, sometimes referred to as **flighting** the advertising. You will encounter some leads who have learned about flighting from other advertising salespeople, and they mistakenly believe that flighting is the way they need to advertise.

Goals Worksheet

	Month		Goal			Avg Order		No of Customers
1)	April	: $	$1,500	÷	$	$1,000	=	2
2)	May	: $	$2,500	÷	$	$1,000	=	3
3)	June	: $	$3,500	÷	$	$1,000	=	4
4)	July	: $	$4,500	÷	$	$1,000	=	5
5)	August	: $	$6,000	÷	$	$1,000	=	6
6)	September	: $	$8,000	÷	$	$1,000	=	8

You already have two long-term sales, you just need one more.

FIGURE 3

We recommend working with that business despite their insistence to flight because, over time, you will have many encounters where you will get the opportunity to help them learn about The Four Keys to Advertising Success® and ultimately help them make a new decision to be more consistent.

You will encounter potential advertisers, who, for whatever reason, cannot implement a long-term consistent advertising plan. There may be a valid reason for you to sell them some short-term advertising. Your Radio station may have some short-term advertising plans linked to events such as high school sports, or county fair advertising that only lasts a month or two.

Even though the consistent annual advertising plan is the best professional recommendation you can make for an on-going business, your list of advertising contracts will ultimately consist of 12-month orders, six-month orders, three-month orders and yes, even some one-month orders.

At this point, we should stop and assess what we have just been discussing. It is crucial to understand the ramifications of poor decision making and the lack of a clear set of goals and how they will affect your profession. We need to talk about time management.

As you start making calls on companies, you will get some initial positive responses. You will even make a quick sale here and there because you just happened to call on a company with an immediate need and you were in the right place at the right time. Don't let that fool you. **Don't start to think, "This is easier than they said!"** You may develop a tendency to forget your training and leave it behind and make the unfortunate decision to start chasing after other short-term easy sales.

In practical terms, it takes contracts of all lengths to build your book of business in the profession of Radio advertising sales. It requires balance. If you only sell short term, one-month advertising agreements, you will overwhelm your time management capabilities.

In our previous worksheet example, you will need to sell 16 clients every month. Sure, some of your customers will go month to month to month. But the workload will become too much. It will create frustration, which will lead to your dissatisfaction with your profession.

You will get excited when you make a sale. Your sales manager will be happy for you. The office and programming staff will be happy for you. We will be pleased for you. Just don't fall victim to thinking that's all there is to this advertising sales business. You can't always be in the right place at the right time.

There is another caveat. When you sell the short-term advertising plan, there is an excellent potential for customer dissatisfaction. The customer is expecting their advertising to generate some short-term increase in sales. That is a challenging task. But even if the advertising does produce some short-term sales increase, you still lose because your customer will want to do it again next month. And when it doesn't generate the short-term sales increase the second or third time, they will conclude they have reached all your listeners, and they will cease to do business with you at all.

In most Radio stations, large or small, you will need to have approximately forty active advertisers on the air every month to make a *professional wage*. If you are overwhelmed with sixteen advertisers each month, how will you ever be able to grow beyond that number?

Forty monthly advertisers at $1,000 a month (our average order in our example), at a 15% commission will earn you $6,000 a month in commission or $72,000 a year. In a larger market, with a larger average order, you could make a six-figure income.

How does the number of active advertisers impact your time management skills?

First, there is the paperwork and the necessary customer contacts to approve the order, the scripts, and the finished commercial. Second, there is the amount of seed work required to cultivate new customers. You must strike a balance. Too much time spent on processing a bunch of short-term orders takes away from the valuable time needed for lead development.

Leads, Prospects, and Customers

The selling business has its language and terms. Several are used interchangeably, even though they don't mean the same thing. Such is the case with the words *prospect* and *lead*. In the next section on the account list management, there is a more detailed definition of leads, prospects, and customers. Account definitions help you define the type and amount of selling activity each definition requires.

A **lead** is an unqualified contact. Any potential client or customer you meet that hasn't been qualified as a prospect is a lead. In professional selling, you first gather names of people or companies that you think might make a good customer. However, at first, you don't have much more than just the name. That is a lead.

A lead becomes a **prospect** after you have met with the lead, you've had a discussion, and the two of you decide there might be some merit in going forward in the sales process. The lead hasn't agreed to sign a contract in our scenario. The lead has shared some information with you, and you have shared some information with them, and it looks like it would be worth your time to have a follow-up conversation with more substance. That's when a lead becomes a prospect.

For a lead to qualify as a prospect, the lead must have **the means** to buy advertising, the lead is authorized to make advertising buying decisions, and there is a match between the lead's business needs and your services. We will go further in-depth about qualifying a lead in a later chapter.

If you happen to be in the right place at the right time, it is possible to take the lead straight to becoming a customer, but those are the rare and far between occurrences.

A **customer** is a company or individual who is actively buying advertising from you. But if they stop advertising, they are no longer a customer; they are now a prospect.

The Sales Process

In the previous section, you learned how to estimate the number of different average customers you will need to sell to reach your sales goals. We used the average figure for our calculations. But you don't want to be average, correct? Certainly not. You have a growth mindset.

In the previous example calculations, you divided the monthly goal of $16,000 by the average customer of $1,000 to determine that you need 16 different average customers to reach the sales goal assigned by the sales manager. Now that you know you need 16 average customers to reach the sales goal, how do you sell 16 average customers when, as a new salesperson, you have few, if any existing customers?

You follow the **sales process**. While the sales process is unique to each company, a sales process is a series of activities performed in sequence to find, sell, and keep customers.

The sales process presented in this training involves six necessary steps, prospecting, qualifying, interviewing, presenting, reaching agreement, and customer service. A detailed description of each step in the process will follow in upcoming chapters. Completing each step in the sales process, according to the plan, builds a rewarding sales career with many happy customers and a big commission check. Skipping a step or taking shortcuts leads to poor sales performance and lower commissions.

The sales process requires specific activities in sufficient quantities. Consequently, you must learn how to plan your time efficiently to complete the sales process with enough companies to reach your sales goals. You need to learn how to set activity goals for every activity in the sales process.

The Sales Funnel and the Sales Pipeline

There are two metaphors used to describe your work during the sales process: the **sales funnel** and the **sales pipeline**. Salespeople often transpose sales funnel with sales pipeline in the conversation about managing the process of sales. We prefer to use the sales funnel as the preferred metaphor for the visual representation of your sales process.

In sales, the funnel (Figure 4) is used to illustrate the process of prospecting for new customers. The funnel has a wide opening to represent that you must contact lots of companies in your initial efforts to find new customers. You fill up your sales funnel with these initial leads.

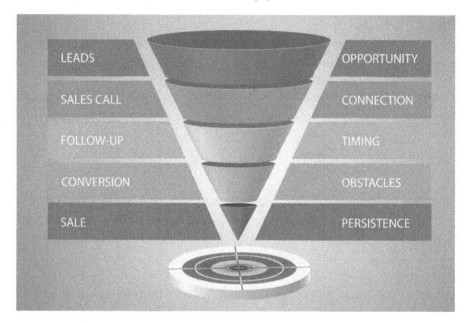

FIGURE 4

As the sales process proceeds, some of the leads you contact will have no desire to engage in your selling efforts, so they don't continue through the funnel. You did not **convert** the lead into a prospect. The funnel narrows from the wide opening to the narrow spout at the bottom to describe **the conversion process**.

You may need to meet with many leads to convert just one to a customer. That is the nature of selling. You may contact as many as twenty new leads to put in your sales funnel, and perhaps only two or three **converts** to a new customer.

Lag Measures and Leading Measures

Sixteen thousand dollars or 16 average customers is the goal. The goal is known as a **lag measure**. When you reach the end of the month, and you don't have 16 customers, you only have 10, you missed the goal, your activities are already in the past. By the time you get a lag measure, you can't fix it. It's history.

The sales funnel is a **leading measurement tool**, primarily used to place an estimated monetary value of your activities based on the current location of each company in your sales funnel. If the calculated value of all the companies you are working within your funnel isn't enough to reach your sales goal, you need to increase your activity levels.

Let's say you want to lose weight; you want to lose 10 pounds. The lag measure is pounds dropped. A couple of leading measures to predict reaching the weight loss goal might be a limit on your calorie intake each day and a specific number of hours of exercise per week.

These leading measures are predictive because they are the specific activities that lead to weight loss; you can predict what the scale (the lag measure) will tell you next week.

In Radio advertising sales, the primary leading measures are:

- The number of daily prospecting calls made.
- The number of appointment set.
- The number of customer needs assessment interviews conducted.
- The number of sales presentations made.
- The number of sales agreements reached.

The lag measure, selling 16 customers, is ultimately the most important thing you are trying to accomplish. But if you are not making enough prospecting calls, you won't set enough appointments; you won't complete enough assessment interviews, you won't make enough presentations and, you won't reach your goal of 16 customers.

Identifying Your Leading Measures

Lag measures are *what you get*. Leading measures are *what you do*. Leading measures are those activities you can control and will have a direct impact on your performance to reach your goal. The only limitation is your commitment level. Remember the growth mindset?

Make a copy of the Goal Setting Activity Planner from Appendix B for the following exercise. Earlier in this chapter, we did the math to determine how many average customers were needed to reach the goal. The goal of $16,000 or 16 customers is the lag measure.

Calculate how many monthly orders you need to sell each month to reach your sales goal:
$16,000 (goal) ÷ $1,000 (average order) = 16 (customers needed)

The number of presentations needed to close a sale is a leading measure. You need a **closing ratio** to make this calculation. If you are new to Radio advertising sales and don't yet have a track record, no need to worry, we will use a 50% closing ratio. That means you close one out of every two presentations you make.

Divide the number of accounts you need to sell each month by your closing ratio:
16 (accounts needed) ÷ .50 (50% closing ratio) = 32 (presentations required)

The leading measure is 32 presentations required to close 16 sales. If you only make 16 presentations, you will only close eight deals. If you don't make enough presentations, you know in advance you won't reach the sales goal.

The next leading measure is the number of customer needs assessment interviews (CNAs) required to make 32 sales presentations. Again, we will use a 50% conversion rate. That means that one out of every two interviews results in an appointment to make a sales presentation.

Divide the number of proposals needed each month by the ratio of CNAs that result in a presentation:
32 (presentations required) ÷ 50 (CNAs to proposal ratio) = 64 CNAs required

The leading measure of CNA interviews is 64 interviews required to set 32 presentation meetings. If you don't make enough CNA interviews, you know in advance you won't reach the sales goal.

The final leading measure is the number of prospecting calls required to set an appointment with a lead.

Divide the number of CNAs needed each month by the ratio of prospecting calls that result in a CNA:
64 (CNAs required) ÷ 50 (prospecting call to CNA ratio) = 128 (prospecting calls required)

When you arrange the leading measures in the order of the sales process, you can see why the funnel is used to represent the conversion process in sales.

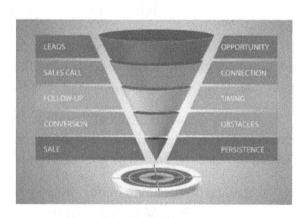

Prospecting calls needed each month: __128__

CNAs required each month: __64__

Presentations required each month: __32__

Sales required each month: __16__

If you want enough sales to come out the bottom of the sales funnel, you must gather up enough leads at the beginning of the sales process to make that happen. A 50% conversion rate in any field of selling is generous. But as we said earlier, you don't have to limit yourself by what Ol' Bill is doing. Your level of success is 100% dependent on you, and on the effort, you apply to **learn and practice professional selling skills**.

The Ideal Day and the Ideal Week

In their book, *The Four Disciplines of Execution: Achieving Your Wildly Important Goals*, the authors write, "The *Second Discipline* is **Act on the Lead Measures**."[7] They call this the discipline of leverage, based on the principle that all actions are not created equal. Some activities will have a more significant impact on reaching your goal than others.

The sales funnel represents the actions with the most impact, but only when taken in the proper order. It is not practical to think you can meet a lead and sell them without first qualifying and conducting an interview. However, it is possible to meet a lead and go through all the six steps in the selling process in one meeting. But it's not practical to expect to go from step one to closing a deal in step six if you skip steps, two, three, four and five.

To put **Discipline 2: Act on the Lead Measures,** into practice, establish and follow a daily and weekly routine with time allotted to all six stages in the selling process.

At the beginning of your profession in Radio advertising sales, you won't have much of a customer list, if any. You must fill your day with lead finding activities. You may need to call on ten, twenty, maybe even thirty leads before you get one person who will agree to meet with you.

As you call to find leads, you will hear objections like "I'm not interested." Don't let that discourage you because that is a training issue. Jeffrey Gitomer, a well-known sales motivator and author, offers this advice when you hear the stall, "We're not interested at this time." Gitomer says, **"If they're not interested, maybe you're not interesting enough!"**

You will learn how to improve your calling skills, so you make better calls that result in more first appointments. You will improve your success rate through training and practice. You can role play with your sales manager or another salesperson. You can monitor what works and what doesn't and refine your telephone script with more of what works.

You can increase the percentage of leads who will agree to a meeting by practicing a telephone calling script. You will learn more about telephone scripts and calling techniques in a later lesson. For now, the lesson is this; you need to call as many leads as it takes to get two appointments each day for a Customer Needs Assessment interview.

As you set some appointments for the Customer Needs Assessment interview, those leads begin to flow down through the sales funnel. You meet to determine if there is a mutual interest in doing business and whether you can convert the lead into a prospect. (You will learn more about how to conduct a Customer Needs Assessment in a later section.)

Meetings with the leads will take time away from your prospecting efforts. You must develop the skill of balancing competing priorities. It is necessary to keep filling the large end of

---

[7] The 4 Disciplines of Execution: Achieving Your Wildly Important Goals (p. 11).

the sales funnel with new leads. At the same time, you must spend time meeting and interviewing your leads.

When you meet with a lead and conduct your Customer Needs Assessment, you have the chance to learn whether your services and the needs of the lead make a good match. You must both reach an agreement to move forward with the next step, a proposal to help the lead with their needs. **If you reach an agreement to move forward with a proposal, you now have a prospect**. The process of preparing a proposal is going to take time away from your lead generation activities. Preparing a proposal is going to take time away from conducting Customer Needs Assessment interviews. You put your time management skills to the test. Leads are starting to flow through your sales funnel, but you must maintain an active lead finding effort.

Fast forward to months from now, when you have several active customers advertising with you every month. How will your day look? You will need to have a balance of the different types of activities necessary to grow your customer list and reach your sales goals. What will an ideal day look like in your profession of selling?

You will get to the office promptly, if not a little bit early. You will go straight to work. You don't spend time around the coffee machine or water cooler. You get straight to your desk and begin your work because as a professional, you know that *your time is your money*.

You have *the Ideal Day* planned. You have at least eight face-to-face appointments scheduled.

- You have an appointment with yourself to conduct lead finding activities and find at least two new leads.
- You have **two CNA appointments** to meet a new lead and conduct a Customer Needs Assessment interview.
- You have **two Presentation Calls**, appointments to meet with a prospect and present your ideas for an advertising plan to meet the needs of the prospect.
- You have **two Closing Calls**, appointments with leads to finalize your agreement and get a signature.
- You have **two Service Calls**, appointments to meet with an existing customer to review their plans, change their commercial, pick up a check, drop off some paperwork, or discuss additional options.
- You have an appointment with yourself to process your paperwork.

There is also *the Ideal Week*. If for some reason, your daily schedule gets changed, you have other days in the week to make it up. Your weekly activity goals should be:

- 10 New leads to call on.
- 10 Customer Needs Assessment appointments.
- 10 Presentation Calls where you present your idea for the prospect.
- 10 Closing Calls where you finalize your agreement and get a signature
- 10 Service Calls

- All your paperwork is up to date before you leave on Friday.

Summary

In this chapter on Goal Setting, we covered the following topics:

- When you know your goals, you can make better planning decisions. You will be able to focus more on what you know is essential.
    - Get your monthly sales goals from your sales manager.
    - Determine what the average monthly order is.
    - Calculate how many **average** customers you need to sell each month to reach your sales goal.
- The sales funnel is used to place an estimated monetary value of your activities based on the current location of each company in your sales funnel. If the calculated value of all the companies you are working within your funnel isn't enough to reach your sales goal, you need to increase your activity levels.
- You learned about the Sales Funnel and calculated the necessary level of activities you need to plan for to reach your sales goal.
- Lag measures are **what you get**. Leading measures are **what you do**. Leading measures are those activities you can control and will have a direct impact on your performance to reach your goal. The only limitation is your commitment level.
- You learned how to define a lead, a prospect, and a customer.
- In the book, *The Four Disciplines of Execution: Achieving Your Wildly Important Goals*, the *Second Discipline* is **Act on the Lead Measures.** Establish and follow a daily and weekly routine with time allotted to all stages in the selling process
    - The definition of the Ideal Day.
    - The definition of the Ideal Week.

"If you go to work on your goals, your goals will go to work on you. If you to work on your plan, your plan will go to work on you. Whatever good things we build, end up building us." – *Jim Rhon,* American entrepreneur. (1930 – 2009)

5

Building Your Account List

In the profession of Radio advertising sales, virtually every category of business can benefit from Radio advertising. Mass media advertising is no longer just for the retail and service categories. There was a time when lawyers and doctors saw mass media advertising as an activity unbecoming the profession. Today, you will see and hear millions of dollars in legal and medical advertising on virtually every medium in your market. Business leaders in every industry see advertising as the path to growth. **The number of business categories and the amount of money spent on advertising is growing every year**.

There is a downside to such a vast opportunity. It can be challenging to get organized and stay organized on who your best prospects should be. The benefit of building an account list comes from the focus a list imposes on your activities. A properly structured account list will narrow your focus on creating and capturing specific opportunities. Self-imposed account list discipline will prevent you from wasting your time on unprofitable activities.

Why is focus so important in your professional sales career? When you try to focus on more than one task at a time, you may be sacrificing your performance on the primary responsibility and distracted by other irrelevant issues. **Time is money**. Discipline helps you protect your time for the most profitable use. In account list management, **that means calling on the right opportunities**.

The Radio station maintains a list of companies called **the master account list**. The account list will include companies that are presently advertising, companies that advertised in the past but not currently, and companies who have never advertised with your Radio station. The account list indicates which salesperson is assigned to sell and service each company. There are some companies on the list that do not have a salesperson attached. That list is called the **unassigned** or **open list**.

Schedule a time to meet with your sales manager to learn how the master account list works in your Radio station. You want to know:

- Does your Radio station have a master account list?
- Does your Radio station use a computer program like the RAB Account Manager, Salesforce, Constant Contact or Excel to manage the master account list?
- Who can access and make changes to the master account list?
- How and when can you get an updated copy of the master account list?
- How and when can you get an updated copy of your account list?
- How many accounts are you allowed to have on your account list?
- Are the companies on your list categorized, i.e., leads, prospects, and customers?
- How can you put new companies on your account list?
- How long can a company stay on your list without you making a sale?
- Will the sales manager ever take companies off your list and why?

Ask the sales manager for a thorough explanation of how your Radio station manages the master account list.

In most cases, you will lose the assignment to a company because you are unable to sell them any advertising or if you commit unprofessional behavior. You might also lose your assignment if the manager feels another salesperson can do better than you can. Sometimes, the management of your Radio station may use account assignment as a management or disciplinary tool.

Ask your manager where the list is maintained and how you can gain access to the list. You want to be able to refer to it often as you build your list.

When you identify a business, you want to call on; you present that business name to your manager for approval. The manager will check to see if that business is assigned to another salesperson. In most cases, if the company is not assigned to another salesperson, you will get the opportunity to sell and service that business. (If your Radio station has a CRM system, explained later, you may be able to check for yourself.)

If that company is currently advertising with your Radio station, the manager is most likely going to leave that assignment with the current salesperson.

If the company is assigned to another salesperson, and the company is not currently advertising, ask the manager when the assignment for that business will be up for review. Tell the manager that you would very much like the opportunity to work with that company.

Ask your manager for a list of the inactive accounts, companies who advertised with the Radio station in the past, but are currently inactive, they are not advertising at present. The inactive list of accounts is a rich source of potential businesses for you to call on. There could be a wide range of reasons those companies are not currently advertising with your Radio station.

Don't let stories from other salespeople deter you from checking out this list. You may hear that those companies are mad at the Radio station for changing the programming or someone messed up the order and the commercials didn't broadcast over the air as intended. You might hear that they didn't pay their bill on time or they have bad credit. If your sales manager is willing, there are ways to deal with these circumstances. If the Radio station made the mistake that angered the customer, ask your manager if you can offer the business a remedy, perhaps a credit on a new schedule is in order. If the account was slow to pay, they could pay in advance with a credit card for future advertising.

Why Use an Account List?

This section describes the basics of account list management. If your Radio station has more stringent policies than those offered in this section, you should defer to those. If your Radio station has a more relaxed policy than our suggestions, we urge you to follow these recommendations if you want to work smarter, not harder, and start making more money sooner.

"Work expands to fill the time available for its completion." That is a proverb coined by the twentieth-century British scholar C. Northcote Parkinson, known as Parkinson's Law. It points out that people usually take all the time allotted (and frequently more) to accomplish any task. You only have so many hours each week for your professional life. You have many competing priorities to accomplish. Account list management is one of those priorities.

When you focus your efforts, they become more productive. Trying to meet too many company representatives all at once is unproductive. If you don't impose some discipline on yourself, you will surely find yourself becoming a **door-to-door advertising salesperson**, jumping from one lead to the next without thoroughly investigating each company because there seems to be an endless supply of other companies. You will surely overlook excellent opportunities.

The net result of becoming a door-to-door advertising salesperson in Radio advertising sales is an account list of short-term, low-budget high maintenance customers. The door-to-door advertising salesperson must work harder than the professional salesperson to maintain their monthly billing. They are more susceptible to high levels of account turnover and monthly billing fluctuations. They don't have a steady income. They are more stressed out. They don't enjoy the benefits of a professional selling career.

How many companies should you have on your account list? Remember the goal-setting exercises you completed in a previous section? How many average customers do you need to reach your sales goal? Was it less than thirty customers? Was it less than forty customers?

Many very successful Radio advertising salespeople make an excellent income with thirty to forty active customers every month. There is also a time management component to consider. Each lead, each prospect, and each customer require a portion of your precious limited time.

Nobody has discovered a way to create more time. Necessary account list management skills help instill the discipline you need to allocate your time wisely among your competing priorities.

Don't consider account list management as a limit on your opportunities. The account list is a tool just like the hammer is a tool for the carpenter or an oven for a baker. The account list is a tool to help you become a successful Radio advertising salesperson.

The Diversified Account List

You want to build a diversified account list beginning with the top advertising categories. First, you want a car dealer or two on your list. The **automotive category** is the single biggest advertising category on Radio. We are a mobile society. We go everywhere in our cars. For many people, their car is likely to be one of their top three assets.

Don't be discouraged if all the new car dealers have already been assigned to another salesperson; there is just as much potential in the used car dealer category. According to the National Automobile Dealers Association, there is more gross profit in used cars than in new.

The **automotive service category** is your next biggest target category. Anything that has to do with automotive service is big business, like a body shop, towing service, auto parts, tire store, quick lube, car audio, car insurance, brakes, shocks, and aftermarket accessories. Cars break down and need maintenance and people listen to Radio in the car, it's a perfect match.

The **financial category** is much more than just banks and credit unions. They are big advertisers. However, don't overlook home mortgage companies and financial planners. Consider pay-day loans and pawnshops in this category.

Advertising for the **medical category** is growing more every day. Consumers feel more empowered about their health care. They have many more options, and medical providers are aware of this. The medical category spends heavily on advertising, especially the high-profit elective services that are not covered by insurance. Doctors, Dentists, Chiropractors, Ophthalmologists, Optometrists, and Plastic Surgeons are spending lots of money on advertising. Don't forget pharmacies.

If all the hospitals in your market are already assigned to other salespeople, look to the walk-in emergency clinics. Don't overlook health spas that sell cosmetic services like Botox.

The **food category** is changing and needs advertising. Everyone needs to eat. Sit down family restaurants, quick-serve restaurants, and grocery stores are facing challenges and responding with many innovations they want to share with the public. Grocery stores now offer online ordering, curbside pickup, and home delivery. The food category is seeing foundational change and growing budgets for advertising.

Home improvement and repair is a fertile category for leads. For many people, their home is the most significant investment in life. In many cases it is more than just a building, it is a home for your family, and you want to take care of it and keep it beautiful. Look for leads in roofing, siding, windows, fencing, flooring, kitchen and bath, painting and interior design, landscaping, heating and cooling, plumbers and electricians. Make sure to include hardware stores, lawn and garden stores, and home improvement stores.

AT&T, Version, and Sprint dominate the **telecommunications category**. However, there is big business in phone accessories, phone and tablet repair

Retail is another top category. Look for leads in furniture, jewelry, clothing, florists, appliances, consumer electronics, pet supplies, sporting goods, and personal services. You will learn more about target categories later in the section on prospecting.

Account List Definitions

The following are standard account list definitions. Your Radio station may have a different list of definitions for much the same purpose. Ask your sales manager to help you merge the two meanings. Regardless of which system definitions your Radio station uses, account definitions lay the foundation of account list management. Account definitions set the stage for the selling activities required in each step of the sales pipeline. Account definitions also dictate how much time should be allocated for moving a company through the selling process.

A **lead** is just a business name or a businessperson you have identified as a possible future customer. You don't know much more than that. In some sales circles, they jokingly call a lead a **suspect**. We recommend you work with no more than 40 leads at any one time. If your Radio station imposes a lower limit, us the lower limit. This limit focuses your efforts to quickly meet the company representative and determine if there is the potential to move the company on to the next level of the selling process. If it takes you more than two contacts to discover the necessary information, that is a good indication that lead isn't going to become a prospect.

A **prospect** is a business contact who has the means to buy advertising from you and has the authority to make those buying decisions. The prospect's business needs, and your Radio station's services must also be a good match. You must be able to speak directly to the decision-maker, and they must have the means to buy the advertising; otherwise; the lead cannot become a prospect. We recommend you work with no more than ten prospects at any one time. Prospects are qualified to become customers. Don't waste any time. The prospect requires your attention to become your next new customer. If you are slow to act, they may buy their advertising from another company, and you will lose out.

A **customer** is a business who is actively buying advertising from you. You should be able to have as many customers on your list as your time management skills will allow.

However, customers still require your time and attention. You will need to see your customers regularly as you **service the account**.

If a customer stops advertising with you, they are no longer a customer. Your Radio station may have a time limit on how long a customer can remain inactive before they force a change in assignment. In this training, if the customer stops advertising with you and you don't have a viable advertising plan for the future, you should reclassify the customer as a prospect so you can restart the selling process.

A **seasonal account** is a company that only buys advertising on a **seasonal** basis like a haunted house or a fireworks stand. Don't fill up your account list with seasonal accounts. The definition system exists to organize your selling efforts. The seasonal definition does not apply to a jewelry store that only buys advertising at Christmas or a hardware store that only buys advertising for the county fair.

The Sales Timeline

In professional selling, the salesperson doesn't wait for things to happen. If you want to be successful, **you must make things happen, and happen on time**. If your Radio station is using a Customer Relationship Management (CRM) program, a sales timeline is likely built right into the software. The sales timeline, sometimes called the sales pipeline, is a reminder to get things done on time. A CRM system won't let companies remain on your account list very long without any sales activities.

The RAB Account Manager from the Radio Advertising Bureau is a CRM program with a sales timeline built into the essential functions. ACT!, GoldMine and Salesforce are CRM tools.

Ten Days to Work a Lead

When you first find a company, you would like to try to sell; you put that company name on your account list in the RAB Account Manager **as a lead**. You have ten days to go and meet your new lead and begin the discovery process. If you don't record any activity with the new lead in the RAB Account Manager CRM system within the first ten days, the system will automatically remove your new lead from your list and return it to the open list.

The action of moving the lead from your list back to the open list if there is no recorded activity within ten days is an example of machine-imposed discipline. Keep in mind; computers don't think on their own. They follow the programmer's instructions. Computer programs are designed to help automate the management philosophy of the company. The design philosophy in the RAB Account Manager assumes no activity within ten days means there is not enough interest or motivation on your part to act quickly. Moving a lead back to the open list after ten days of no activity is not a unique business philosophy. Whether it is ten days or 20 days, it is in your best interest to move quickly.

Professional advertising salespeople don't need a computer program to tell them to act fast. It is a matter of self-discipline. Professional salespeople are not in the waiting business. If you wait more than ten days to make your first contact, some other advertising salesperson is more likely to get the sale than you.

If you find a new company, that new company becomes a lead until you can determine if you can **talk to the decision-maker**, they have **the means necessary to buy advertising**, and **your services are a good match**. You must quickly assess the potential of your new lead. If there is no potential, you want to remove the lead from your list and replace it with another. If you find that you can meet the decision-maker, they have the means, and your services make a good match, that company **changes from a *lead*** and **becomes a *prospect***. The RAB Account Manager (and other CRMs) does not automatically change the designation from a *lead* to a *prospect*. You must always make the change yourself to manage your target of 40 leads and ten prospects on your account list.

60 Days to Work a Prospect

When you record your first activity within ten days and change the designation from a lead to a prospect, the RAB Account Manager will then start another timer. This time, you have 60 days in which to make a sale. If you don't make a sale within 60 days, then the RAB Account Manager will automatically move that business name from your account list and back to the open list. The design in the RAB Account Manager assumes that if you can't make a sale in 60 days, then a deal isn't possible, or you haven't been applying yourself as thoroughly as you should.

The suggested account list target of 40 leads and ten prospects implies that more time should be devoted to developing a prospect into a customer than the time needed to convert a lead into a prospect. If you find that your contact at the company has the authority to enter into an advertising agreement and has the means to pay for it, **and** you make a good fit, you need to proceed with the sales process in quick fashion while the opportunity presents itself. If you wait, another advertising salesperson may get the sale instead of you.

Most CRM systems will notify you of upcoming deadlines. If your 60 days with a prospect is about to expire, you will get a notification that time is nearly up. If you need additional time to complete the sale, you can go and ask your sales manager for an extension. However, before they decide to give you an extension, they will likely check your recorded activities in the CRM system from recent weeks to see if your activity warrants an extension of time.

If your Radio station doesn't have a CRM system, you can self-impose a similar schedule. Ten weeks is a generous sales pipeline for a professional Radio advertising salesperson. Ten weeks will go by in the blink of an eye for the poorly trained and poorly prepared salesperson. You, not them, will make the sale when you exercise discipline and focus.

A Word About Seasonal Accounts

Many Radio stations do a robust business in what they might call **seasonal advertising**. Some seasonal advertising is better than others. A fireworks stand, or a haunted house is a one-time-only opportunity.

Sponsorships to the county fair sold to the local hardware store might offer the opportunity for year-round advertising. Consistent annual advertising customers are what you need to build a successful career in Radio advertising sales.

Seasonal advertising clients may appear to be an easier sale than the annual customer because they want to advertise right now before time runs out.

Don't fall into the trap of moving from one seasonal sales activity to the next. That is the first step on the slippery slope of becoming a door-to-door advertising salesperson. You may think you are making professional progress, but you will quickly find that you work harder than you need to and earn less than you deserve.

Your Radio station may need everyone in the sales department to work on a short-term revenue-generating effort to close a revenue shortfall, and, you need to pitch in. However, always approach any selling opportunity looking for the long-term potential of your efforts. Search for the long-term potential in all you do.

Summary

In this chapter on Building Your Account List, we covered the following topics:

- The Radio station maintains a list of companies called **the master account list**. The account list will include companies that are presently advertising, companies that advertised in the past but not currently, and companies who have never advertised with your Radio station.
- The account list indicates which salesperson is assigned to sell and service each company. There are some companies on the list that do not have a salesperson attached. That list is called the **unassigned** or **open list**.
- How is the company master list curated at your Radio station?
- What are the account assignment procedures at your Radio station?
  - How do you lose a lead?
  - How do you claim a new lead?
  - How much time do you get with each lead?
- The economic benefit of building a diversified portfolio of accounts.
- The benefit of prospecting beyond the obvious retail category.
- The sales timeline or sales pipeline.
  - Customer Relationship Management (CRM) systems
  - How much time should you devote to developing a lead?

- Don't consider account list management as a limit on your opportunities. The account list is a tool just like the hammer is a tool for the carpenter or an oven for a baker. The account list is a tool to help you become a successful Radio advertising salesperson.

"84% of people trust recommendations from people they know. Making them the most influential form of advertising." – *The Nielsen Company*

6

Prospecting

The most critical phase of a professional selling process is prospecting. Without a prospect, all the other steps are mostly useless.

We begin our lesson with the definition of prospecting. Here are some examples for you to consider:

Sales prospecting is the act of recruiting or seeking out new customers for a business. Prospecting is a common role of a salesperson. It is associated with the goal of increasing the customer base of the company and generating new revenue streams.

The search for potential customers or buyers.

Prospecting is the first step in the sales process, which consists of identifying potential customers, aka prospects. The goal of prospecting is to develop a database of likely customers and then systematically communicate with them in the hopes of converting them from potential customer to current customer.

Someone once said 'you have to kiss a lot of frogs before you find your prince' -- and in prospecting, you often need to talk to a lot of people before you find a customer who will buy from you.

Prospecting is a necessary task for many salespeople who need to replace customers who do not return and find new customers to grow and sustain the business.

Prospecting and lead generation is where it all begins in sales. Finding new businesses to call on is the lifeblood of your sales career. Developing efficient and effective prospecting techniques is critical to your success.

In his book, *Fanatical Prospecting*, author Jeb Blount writes:

The path to superstar-level success in sales is brutally simple. Simple, mind you, not easy. It's a Paradox of Basics: A truth that is so blatantly obvious it has become impossibly invisible. A truth that remains frustratingly elusive for most salespeople, causing so many promising, intelligent, talented people to fail miserably in sales, and, likewise, businesses to close their doors and entrepreneurs to crash and burn.[8]

The difference between the top 20 percent of high-performance salespeople and those that struggle just to survive is their ability to out prospect the rest of the field.

While we don't like to think about it, customers will, can and do go away for a variety of reasons. Some go out of business. Some get bought out by a competitor with whom you have no relationship. Some are wooed away by your competitors. However, do everything in your power to never lose a customer through poor customer service.

If you want to be successful in sales and see your income grow, you will need a systematic way of finding and developing new customers. **You must have a growth mindset about prospecting, motivated every day to find qualified prospects**. The top salespeople enthusiastically prospect for new clients by calling on the phone, emailing, networking, sending letters, asking for referrals, and attending Chamber events. They don't make excuses or complain. They don't hesitate to prospect regardless of how good or how bad the economy may be.

Prospecting and lead generation is also the key to an unlimited income in sales. As you develop an account list of active customers, you will find more and more pressure on your time management skills. You will need to sell and service your new customers in such a way to have enough time to get all your competing priorities completed on time. You will learn more about proper time management skills and compatible selling techniques later in another module.

Your Radio station's ratings or your territory are not the cause of sales failure. Your lack of training or experience is not the cause of sales failure. **Poor prospecting and an inadequate sales pipeline are the leading cause of sales failure.** You could work for the number one rated Radio station in your market, you could have the best presentation ever seen, but if you don't have a prospect, you are out of business.

Most people don't like to prospect. They don't like rejection. Prospecting can be hard; you may need to contact a lot of people to find just one good prospect. But that is the tipping

---

[8] Blount, Jeb. *Fanatical Prospecting* (Wiley, 2015) 2

point between the top performers and those that just get by. **Top performers prospect even when they don't feel like prospecting!**

The entrepreneur Jim Rhon once said, **"Don't wish it was easier, wish you were better. Don't wish for less problems, wish for more skills. Don't wish for less challenge, wish for more wisdom."** That is the attitude of a salesperson with a growth mindset.

The exciting thing about being in Radio sales is that your product, **Radio advertising, is and can be used by almost every kind of company**. This widespread acceptance means you have a wider variety of people to call on as opposed to a tool salesperson who can only sell tools to body shops and service stations. Because a wide range of business types use Radio advertising, you can develop a **diversified portfolio of customers** and protect yourself from the ups and downs of the economy.

Just like when you invest your money in the stock market, having a diversified portfolio can help insulate you from the ups and downs in the marketplace. For example, if you were an insulation salesperson for Owens Corning, you might see a decline in sales when the housing market slows down. If you were a salesperson for GoodYear, you might suffer a setback in sales when automotive manufacturing slows down.

As a Radio salesperson, you can sell advertising to a wide variety of business types, so your income isn't directly tied to any one single area of the economy. When you have a diversified portfolio of advertising customers, you are protected from weakness in one business sector by having customers in other business sectors less affected by the economy.

During the Great Recession, a wide range of business categories were affected by the economy, most notably, housing and automotive. However, other advertising categories, like medical and legal, remained quite stable.

When you study the history of advertising, you will find that the very best brands were advertising in both good times and bad. Sure, all categories have their ups and downs, but the most well-known brands realize they must be consistent with their advertising plans. Just like an investor in the stock market, you need to have a diversified portfolio of advertisers. If one sector of business is down, you have customers in other industries that are doing better. You don't want to be *overweight* in any given category. When you have a balanced portfolio of customers, then you will start to see your business in advertising grow consistently.

The 90 Day Rule

You will soon learn that the Radio advertising sales business is a 90-day business. What you are doing today, you will reap in about 90 days. What you are experiencing today is the result of your actions 90 days ago. If you find yourself in a sales slump, you can probably trace the origins of your slump back to the work you were doing three months ago. That's why you need a disciplined daily plan of activities from all phases of the selling process.

When you are new in **Professional Radio Advertising Sales**, you will be prospecting most of the time because you don't have a client list built up. But as you make progress and gain some clients, your day will be filled with other necessary activities. That's when you are likely to cut back or eliminate your prospecting efforts. It won't seem like such a big deal because you're busy with your new clients. But about three months later, 90 days out, you'll start to feel the effects of a dwindling pipeline. You'll find it hard to make sales because you don't have any prospects.

If you're not careful, you could start to lose your enthusiasm for your new job. It will be easy to blame someone or something else for your slump. You will begin to hope for something to happen when you should be getting back to prospecting. Jeb Blount blames this downward spiral on the *Universal Law of Need*.

It states that the more you need something, the less likely it is that you will get it. This law comes into play in sales when lack of activity has left your pipeline depleted. When all of your hope for survival rests on one, two, or even a handful of accounts, the probability of failure increases exponentially[9].

Getting Started with Prospecting

Prospecting for new customers in Radio Advertising Sales is wide open. Almost every company you see in your market could benefit from Radio advertising. The problem is that many of the people you call on for the very first time have had a bad experience with advertising before. As you will learn in the Four Keys to Advertising Success®, many local business owners have tried to learn about advertising the hard way, through the school of hard knocks. They paid dearly for their mistakes because the money lost came right out of their pockets.

Don't be surprised at the adverse reaction you get from some local business owners when you first approach them about advertising. This training will teach you practical techniques for building a bridge with dissatisfied business owners.

Even if you can't build that bridge, don't let that discourage you. There are plenty of local business owners you can call on and still make a very nice living selling Radio advertising.

Referral Prospecting

Unlike other sales training where referral prospecting is something you do after you have some customers, in *Professional Radio Advertising Sales*, **prospecting with referrals is a front-line tactic to accelerate your success**. The return on your activity investment is far higher when you prospect with referrals over other outbound marketing tools.

---

[9] Blount, Jeb. *Fanatical Prospecting* (Wiley 2015) 26

Prospecting with referrals is among the most valuable prospecting methods to generate new leads in Professional Radio Advertising Sales. A sales referral takes place when someone provides you with the name and contact information of somebody; they know that might benefit from your advertising services.

Instead of just cold-calling for leads, calling with a referral allows you to contact the new person while mentioning the name of the referral source, helping you establish a connection that could lead to an appointment.

Selling with referrals is the best way of building trust with new customers. When your customer refers you to one of their acquaintances, that new lead is more likely to trust you and your brand.

The Value of Referrals

According to the Edelman Trust Barometer, **84% of B2B decision-makers start the buying process with a referral**.

The 2015 Nielsen Global Trust in Advertising report indicates **83% of respondents trust recommendations from people they know**.

Heinze Marketing of Seattle surveyed more than 600 B2B companies in North America to learn more about the benefits of referral selling. Those companies with an active referral selling process see impressive results.

- 71% report higher conversions rates.
- 59% report higher lifetime customer value.
- 69% report faster time to close

That's why you want to master the skill of referral selling. Referrals are the best leads you can get. Selling with referrals will speed up your sales pipeline and help you sell more advertising more quickly. You will be way ahead of your competition when you do. The Heinze study found that only 30% of the B2B companies surveyed have a formalized referral program!

If referral selling is so effective, why don't more B2B salespeople use referral selling? In a word, fear. Many salespeople are afraid to ask for a referral. They tell me, "I just feel weird about it" or "It feels too pushy." Some also think a referral request might suggest they're desperate or not doing well.

In her book, *No More Cold Calling*, author Joanne Black writes,

I discovered that there are four reasons that prevent companies from using their most powerful potential sales strategy.

1. It's a new skill. There aren't a lot of salespeople who know how to ask for referrals in a way that gets them immediately in front of the people they want to meet.

2. People are uncomfortable with the idea of asking others for referrals. They feel that they may jeopardize a relationship, that it feels pushy, or that the other person might say no.
3. They aren't aware that there are metrics for referrals, as there is for cold calling, direct mail, and advertising.
4. They don't have a disciplined process or methodology to support referral selling – from incorporating referrals into their sales process to rewarding and compensating people for referral activities.[10]

In Radio advertising selling, when you ask for referrals from your customers, your next new customer could be just one phone call or one meeting away. You want to get into the habit of asking for referrals right from the start of your new selling career.

Don't Be Afraid to Ask

Being afraid to ask for a referral is silly. In the profession of selling, you are always asking, always inquiring. So why is it scary to ask for a referral. We're asking someone to vouch for us. That's why it is so important to follow the path of the professional salesperson. When you build your relationships based on trust, and you deliver what you promise, it's not too much to ask. For people to connect you to others that they know, you must be willing to ask for the referral.

Don't ask for a referral; ask for an introduction. People are willing to help other people, especially when they already know and like you. Start by saying, "I was wondering if I could get your help with something?" When you do that, you set the stage for a productive chat and leave the other person feeling good about helping you out.

Always ask for a referral in person. Don't ask for a referral in an email or through social media. You want to find out how well your customer knows the referral before you proceed. You need to determine if you can help the new prospect in much the same way you helped your new customer.

Be specific about the referrals. Don't just ask your new customer if they know anyone else who could use some advertising. Too many salespeople say, "So who do you know? Who do you think might be interested in what I have to offer?" Don't put the burden on the person helping you. You should be specific about what type of introduction you want. Have a list of high-value prospects you want to meet. Try to determine if your new customer can introduce you to anyone on your list.

Ask for Referrals Every Day

Make referral selling a daily activity. Ask for one introduction per day. Don't think that is a lot of work. How long does it take to ask for a single introduction? You can ask for a referral in just a few minutes. Learn to make asking for referrals a daily activity. Don't cheat. Record and

---

[10] Black, Joanne S. *No More Cold Calling* (Warner Business Books 2012) 18-19

track your referral selling efforts. If you ask for one referral every day, you ask for five each week or 250 per year. How many new customers could you find with 250 referrals?

Keep your referral source in the loop. Your referral source can help you determine how persistent you should be with the person they referred. If you have trouble reaching the referral or they seem unresponsive, let your referral source know. They will help you understand how to proceed without hurting any relationships and will appreciate you considering their perspective.

Leverage Your Entire Network

Consider asking everyone you know for a referral. Don't restrict your search for referrals to just businesspeople you know when you ask for referrals, think about all the people who know you and what you do. Your current advertisers are the first place to look. They are a great source of referrals because they are currently advertising with you. It gives you a reason to stop by or call.

Your past customers, industry connections, former and present colleagues, friends, family members, social acquaintances, friends of friends -- everyone is fair game. The more people you ask, the more referrals you'll get, plain and simple.

Never take referrals for granted as an *easy* sale. Remember that relationships are very personal, and making deep connections takes some hard work. Referral skills should be treated as a business asset, and you should work toward improving your skills.

Always send a handwritten thank you note to the referral source for the introduction. Little things mean a lot, and they do make a difference.

Referrals for the New Salesperson

You're brand new to the Radio station. You don't have any current customers. How do you start prospecting by referrals? Author and sales trainer Joanne Black writes, "You are your own channel for more business."[11] You can activate your own referral network by first referring a lead to someone else. Maybe you refer your dry cleaner to a friend because they stained their new blouse. Perhaps you refer your accountant to someone who is having trouble with their taxes. Starting the referral process will encourage other people to refer people back to you who might need advertising. It's the **Law of Reciprocity**.

My friend Jerry Adams was a salesperson in Wichita, Kansas at KFDI AM & FM. Jerry came to the sales department from the programming department. Jerry was an expert at referral prospecting. He had collected more business cards than just about any other salesperson I know. If Jerry was on a sales call and his prospect had a need unrelated to advertising, Jerry was quick to offer a referral to one of his other contacts who could help. In addition to being known as a good guy and a referral source, I came to realize that Jerry was sometimes clearing the way for

---

[11] Black, Joanne S. *No More Cold Calling* (Warner Business Books 2012) 46

his original prospect to say "Yes" to his advertising proposal, once the other business issue was resolved.

Jerry realized that when he heard a "No" from a prospect, it might just mean "No, not now." Sometimes other pressing business needs take so much of the prospect's attention; they can't decide about his advertising proposal until the other issue is cleared up. Since Jerry helped resolve the issue, the prospect saw Jerry as a problem solver, not just a salesperson.

Jerry wasn't expected to be a success at sales when he started, but he surprised everyone with his tenacity and held a top position in the sales department year after year. Prospecting with referrals was one of his strong suits. You can make prospecting with referrals one of your strong suits if you learn how at the beginning of your new profession.

Networking

Perhaps you have heard people say that selling involves a lot of cold-calling. In some selling jobs that is true. In Radio advertising sales, it doesn't have to be that way. You are selling B2B (business to business) advertising services to companies in your community. You can attend business events and network with people in your town, allowing you to meet other local businesspeople outside of their office, where you might get the chance to introduce yourself. Next time you call, you won't be a stranger.

Selling is about making connections. Your success as a salesperson depends on your ability to interact with others. Networking generates business leads and yields significant rewards. The salesperson who invests time to networking finds they can make lots of first-time sales calls without the need to cold-call.

Networking lets you meet other businesspeople in your community, but it can also help you become known for what you do — volunteer with publicity and other activities in the groups which you belong.

It might take a long time to nurture a new contact into a new customer. Other times, you might meet someone who is in immediate need for some marketing help. The key benefit of networking is the prospect has met you face-to-face. You have some credibility when you call for an appointment. Just make a regular commitment to networking activities, even if they are outside of your daily work hours. Networking will open doors and help you build relationships.

Tips for Networking

Effective networking requires that you be outgoing and willing to meet new people, get out of your comfort zone. If this scares you a little, think about what you bring to a networking event. Why do businesspeople attend networking activities? They want to meet **new leads**! What business are you in? **You are in the new leads business!** Every other person at the networking event represents only one possible connection. But in your case, you represent thousands of new business connections, the people listening to your Radio station.

When someone asks what you do, tell them you're in the new leads business. "How many new leads would you like?"

Companies are always looking for new business leads. There is an entire industry of lead list vendors selling lists of leads to local companies. They buy a list of leads, and then they must reach out with a telephone call, a letter, or an email.

But your list of leads is much higher quality. **The leads on your list like your Radio station. They trust your Radio station. They respond to what your Radio station tells them.** And for a small fee, you'll be happy to tell your audience about your new networking friend's company.

Be sure to smile and make eye-contact. That puts other people at ease when they look your way. Invest in a professional-looking name tag and wear it where it can easily be seen. If someone recognizes your face from a previous event, but can't remember your name, they won't feel so awkward.

Dress professionally. First impressions last a long time, and they do make a difference.

Don't come on too strong. You're not there to sell. You're there to network. Enjoy yourself and see what happens.

Zig Ziglar reminds us, **"Selling Isn't Telling."**[12] That's especially true at a networking event. There will be plenty of time later for a sales presentation. For now, at the networking event, you are on a mission to meet people and learn about them. Listen! Ask genuine questions and then, listen. People love to tell their stories. Turn off your need to tell your story. The story you hear at a networking event is the material you can use later when you call and try to get an appointment.

Ask for business cards, but only offer your card if someone asks for it.

Join the Chamber of Commerce

Joining the Chamber of Commerce should be your first step in prospecting. The Chamber of Commerce in your market is organized to promote economic growth. Advertising supports economic growth. Chamber members tend to be the most active businesspeople in your community.

Once you join, you need to participate. Go to the ribbon-cutting ceremonies. Attend the lead exchange groups. Take part in seminars and workshops. Go to the after-hours social mixers.

---

[12] Ziglar, Zig. *Secretes of Closing the Sale.* (Revell 2003) 313

Just by participating, you will meet businesspeople who know other businesspeople. Better yet, those businesspeople will get to know you.

Join a Networking Group

Networking is such a useful tool for meeting new business contacts; networking groups have formed to facilitate the process. Some of these groups will meet once a week, perhaps at breakfast or lunch. Part of the meeting involves each member standing and offering a tip on a new business they have encountered. Most networking groups only allow one member from each industry, so you probably won't see any of your competitors in the group.

Prospecting in Civic Groups

Businesspeople join civic groups as a way of giving back to the community and networking. You must give something first before you can take something from membership in a civic group. If handled poorly, you will be perceived as a user, not a giver, and you will quickly be ostracized from the group.

If you join a civic group with networking in mind, make sure you join a civic group, you would join even if networking were not a benefit. You need to belong to a group that you genuinely want to belong to for the mission of the group and nothing else. Networking in a civic group takes time and must be done with finesse.

Prospecting Who and What You Know

There is nothing wrong with prospecting companies where you know the owner, or you are currently a customer. That's a great place to start.

Don't overlook your personal experience. If you grew up in a family business or you've worked in a field before, that previous experience could be very beneficial for you. However, be careful not to fall into the trap of telling the customer what to do just because you have some experience in that field. You will lose all credibility. They are still in that line of business, and you are not. Your previous experience can help you understand what the prospect is going through more than anything. The prospect won't see you as an expert in the field; they will see you as an advertising expert that understands his business better than the other advertising salespeople.

Prospecting by Category

Even though virtually every business category uses advertising, there are some categories more inclined to buy Radio advertising. We discussed this earlier in the chapter on building your account list. The concept of prospecting by category begins with identifying the most fruitful categories for Radio advertising and then digging deep within that category for new leads.

The biggest spending category for local Radio advertising is automotive. You can segregate the automotive category by cars or trucks, foreign or domestic, new or used. As a new salesperson, you may find that the biggest names in the automotive category are already spoken for by another salesperson. But by digging deep within the category, you will discover leads to call.

It is to your advantage to dig deep into the valuable categories first before searching for leads in more obscure and less valuable categories.

Automotive service is also a big-spending category for Radio advertising. You can divide the automotive service category into many different subcategories, engine, and transmission, tires and suspension, body repair, maintenance, car stereo, and more.

Home Depot was the single biggest advertiser on Radio in 2018. For a homeowner, their home represents an immense investment, both financially and personally. Consequently, homeowners spend money on home improvement and maintenance. You can subdivide **the home improvement category** into general contractors, roofing, siding, window, fencing, flooring, kitchen, and bath remodeling, basement repair, landscaping, and more.

The medical category is a growing category for Radio advertising. You can break this category down into services covered by insurance or elective services, meaning the patient pays for the entire cost of the procedure. Elective procedures such as cosmetic dentistry are very profitable for the dentist, and the category spends vast amounts of money on advertising. Purchases within the elective medical procedure category tend to be emotionally driven by the consumer's desire to improve their physical appearance.

The Radio Advertising Bureau has a weekly report for subscribers called the RAB Prospecting Report. The report summarizes member category research on the site. This report gives you an idea of what other Radio salespeople are looking for at www.rab.com.

Another member-only report is the RAB Top 40 Business Survey. The survey uses a three-year average of the US Department of Commerce data to show business trends for 40 key advertiser categories. The document identifies the monthly percentage of business transacted by category.

Prospecting Online

In prospecting, it's not necessarily who you know that is so important, it is more **who knows you** that takes priority. But take that thought to the next level and adopt for yourself this guiding principle in your networking efforts, it is **who knows you and who knows what you do** that is the most profitable strategy.

With the Internet and social media, it is common practice to **check people out online**. People that you meet will inevitably look for you on social media to learn more about you. Make sure your online presence is professional enough to leave a positive impression.

LinkedIn is a social network for business professionals. It has many of the same features as other social media sites, but **professional businesspeople use LinkedIn for business networking**.

LinkedIn is the online equivalent of attending a traditional networking event where you attend to meet other businesspeople. You can search for leads on LinkedIn and find out a little bit about them before you make your first initial contact. The first thing you see beneath their profile picture on their home page is a section called Highlights. Here you will find the mutual LinkedIn connections you and that person share. It's like playing the game *Six Degrees of Kevin Bacon*. In many cases, you and the person you're researching know some of the same people.

Many people on LinkedIn list the university they graduated from, the professional associations they belong to, and specific business interests. This information can be beneficial if you're looking for something you may have in common. As you scroll down their home page, you will see their previous work experience, skills, endorsements, and interests.

You connect with other people on LinkedIn using the connect button located in the profile section of the user's home page. This process allows you to introduce yourself with a brief personalized message, more than just the standard greeting provided by LinkedIn. With LinkedIn's private messenger, you can connect with other professionals and even talk a little about what you do.

Anyone interested in advancing their professional life, looking for new opportunities and connect with other professionals should be using LinkedIn.

Take some time to polish up your profile with a new professional looking photograph. Update your work experience, education, and interests. Ask some of your connections to endorse you for the skills you want to promote. Return the favor. Write a recommendation for some of your contacts so they will write one for you. RAIN Group research found **82% of buyers look up a vendor on LinkedIn before they respond to their outreach efforts**.

LinkedIn offers the opportunity for you to publish an article. **You can use LinkedIn as a blogging platform**. The article function is different than short posts to your timeline. At the top of your page, just below **Start a post**, you will find a link to **Write an article**. Writing an article or using LinkedIn as a blogging platform helps you establish an online presence as an expert in your field. If you are prospecting a new lead, check and see if that person has posted any articles. Knowing that could be an **icebreaker** when you make your initial contact.

LinkedIn provides users the ability to start and join special interest groups, where members congregate around specific topics. These special interest groups are a place for you to meet with people and get to know their interests.

Keep in mind; computer programmers want your eyes glued to the computer screen for as long as possible. That's how they make money. Regulate your time spent on LinkedIn to a specific time of the day and only for as long as you have planned. The seductive nature of social media can pull you in, and before you know it, hours have passed. As with everything you do in your professional advertising sales career, carefully guard your time because you have many competing priorities to manage. **Don't let LinkedIn become a drag on your time**.

Prospecting Sources

Where do you prospect for new leads? Here is a list of suggestions.

- Newspaper
- Broadcast TV
- Cable TV (there is a difference)
- Direct Mail (you get a lot at home)
- Billboard
- Radio
- Referrals from existing customers
- Referrals from non-customers
- Linked In
- Facebook

- Google
- Yelp
- YP.Com
- Radio Advertising Bureau
- Yellow Pages
- Lead groups
- Civic organizations
- Category Specific
- Shoppers – Thrifty Nickle
- ValPac

Can you think of any additional sources?

Just because a business is advertising in the newspaper or another medium, doesn't mean they will be eager to buy Radio advertising from you. Many times, the business owner has settled into advertising in a medium as a result of their previous costly advertising efforts. They have decided through their own experiences that the current advertising they are doing is the right advertising for them. They don't want to be convinced that something else is better because they have been down that road before; they spent their money and didn't get the results they were expecting.

As your training progresses, you will learn practical techniques for building a bridge with these business owners that can lead to them making **a new decision** about Radio advertising.

Remember the diversified portfolio concept when prospecting. You want to strive to have at least one business from all the major advertising categories on your active account list. You want a car dealer, a bank, a credit union, a furniture store, a grocery store, a doctor, a lawyer, a restaurant and so on.

Summary

In this chapter on Prospecting, we covered the following topics:

- Sales prospecting is the act of recruiting or seeking out new customers for a business. Prospecting is a traditional role of a salesperson.

- Prospecting is associated with the goal of increasing the customer base of the company and generating new revenue streams.
- The concept of prospecting by category begins with identifying the most fruitful categories for Radio advertising and then digging deep within that category for new leads.
- Prospecting for new customers in Radio Advertising Sales is wide open. Almost every business you see in your market could benefit from Radio advertising.
- Networking generates business leads and yields significant rewards. The salesperson who invests time to networking finds they can make many first-time sales calls without the need to cold-call.
- Joining the local Chamber of Commerce.
- If you join a civic group with networking in mind, make sure you join a civic group that you would join even if networking were not a benefit.
- There is nothing wrong with prospecting companies where you know the owner, or you are currently a customer. That's a great place to start.

"A lot of times, people don't know what they want until you show it to them." – *Steve Jobs*, Entrepreneur. (1955 – 2011)

7

Qualifying a Lead

You've done some prospecting, and you made a list of some business names you think might make a good lead, now it is time to see if the lead is qualified to buy some advertising from you.

What do you know about this lead? Are they the decision-maker? Do they have the authority to enter into a binding advertising agreement? Do they have the financial means to buy your advertising proposal? Have you uncovered a specific reason for the lead to advertise? These are critical fundamental questions to which you need answers. You need to gather as much of this information before you make your first approach.

Without some basic information about your lead, you could waste valuable time chasing down a bunch of dead ends, all the while thinking you are productive in your qualifying efforts. But where do you start?

Start with name, address, phone number, email, website, LinkedIn, Facebook, Instagram, and a basic Google search.

Earlier, you learned that there are leads, prospects, and customers. You also learned that lead and prospect are sometimes erroneously interchanged. We will review each one again.

Review, Lead, Prospect, Customer

A **lead** is just a business name or a businessperson you have identified as a possible future customer. You don't know much more than that. In some sales circles, they call a lead a suspect.

A **prospect** is a business contact who has the means to buy advertising from you and has the authority to make those buying decisions. A good prospect's need and your Radio station's services must also be a good match.

A **customer** is a business who is actively buying advertising from you. If a customer stops advertising with you, they are no longer a customer. They are now a prospect again. They remain a prospect until they buy from you again.

You must be able to speak directly to the decision-maker; otherwise; the lead cannot become a prospect. The lead must have the means to buy the advertising; otherwise; the lead cannot become a prospect.

The Consequences of Poor Qualifying

You will find in advertising sales that many leads appear as if they have the authority to make buying decisions when, in fact, they don't. They may even have a title that signifies some authority when, in reality; they are just a gatekeeper with a title. It is their job to say "No." They can't say "Yes" without permission. That is not a lead that is authorized to make buying decisions. You must develop the discipline to recognize the lead is not going to become a prospect. You must be talking to those who have the authority to sign on the dotted line.

Having the means to buy advertising from you is essential to becoming a qualified prospect. They must have enough money to buy the right advertising plan from you. They must have enough money to buy a consistent schedule with enough reach and frequency, combined with an emotionally engaging commercial, that will build their brand name and attract new customers.

The poorly trained and poorly organized salesperson who doesn't recognize this fact will attempt to create a very small advertising package to fit the lead's so-called **advertising budget**. They are just filling orders instead of proposing solutions. This practice leads to a lot of very small contracts and lots of service work, which in the end will prevent you from ever reaching your desired income goals.

That's why you were asked in an earlier chapter to ask your sales manager for the Radio station's average order.

Qualifying Research

Before you attempt to make your first contact with a new lead, recognize this unfortunate fact; far too many salespeople just pick up the phone or walk into the business, and start making their pitch and citing one reason after another why the lead should buy some advertising. Most salespeople don't devote the time necessary to **develop a *why* for the call**.

Sales trainers like to talk about closing the sale. **You can't close something that has yet to open**. You will find that many leads are closed to the idea of buying advertising. An unprofessional approach, an approach without any fundamental research, only locks that lead's door to advertising even more.

Your pre-call research is the key that can help you unlock the door to that lead and possibly begin a conversation that leads to a new customer. The goal of doing your research is to develop a valid reason for your call. Why are you calling? Why should the lead give you the time of day? Without a good **why**, it's easy for the lead to say they are not interested and rebuff your approach. With a good **why**, you trigger the lead's interest in hearing you out. You can get an appointment. They may even buy some advertising.

In House Research

Start by checking the Radio station's master list to see if someone has been in contact with the lead in the past. Double-check with your traffic and billing department and ask if they know anything about the lead. If the lead has previous experience with your company, they may be able to share with you any past business history.

If there is a previous history, you want to know about their previous contracts. You want to get copies of their previous commercials. You also want to learn if anyone knows why your lead is no longer a customer. Did the relationship fall through the cracks because of a change in a salesperson? Did the Radio station mess up the advertising schedule? Was there a problem in billing? Did they pay their bill?

If you find there is a story behind your lead's previous business experiences with you Radio station, don't be too quick to discard the lead out of fear or reliving those past bad experiences. Perhaps the previous salesperson is to blame for whatever the situation is, and the lead is fully qualified and willing to buy advertising from you. Nobody has bothered to ask.

In most Radio stations, there are former customers that salespeople don't call on out of fear of rejection based on their fear of the past circumstances between the lead and your Radio station. Before you know it, years have passed since the last attempt to contact your lead. Try to gather as much information as possible and try to make your own decision.

Many successful salespeople earn big commissions by focusing on previous advertisers who, for whatever reason, stopped advertising with your Radio station. The previous activity is an excellent reason to be calling your lead. You have at least one subject that you can discuss, the previous business relationship. It can be very informative for you to go and talk to this lead. You may find that the lead hardly remembers the incident that caused the relationship to end. You may find that they still want to advertise. It was the previous salesperson that blew the incident out of proportion. Maybe there is a new decision-maker.

Your pre-call research within the Radio station may uncover many legitimate reasons to pass on this lead. As it turns out, it may require too much effort to rehabilitate the relationship between the client and your Radio station. Perhaps your Radio station had to use legal means to collect the bill. Maybe the Radio station never got paid at all. Perhaps the lead doesn't have any money to advertise.

It is possible, despite the adverse reports, your sales manager has a plan for that lead, and all they've been waiting for is a new salesperson like you to work up the courage to call on the lead and work a plan to reestablish the business relationship and start doing business again.

Pre-Call Research by Category

Earlier, you learned about building your account list based on categories such as car dealers, auto service, medical professionals, etcetera. By prospecting for leads within certain categories, your pre-call research for one lead in the category is all pre-call research for other leads in the same category.

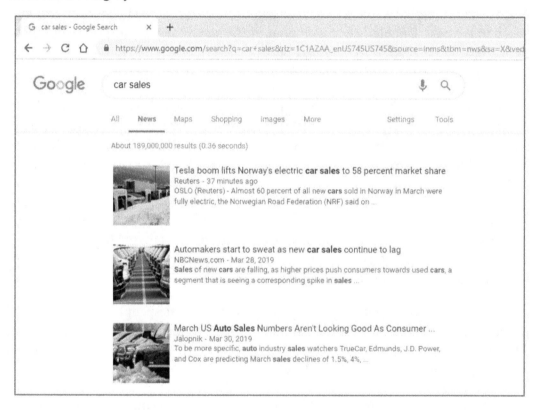

FIGURE 5

Pre-call research has never been easier. With the Internet, you can quickly search for industry and lead specific research. Google even has a search function that will scan just for news articles based on your search criteria.

You type in a search term, it this example, the term is *car sales* and press enter. The first list of results will be under the **All** tab. The **News** tab is just to the right. When you click on that, Google returns a list of news articles (Figure 5). The more specific you are with your original search term, the more precise the results you'll get back from Google.

Go to the lead's website. The website is an electronic brochure. The company is trying to put its best foot forward on their website in hopes of attracting new customers. Their website is their sales pitch in an electronic form. Check the site for recent press releases. Many websites have a page labeled *About* that contains some background about the lead and the company. Look at the *Contact Us* section to make sure you have the correct address and phone number. Make sure you're calling the right person. You can learn a lot about what is important to your lead from looking at their website.

As you gather your initial research about your new lead, **you should be developing your** *why* **for making your initial contact**. You need to assemble enough basic knowledge about the lead and their business to have a foundation for a conversation. Your foundational knowledge will give you the mental strength to talk **with** and **not to** your lead.

You will see that your pre-call research pays off as the conversation goes beyond the initial greetings and starts to become a true interaction because you appear to have some working knowledge of what your lead is experiencing. You seem to be informed, and that helps you open the door a little bit more for an appointment, the Customer Needs Assessment interview, the presentation, and the eventual sales agreement.

The time you invest in your pre-call research will pay handsome dividends down the road. You will be building an account list of companies that come to trust you as an advertising resource they can rely on for help instead of just some person who sells Radio advertising.

Summary

In this chapter on Qualifying, we covered the following topics:

- You've done some prospecting, and you have made a list of some business names you think might make a good lead, are they qualified to buy some advertising from you?
- Without some basic information about your lead, you could waste valuable time chasing down a bunch of dead ends all the while thinking you are productive in your qualifying efforts.
- A **lead** is just a business name or a businessperson you have identified as a possible future customer. You don't know much more than that. In some sales circles, they call a lead a suspect.
- A **prospect** is a business contact who has the means to buy advertising from you and has the authority to make those buying decisions. A good prospect's need and your Radio station's services must also be a good match.
- A **customer** is a business who is actively buying advertising from you. If a customer stops advertising with you, they are no longer a customer. They are now a prospect again. They remain a prospect until they buy from you again.
- The salesperson with poor qualifying skills will write smaller short-term orders and make less money than the salesperson with good qualifying skills.

- Start by checking the Radio station's master list to see if someone has been in contact with the lead in the past.
- Pre-call research has never been easier. With the Internet, you can quickly search for industry and lead specific research.

"The secret of getting ahead is getting started." - *Mark Twain,* Writer, humorist, entrepreneur, publisher, and lecturer, (1835 – 1910)

8

The ABCs of Qualifying a Prospect

You arrive for the presentation. You set up your materials. You stand and deliver one of your best presentations ever. The prospect nods in agreement throughout. You get positive feedback to all your trial closes. You feel like the sale is a sure thing. You ask for the order, and the prospect will say, "It's a great presentation. I need to send it to the Regional Manager for their approval."

You instantly realize you've just wasted one of your very best presentations on someone who can't say "Yes" to your proposal. You desperately try to recover and ask if you can see the real decision-maker. You are politely told that they are busy, but don't worry, your presentation will be delivered to them with a glowing review.

A few days later, when you call back, the prospect tells you that they're not interested. You ask why and they tell you an excuse you could have easily answered if you could only have some face time with the real decision-maker. You ask for an appointment, but you are told the company has selected another vendor.

As you hang up the phone, you start to think about how to avoid this rejection on your next presentation. You instantly realize that you didn't have **ALL** the decision-makers present for your presentation.

You arrive at your next prospect's office fully prepared with your flip chart and supporting materials. This time you made sure that all the decision-makers are present — the prospects nod in agreement throughout the presentation. You get positive feedback to all your trial closes. You feel like the sale is a sure thing. You ask for the order, and the prospect says, "It's a great presentation. We don't have it in our budget right now."

You instantly realize that you've just wasted one of your best presentations on someone who doesn't have the **BUDGET** for your proposal. You try to probe for when a budget is available, and they just tell you they haven't made any plans yet.

As you leave the office, you start thinking about how to avoid this rejection in your next presentation. You realize it would be helpful to know if the prospect has a **BUDGET** for advertising.

You arrive at your third prospect's office prepared this time. All the decision-makers are present. You've ascertained that they have the budget for your proposal. You give your finest performance to date. The prospect nods in agreement throughout. You get positive feedback to all your trial closes. You feel like the sale is a sure thing. You ask for the order, and the prospect will say, "It's a great presentation. We're just not doing anything until the third quarter."

By now, you're feeling low. You've made three dynamite presentations with no success. You start thinking about how you can avoid this rejection on your next presentation. During this presentation, you learned that the prospect didn't have a **COMMITMENT** to advertising at this time.

As you review your performance, you realize the in the first presentation; you didn't ensure that **ALL the decision-makers** were present. On the second call, the prospect didn't have the **BUDGET for your proposal**. During your third presentation, you realized the prospect **didn't have a COMMITMENT** to the services you were offering.

Before you know it, you start to see a pattern. You begin to realize that your closing ratio would have been dramatically better **if you had only done a better job in your preparation**. You could have ensured that **ALL** the decision-makers were present for the meeting. You would have known whether the prospect had a **BUDGET** for what you were proposing. You would have known whether the prospect had a **COMMITMENT** for what your service could provide.

If only you had followed the *ABCs of Qualified Presentations*, **ALL** the decision-makers are present, the prospect has a **BUDGET** for your products or services, and they have a **COMMITMENT** for the benefits your help can provide, you could be dining on caviar and champagne instead of rice and beans.

There is a direct correlation between the quality of your sales performance and the quality of your preparation. You sell better when you prepare better. Regardless of what you call it, the Pre-call Diagnostic or the Customer Needs Assessment, the more research and discovery you do with your prospect before the presentation, the higher your closing ratio will be.

While there may be many more key factors to learn about the prospect's needs than just what the *ABCs of Qualified Presentations* require, the ABCs are certainly among the top bits of information you need to know before you proceed with a presentation.

When you have this critical information, your presentation appears to be much more customer-focused. If you do an excellent job of interviewing the prospect about what the prospect needs and wants, the prospect feels more connected to your solution because you are addressing their most essential needs exactly as they feel they should be. In other words, the proposal makes sense to them. It fits nicely into their paradigm.

Your interview with the prospect should be so complete that you could summarize the meeting in a way that gains initial agreement to proceed. You might say something like; "From what we've discussed, you and Mr. Jones can make this decision, true? Your top priority is to increase your inventory turnover from two to three times per quarter, and you have allocated $15,000 per quarter to drive new sales, is that true? And is it also true that if you found a solution that felt good to you, you would be willing to get started right away?"

If you can't get an affirmative answer to those three questions, then you are not ready to proceed with a proposal. If you do, you are committing **the classic error of Ready, Fire, Aim**. You don't even know at what target you're shooting.

You may feel confident enough to barge forward and make a presentation in hopes of hitting the mark, but you risk damaging your chances with that prospect for a long time if your presentation creates the wrong perception of what you and your company can do for them. They may feel as if your company doesn't have the right answer for them even though you may very well have the best solution. In her book, *SNAP Selling*, Author Jill Konrath says you may be sent to **the dreaded D-Zone**. "When you are in the D-Zone, your sales are Delayed temporarily or Derailed permanently, as customers Default to the status quo. You are Dismissed or Deleted. Your prospects Disappear, or they're Dead to you completely."[13]

The prospect puts you in their **mental penalty box** based on the perceptions they form in a poorly prepared presentation.

There is one final component to the *ABCs of Qualified Presentations*. In addition to ensuring that **ALL** the decision-makers will be present, knowing that the prospect has the **BUDGET** for your proposal and that they have a **COMMITMENT** for taking action, you need to make sure you can get a **DECISION** within a reasonable time frame. Set your limits. If you don't get a firm decision, yes or no, after a while, you must assume the answer is no, and it's time to move on and reset your efforts with that prospect.

When trying to establish yourself as a serious business consultant, **to be known for what you won't do can often be more important than being known for what you will do**. Your prospect may ask you what you are currently working on and thereby make a judgment based on what you say.

Slow down and do a thorough job of preparation. Do some research but don't try to impress the prospect with a bunch of quickly learned facts about their business. Zig Ziglar reminds us, **"They don't care how much you know about their business until they know how much you care about their business."**

---

[13] Konrath, Jill. *SNAP Selling*. (Penguin Publishing Group 2012) 20

Summary

In this chapter on the ABCs of a Qualified Prospect, we covered the following topics:

- There is a direct correlation between the quality of your sales performance and the quality of your preparation. You sell better when you prepare better.
- While there may be many more key factors to learn about the prospect's needs than just what the *ABCs of Qualified Presentations* require, the ABCs are certainly among the top bits of information you need to know before you proceed with a presentation.
    - A=All the decision-makers are present.
    - B=Budget, you have determined the prospect has the budget for your proposal.
    - C=Commitment, you have determined the prospect has the commitment to solve the problems identified in the *Customer Needs Assessment* interview.
- An unprepared presentation may land you in the **dreaded D-Zone**. You might end up in **the mental penalty box** with no future options.
- There is one final component to the *ABCs of Qualified Presentations*; you need to make sure you can get a **DECISION** within a reasonable time frame.
- Don't try and impress your prospect with how much you know. **They don't care how much you know until they know how much you care.**

"If you can't fly, then run. If you can't run, then walk. If you can't walk then crawl, but whatever you do, you have to keep moving forward." – *Martin Luther King, Jr.*, Baptist minister, and civil rights activist. (1929 – 1968)

9

Setting Appointments

Working by appointment is not only the most professional, but it also the most productive way to grow a successful career in Radio advertising sales. When you work by appointment, you present yourself to your leads as an organized professional, someone who recognizes the value of time and uses time wisely. Working by appointment is the key to successful time management and the best way to get more done in less time.

Setting appointments over the phone is the most time-efficient way to set appointments because you can call many more prospects in an hour than you can see in person. You can call twenty different leads in an hour. In-person, you might be able to see two or three different people.

SNAP Selling

In her book, *SNAP Selling*, author Jill Konrath writes, "The people you're calling on suffer from a severe case of *Frazzled Customer Syndrome*, a debilitating condition brought on by excessive workloads, 24/7 availability, information overload, lack of sleep, and job-related stress."[14] When you call for an appointment, you are often seen as just one more interruption to an already hectic day. Traditional cold calling, presentation, and objection-handling sales techniques can make matters worse. That's why *SNAP Selling* is effective.

The basis of *SNAP Selling* is the following:

1. Keep it Simple (S).

---

[14] Konrath, Jill. *SNAP Selling*. (Penguin Publishing Group. 2012) 14

2. Be i**N**valuable (N).
3. Always **A**lign yourself with their needs (A).
4. Raise **P**riorities (P).

As you prepared your appointment setting script, try to discover how you can simplify your message. Prospects don't have time to be dazzled by how much you know about your Radio station. How can you help someone with no Radio knowledge and little advertising training quickly understand the value you offer? **You must find a way to Simplify your message**. Start by eliminating Radio and advertising jargon from your vocabulary. That can be difficult for the new salesperson because you're excited about your new job and you can't wait to share what you have learned.

Prospects suffering from *Frazzled Customer Syndrome* seek out vendors who are knowledgeable and bring them fresh ideas on a regular basis. When you approach Radio advertising sales as a professional, when you devote time to ongoing personal development, when you start to learn and understand the business world better, you come to be known as a resource and not just a salesperson. In addition to learning everything you can about advertising, you must learn the business of business **AND** the language of business. When you have a better grasp of the world of business and the role you and your Radio station can play, **that's when they begin to see you as iNvaluable**.

The **A** in *SNAP Selling* stands for **Alignment**. Are you perceived as a good fit? Are your services seen as relevant to your prospect's issues and objectives? Does the prospect feel you understand what they are going through? You could make a better impression on the prospect when you call for an appointment if you completed enough qualifying research before you called. **Don't skimp on qualifying research**.

Finally, the **P** in *SNAP Selling* is to **Raise Priorities**. This means you must keep the focus on the prospect's priorities and succinctly craft your message around those priorities so the prospect will see your solution as their best option. Stay focused and stay on message.

The Value of Using the Phone

The RAIN Group is a global sales training company. Their 2018 report, *Top Performance in Sales Prospecting*, details what works in prospecting today.[15]

- 69% of buyers have accepted phone calls from new providers in the previous 12 months.
- 57% of C-level (corporate level) and VP buyers prefer to be contacted by phone.
- Only 5% of sellers say sending bulk emails is effective.

---

[15] Mike Schults, Bob Croston, Mary Flaherty, *Top Performance in Sales Prospecting Benchmark Report*, RAIN Group (2018)

Call Reluctance

The thought of picking up the phone and calling a stranger for the first time, to set an appointment, is enough to cause some salespeople anxiety. This anxiety in sales is real. There is even a term for it, ***call reluctance***. If the thought of making calls to strangers to try and persuade them to give you an appointment is causing you some anxiety right now, you're just like everyone else.

When you add a lack of proper training to your anxiety, you now have a paralyzing formula that will only lead to sales failure. Your first course of action is to develop your telephone skills and gain some personal confidence in your efforts. Time will help you lose your anxiety as you realize for yourself that calling strangers for appointments works. But you need to train and practice until you develop your calling skills to the professional level. It takes more than just memorizing a script. It takes interpersonal skills. It takes question-asking skills. It takes listening skills. It takes thinking skills.

Using the telephone to prospect, qualify, and set appointments with leads is not optional in today's over-communicated society. Using the phone is the most interactive way to prospect for and qualify new leads. Emails and direct mail are marketing tools to help you generate leads, get referrals, and seed the lead with information about you before you call. These are great resources, and you should **use them as much as *practicable***. But don't let these activities take away from your valuable time on the telephone, interacting with your leads. Emails and direct mail are quickly deleted or tossed in the trash without a second thought. It's easy for your lead to ignore a letter or an email. It's more difficult to ignore someone calling on the telephone.

We've seen too many good people let their call reluctance get the better of them. They dutifully send out hundreds if not thousands of emails and letters and don't get a single response. They think they are productive, but they are just busy, not productive. They are only communicating in one direction, outbound.

With the telephone, you have a two-way conversation. You and another person are communicating with each other, exchanging information and ideas. This two-way conversation creates many new opportunities that an email or a letter cannot do. You may be in the right place at the right time. Your lead is already in the process of considering advertising, and you have a chance to enter the process.

With a well-planned approach, a thinking approach, your telephone contact could develop into future opportunities. "No" doesn't always mean "No, not ever." It very often means "No, not right now." Wouldn't that be nice to know?

Don't shy away from using the phone to set appointments just because you get turned down. **Don't convince yourself that you're more effective setting appointments in person**. When you start to think that way, you are headed in the wrong direction, and your sales career is in jeopardy. Your sales pipeline will tell you the truth about your prospecting success.

Your high value leads, people who have money to spend on advertising are usually very busy and hard to reach. They are busy running their company. The more money they have for advertising, the harder they are to reach. Leads with little or no money are usually not very busy, and they are easy to meet.

Best Time to Call

CallHippo is a company specializing in virtual telephony and workflow automation. They help companies build out their call centers. They conducted a research project that covered 24 weeks, 13,750 call attempts, and 1,350 successful conversations.

- The best day to call (in order), Wednesday, Thursday, Tuesday, Monday, Friday.
- The best time to call, 4:00 pm to 5:00 pm, 11:00 am to 12:00 pm.
- The minimum attempts to call your lead should be six times. [16]

Knowing when to pick up the phone to call a lead for an appointment takes some strategic planning. Don't call a restaurant in the hours before noon; they are too busy getting ready to serve their customers.

Calling before 8:00 am is an effective way to reach the decision-maker at companies that sell their daytime hours, i.e., HVAC, plumbers, and remodelers. They are out of the office providing their services.

For some business categories calling over the lunch hour can be productive. Most other salespeople are having lunch, and busy executives often have their lunch brought in.

If you are having difficulty reaching the decision-maker between 8:00 am and 5:00 pm, politely ask the receptionist for the best time to call.

Keep your lead list handy. Start trying to make phone calls to your hard to reach leads at odd times throughout the day. You should always be prepared to fill in any slow time in your day with more prospecting and appointment setting telephone calls.

First Impressions

You can't expect to walk in, unannounced, at a high value lead like a car dealer, and hope to see the owner of the dealership about advertising right away. Even if the owner of the dealership does take a moment to be courteous to you and comes to the showroom to meet you, you're on shaky ground to begin a professional conversation about advertising.

You have just interrupted a big lead and they put down whatever they were working on at that moment to meet you. You better have a darn good reason for the interruption, or they will

---

[16] CallHippo.com May 2017 *The Best Day and Time to Make a Business Call*
<https://callhippo.com/seo/best-day-time-make-business-call>

likely be annoyed with you. You could end up in the dreaded D-Zone, the mental penalty box.

The American Humorist, Will Rogers said, **"You never get a second chance to make a first impression."** You should heed his advice because there is strong science behind his humorous observation.

First impressions are compelling and hard to change. Human beings are quick to make a snap judgment based on first impressions; it is human nature. In the very early stages of human history, we developed an evolutionary need to make a quick decision about an approaching stranger to determine if the stranger posed a threat. Our ancestors knew how to quickly recognize the expression on a stranger's face and the intent of their posture to determine if it meant the difference between friend or foe.

If your first contact with an essential high-value lead is an interruption, you're not starting on a positive note. Even if you have something of value to offer, **the mere fact that you interrupted the lead clouds your message**.

It may take you several professional telephone calls to finally get an appointment with high-value leads. You may need to cultivate a phone relationship with the lead's gatekeeper to learn how best to reach the lead. This new relationship can be very productive. The gatekeeper can decide to put your message on the top of the list for callbacks.

Don't fall for any of the old stories about telephone sales. "It's a numbers game." "You need to love rejection to be in sales." "For every *no,* you hear means you're one call closer to a *yes.*" The odds are for gamblers. You have chosen to be a professional salesperson. You are not planning on leaving your future to chance. You are focusing on the quality of each of your calls.

Don't get discouraged in the beginning. You are building the foundation of your profession in advertising sales. It is the crucial, high-value accounts that make a financially rewarding career.

On the Phone vs. In-Person

There is always a chance that you will get lucky and get an appointment with that high-value lead in person, but the odds are against you. In many cases, you'll make a pest of yourself and damage your image as a professional. Learning to use the telephone effectively as your primary appointment setting tool is the most efficient way to build a successful career in Radio advertising sales.

To be sure, there will be circumstances where making appointments in person is appropriate. But don't fool yourself into thinking that in-person is more effective than using the phone. Trying to set appointments in person is much more time consuming than using the telephone. You can't possibly see as many people in person as you can call on the phone. The people you can see on the spur of the moment are probably not busy and don't have any money to spend on advertising.

If you learn to use the phone effectively, you set more quality appointments with high-value leads.

Appointment Setting Tools

Setting appointments with your leads is a multifaceted process involving many tools and multiple efforts to secure an appointment. Emails and letters are just that, tools to help you set the appointment. Emails and letters are not a substitute for making the call yourself.

Email marketing has become so overwhelmed with email spam that your email may become lost in a spam filter or just ignored by the recipient. Direct mail is inundated with unwanted offers; it has earned the name *junk mail* for a reason. A professionally written and addressed business letter sent through the U.S. Postal Service is such a rarity today that it might stand a better chance of reaching the lead.

Be sure you know how to print the address on the envelope using a printer or a typewriter. Don't undercut the positive impact of your professionally prepared letter with a hand-written envelope. Some have argued that the hand-addressed envelope is more personal. If that is indeed the case, handwrite the entire letter. Better yet, get a nice card and hand write your message. If you don't know how to print an envelope on your printer, learn how. **A professionally printed envelope says *business* when it arrives**.

Regardless of which you chose, email or U.S. Postal Service, announce in your communication that you will be calling and then make the call when you said you would.

Your Value Proposition

Your approach to setting the appointment must quickly demonstrate a compelling reason to make time for your appointment. The lead must view your request for their time as a benefit to them. They need to know **what's in it for them** before they will set the appointment with you. The lead needs to know that they will gain something from the meeting. **Your opening message is often called a value proposition**.

Your lead is also a lead for many other salespeople representing a wide array of business products and services. If you don't have a well-formulated value proposition, they can easily view your attempt to set an appointment, whether in person or over the phone, as an interruption to their busy day and they will try to brush you off.

Most companies can benefit from additional customers. The fundamental value proposition of Radio advertising is this; **according to the Nielsen Company, more people listen to AM & FM Radio than any other medium**[17]. With Radio's low cost, your local advertiser can reach more people, more frequently than they can with any other advertising

---

[17] RADAR 138 Sept 2018 © Nielsen Total Audience Report: Q1 2018

choice. You should say it this way to your lead; **"Your commercial will be heard by more people, more often, for less cost than any other medium."**

Even if your Radio station is not the highest-rated Radio station in your market, **you are in the business of bringing buyers and sellers together**. Your Radio station's listeners are the **buyers**, and your lead is the **seller**. Your listeners listen to what your Radio station tells them. They pay attention to the commercials. They shop with the advertisers that support their favorite Radio station. Even a small Radio station has more than enough potential buyers for any lead you may find.

The other component of your value proposition is this; according to the Nielsen Company, **Radio has a positive impact on product sales, driving an average of a 10 to 1 return on advertising investment**[18]. That is the average; some product categories saw a 23 to 1 return on advertising investment.

Many Radio stations now offer some digital marketing tools. The most common are display ads on the station's website or mobile app, streaming commercials on the station's Internet stream, email marketing and sponsorship commercials in a podcast. With these digital marketing tools, the new value proposition for a Radio station can be, **"We help companies like yours see more in-store customers, more website visitors and more subscribers to your email list."**

These and other powerful *Why Radio?* tools can be found at the Radio Advertising Bureau's website. Be sure to check the site often for new and updated sales tools.

Your value proposition is not your appointment setting script. We use that information to help you form, in your own mind, what your value proposition will be. As a Radio advertising salesperson, you should never take a back seat to any other medium based on Radio advertising's ability to deliver a higher return on investment than other advertising choices.

Advertising is a growing business. Every year, companies spend more money on advertising than the year before, and experts don't see a slowdown soon. The advertising pie continues to grow but so does the competition. Radio can out deliver all the other advertising choices when done correctly. That is your value proposition.

You can't just come right out and say that to your lead because it is only a claim at this point. A claim just like all the other claims they will hear. A claim is just a statement like "We sell the best tacos in town." Before you can craft your appointment setting script, you must feel it in your gut that you have a great product to sell so you can always bounce back when faced with some stall or objection.

Many salespeople initially resist the idea of using a script. You may think that a script won't sound natural and you will sound like all the other salespeople using scripts.

---

[18] Nielsen ROI Studies 2014 - 2016

Think of your favorite movie or TV show. Those actors are using scripts. They seem natural. They don't sound *scripted,* do they? **Professionals use scripts**.

It's not the script that sounds canned, it is the unprepared, and consequently, unprofessional delivery of a script that sounds canned. The critical difference between the highest-paid salespeople and the lowest paid is the level of preparation involved.

The Basic Appointment Setting Script

As you prepare your appointment setting script, you must go back to the pre-call research you did on your lead to help craft your opening line. What did you learn about the lead in your research? In this first example, we'll assume the lead had a banner ad on their website offering a special Three-Point Inspection Plan for homeowners.

> "Jane, I'm Spike Santee from the local Radio station WXYZ. I was on your website, and I see from your banner ad that you are looking for homeowners who could benefit from your Three-Point Inspection Plan. My company has been helping local business owners drive more traffic to their websites. We also can help reduce your customer acquisition costs. I have some ideas for you and was calling to see if you'd like to take a closer look?"

Your call opens with a greeting, and then you demonstrate you took a little time to research their website by bringing up the banner ad for the Three-Point Inspection Plan the company offers. You also did some research at the Radio Advertising Bureau and found that **Radio can drive up internet search results an average of 29%**[19].

Since this lead appears to be looking for homeowners or future homeowners, don't forget to do your category research. Home Depot was the single biggest Radio advertiser in 2018[20] placing 2.57 million Radio commercials. Many of those Radio commercials ran on your local Radio station. Lowe's was the fifth largest Radio advertiser.

In this example, you are getting your car serviced, and you noticed a lot of signs in the window and on the marquee for different products and services. And the best you can determine, surveying other local media, that's about all the advertising they are doing. You might craft a script like this:

> "Bill, I'm Spike Santee from the local Radio station WXYZ. I was in your store the other day getting my oil changed, and I noticed you have a lot of specials posted in your store, but I don't recall seeing any mass media advertising. Radio has a track record of increasing in-store traffic 22% on average. While I was waiting on my car, I came up with some ideas that might help and I'm calling to see if you would like to look at them."

---

[19] RAB Radio Drives Search, Sequent Partners, Media Monitors, In4mation Insights 2017
[20] Media Monitors 2019

In this example, we're using a similar template only this time you are informing the lead that you are a customer! That will surely gain you some small advantage. You also did your research, and you know that by adding Radio advertising to a campaign, Radio can drive a 22% incremental increase to in-store traffic[21]

By devoting some time to planning your call, you can collect some information, and your thoughts, to place a well-planned and more professional call.

Objections and Stalls

Regardless of how well planned and professional you are, you will inevitably face some questions after your opening statement. These questions should be expected because your opening statement proposes some exciting ideas. Once again, be prepared. Keep in mind, **the sole purpose of your call is to get an appointment!** If you get an appointment, **then** you can show your ideas and ask if they would like to proceed to the Customer Needs Assessment interview.

You will feel compelled to explain it all on the phone, divulging the details and the price. It's a cat and mouse game. The lead wants you to tell them all about it on the phone, so they can then say "Thanks, but I'm not interested" or some other reason for not meeting you in person.

Remember, you have done some research about the lead's business. You have discovered something that appears to be important to your new lead, and you think you have some ideas that could help. You want to find out if they would like to look at your ideas. You are not seeking a commitment to make a buying decision on the phone. You have some ideas, based on what you see the lead trying to do, and you think you could help them out. **That's exactly why you are calling**.

When you get a stall or an objection, respond by saying, "That's exactly why I'm calling." At first, you may question why that is the best way to respond. It allows you to set up your response. Your response should follow this formula; **Acknowledge, Respond, Continue**.

"I'm not interested."

ACKNOWLEDGE: "That's exactly why I'm calling. I understand what you're saying."

RESPOND: "This is not a sales call; it's an appointment call. I did some research on your business, I saw you were advertising in-store specials, and I came up with some ideas that might help you out. I'm just calling to see if I can stop by and show them to you."

CONTINUE: "Could we meet for a few minutes this week?"

---

[21] Radio Drives Store Traffic, RAB DialReport 2018

Another approach could follow the **Feel, Felt, Found** response. I know how you feel, my other customers felt that way, but when they looked, they found the ideas fascinating.

"I'm not interested."

ACKNOWLEDGE: "That's exactly why I'm calling. I hear what you're saying. I've heard that before."

RESPOND: "A lot of my current customers said they weren't interested at first. But once they looked at my ideas, they found them to be very interesting, and very helpful. That's why I'm just calling for an appointment."

CONTINUE: "Could we meet for a few minutes this week?"

You need to be prepared to stand your ground and ask politely for the appointment. But it is a delicate balance. You must carefully listen to the lead for meaningful feedback. It may sound like a canned stall or objection, but the response could contain essential information that can lead to a more meaningful contact in the future. **When you hear "No" from a lead, it rarely means "No, not ever," it probably means "No, not now."**

In our workshops, the first stall or objection attendees want to know how to handle is the "How much does it cost" question. Remember, this is not a sales call but an appointment call. We recommend when you get the "How much does it cost" question, you say, **"If it's not what you're looking for, it won't cost you a thing."**

You'll find a complete list of possible objections and stalls, plus recommended responses in Appendix D.

Summary

In this chapter on Setting Appointments, we covered the following topics:

- Working by appointment is not only the most professional, but it also the most productive way to grow a successful business in Radio sales. When you work by appointment, you present yourself to your leads as an organized professional, someone who recognizes the value of time and uses time wisely.
- What is call reluctance and how to respond?
- Using the telephone to prospect, qualify, and set appointments with leads is not optional in today's over-communicated society. Using the phone is the most interactive way to prospect for and qualify new leads. How to use various appointment setting tools?

- The lead needs to know that they will gain something from the meeting. **Your opening message is often called a *value proposition*.**
- You learned a basic calling script and the necessary components.
- You were introduced to a formula for handling objections and stalls: acknowledge, respond, and continue.

"Ask, and it will be given to you; seek, and you will find; knock, and it will be opened to you." – Matthew 7:7

10

Customer Needs Assessment

Companies rarely buy advertising from you just because they like you or your Radio station. **They buy advertising from you because they have a problem to solve and they believe you can help them.** The degree to which they believe this depends on the level of confidence and comfort they have with you and your product.

The professional Radio advertising salesperson is a problem solver. You solve problems for your customers. Zig Ziglar reminds us that; **"We can have everything in life we want, as long as we help enough other people get what they want in life first."**[22]

Most business problems can be solved with a greater supply of customers. The professional Radio advertising salesperson is in the business of bringing buyers and sellers together. Your listeners are buyers, and your customers are sellers. You bring the two together with advertising and promotions on your Radio station.

The Customer Needs Assessment (CNA) implies that the customer's real needs will be identified in the interview. Unfortunately, because of a salesperson's internal requirements and motivation, the poorly trained salesperson may be motivated by selfish needs and conduct a cursory Customer Needs Assessment that doesn't investigate the needs of the customer. Worse yet, they begin the interview with the end already in mind. They are merely going through the motions of an interview, faking empathy to sell the lead a pre-determined package.

To propose an advertising solution to solve your customer's problems, you must determine what problems they have. This is the time for specifics.

---

[22] Ziglar, Zig. *Secrets of Closing the Sale*. (Revell 2003) 11

Your job is to help your clients solve their business problems using the various tools at your disposal, the most effective of which happens to be your radio station.

The Customer Needs Assessment interview, where you learn about the lead's exact needs and desires, **requires you to have a curious mind,** because the lead may be hesitant to answer direct questions about proprietary business information. You can't just barge into someone's office and ask, "What is your average profit margin on your best-selling item?" You haven't set the stage to ask such a question, and you will appear to be rude and unprofessional. Nonetheless, you still need to learn what is the average profit margin on the best-selling item.

Conducting an effective Customer Needs Assessment is a nuanced process in which you must avoid becoming an unpaid conversationalist. You must learn how to make a sound, professional, first impression to set the meeting atmosphere for an exchange of information and ideas. You must stick to a fact-finding agenda, all the while recognizing that no two Customer Needs Assessment interviews will ever be the same.

Now is the time to ask questions and *listen*. "Selling isn't Telling."[23] **You are there to *learn* if the lead has a problem that is bothering them so much that they would be willing to spend some money with you to solve it.** You cannot establish a mutually beneficial business relationship without the process of identifying the needs and gaining agreement that the lead must do something about them.

Empathy, Not Sympathy

In many training courses, you are taught the purpose of the Customer Needs Assessment is to **demonstrate a sincere empathy for the customer's problems**. The keywords here are sincere empathy.

Empathy is defined as the ability to understand, being aware of, being sensitive to, the feelings, thoughts, and experience of another.

The goal of the Customer Needs Assessment interview is to find out if the lead has some business goals they want to achieve or challenges they want to overcome. You also want to learn how badly they want to follow through on those goals or challenges. It's one thing for the lead to say they would like to increase their business. It's another thing entirely for them to take the actions necessary to grow their business. You want to learn how badly they want to find a solution. Are they willing to tell you these things and will they let you come back with a solution?

We believe that sincere empathy begins when you genuinely believe that your product, Radio advertising, when done correctly, can help cure business problems better than anything else available. Selling is a transference of emotions. You must feel sincerely excited about your product and what it can do for the customer if you want to have genuine sincerity. If you don't

---

[23] Ziglar, Zig. *Secretes of Closing the Sale.* (Revell 2003) 313

feel like Radio advertising is the best solution for the customer, you can fall victim to having sympathy for your lead instead of empathy.

Here's what will happen when you have sympathy instead of empathy. You make an appointment with a lead to conduct the Customer Needs Assessment interview. As the conversation begins, the business owner tells you just how bad his business has been. There is a big new national chain store out at the edge of town selling the same products as his but at a considerable discount price. His best salesperson just quit to go work for the new store. The landlord just raised the rent, insurance costs more, his kids don't want to take over the store, he can't afford to advertise, he can hardly pay himself. Man, he's in sorry shape.

If you have sympathy for the business owner, you're likely to say, "Yea, I know what you mean. I've got a discount competitor; my insurance has gone up, and I can hardly pay my rent too. Yea, times are hard, aren't they? Oh, by the way, you wouldn't want to buy some advertising, would you? No? I didn't think so."

With empathy, you can stay emotionally detached from the customer's problems so you can offer solutions. Remaining detached allows you to move from your side of the desk over to the customer's side of the desk and begin to see his problems from his point of view. Then, you can offer solutions because, in your heart of hearts, you know advertising done correctly on your Radio station can help this business owner find new customers, sell more products, increase revenue, pay his bills, and even have more money left over for themselves.

Your objective in the Customer Needs Assessment interview is to listen. You are not there to list off all your Radio stations, your packages or your prices. **You want to ask questions that cause the customer to talk.** Author Jill Konrath says, "Prospects consider you to be irrelevant when you present information about your product, service, or solutions before you understand their business directions and challenges."[24]

The secret to successful interpersonal communications is this; the person who is asking the questions is controlling the conversation. It is difficult for someone to remain silent when asked a question. If you are doing all the talking, the customer can just sit there and listen. You won't learn anything.

Preparation and Research

Some sales organizations will have a Customer Needs Assessment interview form with a list of questions to ask. That's a good start. Don't rush into your customer's store without any preparation, pull out your sheet, and ask, "How many years have you been in business?" Do some research! How many of the standard questions on your CNA sheet can you answer from research alone?

---

[24] Konrath, Jill, *SNAP Selling*. (Penguin 2010) 28

We recommend following the guidelines from the Radio Advertising Bureau (RAB). They have a comprehensive pre-appointment research checklist to get you started. Start with the lead's website. That's a rich place to learn what they are trying to say to the public. Look for them on social media. Find the website for their trade association. The RAB's Instant Background Reports is an essential pre-appointment research tool. The report describes the business category and relevant consumer information such as, who buys, what they buy, when they buy, how they buy, why they buy, and so much more.

The RAB Instant Backgrounds contain recent trends about your lead's business category. You can learn about the industry issues that may be affecting their business. This information can be helpful as a conversation starter when you begin your meeting.

The RAB also maintains a library of news stories organized by product category. This is a wonderful resource for up-to-date category news and information.

If your company is not a member of the RAB, you can still learn many things about the business and their industry using the Internet.

When you begin with a general knowledge of the business and the industry, then you can start to create some custom questions to use in your Customer Needs Assessment Interview. Remember, no two interviews will ever be the same. Never begin a Customer Needs Assessment interview without doing your research.

Spin Selling

SPIN Selling is a book by Neil Rackham. Based on the Huthwaite Corporation's massive $1 million, 12-year research study into effective sales performance, the 1988 book has become a best seller and essential reading for the professional salesperson.

SPIN is an acronym for the four different types of questions: **Situation**, **Problem**, **Implication**, and **Need/Payoff**.

Situational Questions (The <u>S</u> Questions)

Questions like "How long have you been in business?" or "What advertising are you currently doing?" are Situation Questions. According to Rackham; "Situation Questions are not positively related to success,"[25] and "Buyers quickly become bored or impatient if you ask too many Situation Questions."[26]

While you need this information, you must realize that Situational Questions **benefit you most** and if your lead is busy, they will grow tired of providing you with details you could have easily looked up before the interview. **Do your pre-call research**.

---

[25] Rackham, Neil. *SPIN Selling* (McGraw Hill, 1988) 68
[26] Rackham, Neil. *SPIN Selling* (McGraw Hill, 1988) 69

The Situational Question gives you the context you couldn't get through research and helps you better qualify the lead.

Problem Questions (The **P** Questions)

The experienced salespeople in Rackham's research were more likely to ask Problem Questions like "Are you satisfied with the number of visitors to your website?" or "Is it difficult getting new subscribers on your email list?"

These questions are probing for problems or **Implied Needs**. Rackham concludes, "Problem Questions are more strongly linked to sales success than Situation Questions are."[27] That is easy to understand. If you can't solve a problem for your customer, why would they need to buy any advertising from you?

The Problem Questions show you what is foremost on the lead's mind and what their most important needs are.

Implication Questions (The **I** Questions)

Radio is an intangible product. It is difficult for the lead to understand the value of advertising without a compelling value proposition. You can quantify advertising with things like Cost Per Thousand or Cost Per Point, but those metrics don't mean anything to the business owner. They only encourage the lead to treat you more like a commodity than a problem solver.

An Implication Questions is a **How Bad Does It Hurt** Question. For your lead to decide to spend money with you, they must perceive the reward of your advertising campaign to be higher than the price of your advertising proposal.

Here is an example of an Implication Question, "Are your sales negatively impacted by a low number of website visitors, and by how much?"

If you propose a $5,000 advertising plan without supporting evidence, the lead may doubt the value of your proposal and say, "No." But had you learned that each new customer is worth $1,000 to the company, you could have made the case that your plan could efficiently deliver five new customers.

The Implication Question helps you determine the urgency the lead has for solving the problem.

Need-Payoff Questions (The **N** Question)

The Need-Payoff Question focuses the lead's attention on the possible solutions and encourages your lead to tell you what the benefits of solving their problem will be. A Need-Payoff Question is a **How Will You Benefit** Question. At first, you may wonder, what is the difference between an Implication Question and a Need-Payoff Question? Implication Questions

---

[27] Rackham, Neil. *SPIN Selling* (McGraw Hill, 1988) 70

are about the problem and why the problem is bad for the company. A Need-Payoff Question is focused on the possible solutions and the value of solving the issue identified with the Implication Question.

There is an interesting reward in asking Need-Payoff Questions. Since the Need-Payoff Question is asking the lead about the possible solution, the lead is selling themselves on the benefits of your proposal. By asking the lead to tell you how they will benefit from the proposal, you're building buy-in, and you reduce possible objections.

Here is an example of a Need-Payoff Question, "What would happen if you were able to increase your website visitors, how much would your sales go up?"

As someone with a growth mindset, this is a tipping point in your professional training. Without learning how to ask the Implication and the Need-Payoff Question, you may find yourself chasing after small, short-term advertising deals. At first, you won't see the impact on your career because it seems like it's easy to make a $500 sale. But revisit the ***Goal Setting*** section of your training. You must learn how to ask the Implication and the Need-Payoff Questions to build a strong case for why your customers should spend $1,000 or even $5,000 a month with you on advertising.

The Need-Payoff Question helps you determine the lead's interest in solving the problem in general, independent of your proposal, conditioning the lead to accept your features and benefits as the solution.

The First Question

The first question in your Customer Needs Assessment is always the most awkward. You may be nervous, and the lead may be apprehensive. A little small talk is only suitable for a short while. The lead expects you to get down to business. So, don't be afraid to jump right in.

When you have done your homework, when you have prepared for the meeting, you can start the meeting with an opening phrase like:

"Before I meet with a new customer, I like to do some homework, and guess what I found?"

Well, what do you think the lead is going to say, "No, I'm not interested?" Sure, they want to hear what you found. Tell them and then ask, **"Can you tell me a little bit more about that?"** The interview has begun, and the lead is telling you more about what you found? How great is that?

Another approach could sound like this:

"When I did some research about your business, I had a feeling I could write a good creative commercial for you, but now that I see your store in person,

I'm convinced I can write a **great** creative commercial for you. Can you tell me more about what you want people to know about you?"

This approach initiates a discussion about what kind of message the lead would like to send out to people. You are also putting the focus on the eventual commercial you will write, and that gives your overall presentation more tangibility. The lead can relate to a written or recorded commercial easier than they can relate to the details of the advertising schedule.

Also, when you introduce your lead to the creative process early, when it comes time to review the finished commercial, you have a chance for a trial close. After you read or playback your commercial to the lead, you can say, "Could we run a commercial like this?"

Regardless of how you begin the Customer Needs Assessment interview, you need your curiosity. You don't know exactly where the conversation is going to lead. You need to listen carefully to what the lead is telling you and take it from there. You can't be robotic and simply ask one question after another from your list. If the conversation is revealing relevant issues and feelings, you may need to pursue that line further than you anticipated. If the conversation is getting off track, your research and prepared questions can help you get back on track.

Drew Carey is an American actor, comedian and game show host of *Whose Line is it Anyway?* It is a game show consisting of improvisational actors and comedians who must perform without any advance notice of what the games are going to be. One segment is called *Questions Only*. The contestants must speak only in questions. If they can't respond to a question from the other actor with their own question, Carey rings the buzzer, and they must sit down. You can find examples on YouTube if you search for *Drew Carey* and *Questions Only*. You should watch a few. They are entertaining **and** helpful to learn just how powerful questions can be in a conversation.

The person asking the questions is the person who controls the direction of the conversation. Not only does the other person need to respond, but they also have a natural desire to talk about themselves and what they think is important. Everyone enjoys expressing their opinions and feelings. It is psychologically rewarding to have someone else interested in what we have to say. This is the time when your sincerity begins to play a role. If you truly believe that by helping people get what they want, you can get what you want, your questions will be heartfelt, and your lead will be more inclined to honestly engage with you.

Get Down to Business Early

Any list of possible Customer Needs Assessment interview questions will need to be considered well in advance of your appointment. Some questions are better than others. Some go straight to the point. Others not so much. Don't lose sight of the goal of the interview. **You want to find out if the lead has a need that you can help them overcome or a goal you can help them achieve.** So, get to the point.

"Thanks for meeting with me today. My company has a successful history of helping local businesses find more new customers while at the same time, helping them keep their advertising costs down. My goal today is to learn more about what you're trying to do and see if I can help. I don't have a presentation planned today; I just want to find out if together we might able to help your business. Could I begin by asking you a few questions?"

This opening statement, ending with a question, is straight forward and sets the stage for a business discussion, not a social visit. It's a nice transition from the pleasantries of the opening small talk and sets the direction of the meeting. You also show courtesy by asking if you may proceed. You have signaled that you don't have a planned presentation for the meeting. The purpose is to determine if there is a possibility of working together if the two of you find some business need with which your Radio station can be of assistance.

"Could I start with some big-picture questions? Could you give me an idea of where you stand today in relation to where you want to be at this point in terms of sales, customer counts, margins? What can you tell me about that? Are you pleased, are there some areas for improvement? How do you feel about those things?"

Sure, that is four questions in one paragraph. There are four questions, but just one *conversational* paragraph. However, look at the construction of the paragraph, it begins with a question about the scope of the questions, big picture, broad brush, general questions are coming. The second question begins to narrow the focus of the big picture question to sales, customer counts and margins, three things essential to every business. The third question asks for an assessment, and the fourth question asks the lead to respond.

In practice, the conversation would sound like this:

You: "Could I start with some big-picture questions?"

Lead: "Sure."

You: "Could you give me an idea of where you stand today in relations to where you want to be at this point in terms of sales, customer counts, margins?"

Lead: "Uh-Huh."

You: "What can you tell me about that? Are you pleased, are there some areas for improvement? How do you feel about those things?"

Lead: "Okay, well...." Then let the lead respond.

Don't worry if the lead is slow to respond; you've just asked a big question, a question that gets to the point about the purpose of your visit, "How's business?" Start listening. Don't be too quick to ask for a follow-up. Don't let a pause in the conversation cause you to jump ahead; the lead is just thinking about what to say next. Your patience will cause the lead to elaborate.

Don't Try to Rebut or Counter

As your Customer Needs Assessment interview continues, the lead is bound to say something that will trigger in you a compulsion to refute or counter what they just said. Under no circumstance should you allow yourself to fall victim to this amateurish impulse. Your goal in the interview is not to argue with the lead or try to prove a point. There will be plenty of time for that in your presentation. If you attempt to refute or counter what your lead is telling you in the interview, you may not get the follow-up appointment and the opportunity to present your ideas.

If the lead says something that you find unflattering about your Radio station or Radio advertising in general, just nod your head, say you understand, and ask them to elaborate more. When you come back to make your presentation, you will already know how the lead feels about your Radio station or Radio advertising, and you will be able to give them a much better response at that time.

Here is an example of how you will be able to refute an issue later in your presentation meeting. Don't be anxious to deal with it in the Customer Needs Assessment interview.

"In our last meeting, you told me that you didn't think people listened to Radio anymore, especially young people. I did some research with the Nielsen Company, maybe you've heard of them, they are the world's largest consumer research company, they do the TV ratings. In their most recent survey, they found that 249.7 million people listen to the Radio every week! [28] That's nine out of ten people walking past your store. Isn't that surprising?

The consulting firm Deloitte estimates that by 2025, more adults between 18 and 34 will be listening to more Radio than watching traditional TV [29]. That's a significant change, wouldn't you say?"

In the Customer Needs Assessment interview, you are there to gain knowledge, not prove a point. You are there to learn if and how you can help the lead.

Listen carefully to what the lead is telling you. Process the information, take notes, hear what they are saying. This information is news to you. You must judge whether to probe further or if it is time to move on to another subject.

The Gross Margin Question

One of the most critical issues and one many advertising salespeople avoid is the conversation about sales and gross margins. Gross margin is the sale price of an item minus the cost of acquisition. In other words, if a tire store sells a set of four tires for $500 but the tire store

---

[28] Nielsen Company RADAR 140, March 2019 Persons 12+
[29] Deloitte Insights, Technology, Media and Telecommunication Prediction 2019

paid $250 to the supplier, they have a $250 gross margin per sale. These numbers represent a 50% margin.

You need to learn how to quantify accomplishing the goal or overcoming the challenge in terms of the price of each sale and **gross profit margin** left over after the sale. You will need this information for your presentation when you estimate a possible Return on Investment for your proposal. How many widgets will the lead need to sell to pay for the advertising and put some extra in the bank?

Follow Up Questions

Follow up responses are designed to encourage the lead to tell you more. You want to learn how strongly the lead feels about that subject. If they feel very strongly about it, you want to encourage them to elaborate on why they feel strongly about it, what are they doing about it and are they satisfied with their progress. If they are unsatisfied, you may have just uncovered the first area of need where you might be able to help the lead. However, don't go there yet; just make a note. The lead is talking! Let them keep talking.

Follow up questions tend to be shorter in length than the opening question because you want to stay on topic but at the same time, discover more about the lead's deeper feelings on the subject. Follow up questions could sound like this:

"How do you feel about that?"

"Has it been an issue for a long time?"

"What is the impact of that?"

"What are you doing about that?"

"Does it seem to be working?"

The goal of the Customer Needs Assessment interview is to determine if the lead has a business goal or challenge; you could help them achieve or overcome. In addition to identifying a need or problem, you must learn more about their feelings and perceptions of advertising and their many choices. This information will be required as you prepare your proposal. Don't just ask what kind of advertising they are doing. Do your homework. One of the pre-call checklist items is to conduct an inventory of their current advertising by checking their website, OOH (out of home) advertising, read the newspaper, watch your local TV and cable channels and of course, listen to other Radio stations.

"Before I decided to call on you, I tried to survey the different advertising choices in the area, and I saw a couple of your billboards, some TV ads, and your ad popped up on my phone when I was reading the news. Would you tell me how those are working for you, what do you like, what don't you like?"

This type of question sets you up for another part of your presentation, the strengths and weaknesses of Radio advertising and other media choices. Once again, turn to the competitive media section of the Radio Advertising Bureau's website. There you will find an overview of the critical media categories, a list of the positives and negatives and suggestions on how combining Radio with the lead's other media choices can make those other choices more effective.

Resist the urge to refute and counter what the lead tells you in the Customer Needs Assessment interview. You will ruin your chances of making a new customer. You will come off as argumentative, and you don't want that. You want to learn about the business and determine if you can help them in some way. You want to get that second appointment for the presentation. You want time to go back to the office and prepare a professional presentation that provides answers and solutions to the needs of the lead. So, bite your tongue.

Remember the "I think I could write an outstanding commercial for your company," opening statement approach? If not, go back to the beginning of this chapter and reread it. Here is a follow-up question to use near the completion of the Customer Needs Assessment interview.

"Before I set an appointment to come see you, I was pretty sure I would be able to write a good creative commercial for you, but now that we've talked, I'm even more excited to give it a shot. Would you please tell me more about what you would like the public to know about your business?"

Now you want to be a stenographer. You want to write down everything the lead tells you about what they would like to hear in their commercial. Read it back to them to make sure that's what they would like their commercial to communicate to the public. Ask if there is anything else that comes to mind.

The Wrap Up

As you collect the information from the lead and you sense you have what you need to get started, you want to professionally **wrap up the interview and set an appointment to come back with a presentation.** Your wrap up should include a review of the critical issues discovered in the interview, the goal or challenge, how badly the goal or challenge is needed, what it means to the lead, their perceptions of advertising and the beginnings of a commercial.

In this example, the lead is an automotive service department at a local car and truck dealership.

"This has been a fascinating meeting. Based on what you have shared with me, you have ten bays in the service shop and that you're running about 60% of capacity each week. That means that four of the service bays are underutilized. You're set up to do 350 service jobs a week, but right now that is about 210 jobs.

You said you want to run at about 80% of capacity each week. You're already paying a staff to handle 80% capacity. That extra 20% capacity is about 70 additional service jobs a week at an average of $298 each. After parts and labor, your gross profit margin is about $137 on each job[30]. Is that about right?

I feel like we can write a really great commercial too. May I come back next week at this same time and show you what I come up with?"

The wrap up is not complete without an appointment for a return meeting to present your proposed solutions. If the lead can meet with you at this time for the Customer Needs Assessment interview, perhaps, the same time next week will work again. If the lead becomes a customer, this might become your regular meeting time.

Securing an appointment to come back with a presentation is the tipping point when your lead becomes a prospect.

Summary

In this chapter on the Customer Needs Assessment interview, we covered the following topics:

- The goal of the Customer Needs Assessment interview is to find out if the lead has some business goals they want to achieve or challenges they want to overcome with which you might be able to help.
- Learn to practice empathy, not sympathy.
- Always do your preparation and research. How many of the standard questions can you answer from research alone?
- In *SPIN Selling*, SPIN is an acronym for the four different types of questions: **S**ituation, **P**roblem, **I**mplication, and **N**eed/Payoff.
- Learn how to get down to business with the first question. Don't waste time; get down to business early.
- Don't try to refute or counter in the CNA interview. Your goal in the meeting is to learn, not to argue with the lead or try to prove a point.
- Be sure to ask the gross margin questions. Gross margin is the sale price of an item minus the cost of acquisition.
- Be prepared and always ask follow-up questions.
- The wrap up is not complete without an appointment for a return meeting to present your proposed solutions.

---

[30] 2018 National Automobile Dealers Association Dealer Profile

"Advertising people who ignore research are as dangerous as generals who ignore decodes of enemy signals." *David Ogilvy*, Founder, *Ogilvy & Mather*, known as the "Father of Advertising." (1911 – 1999)

11

Co-Op Advertising

Co-op advertising is a system where manufacturers and distributors establish reimbursement plans to help a local business pay for a portion or sometimes, all their advertising costs.

Co-op advertising programs have many requirements the local companies must meet to qualify for co-op advertising funds. The rules can be complicated so you must do your homework to get paid.

One of the many benefits of membership in the Radio Advertising Bureau is the online co-op library at www.rab.com. The database is updated regularly with the latest co-op advertising plans from thousands of manufacturers. There is an extensive Guide to Selling Co-op. Plus, you have access to the RAB staff for additional help if necessary.

If your Radio station isn't a member of the RAB, you will need to work with your advertiser to get the name and number of the co-op advertising contacts at their suppliers. You will have to do a little more research on your own to learn what is available. The co-op coordinators will be happy to work with you once they know you have been authorized by your customer to call and get the program information. Manufacturers want their dealers to spend co-op advertising dollars because it benefits the dealer and the manufacturer.

Benefits of Co-Op Advertising

Co-op advertising is essentially free advertising for your local advertiser, offered by the manufacturer or distributor. Your customer has earned this advertising help through their purchases. The co-op advertising will help extend your customer's advertising purchasing power beyond what they can afford on their own, bringing in more new customers, which means more business for the manufacturer, which means more co-op dollars and more advertising.

Co-op advertising funds help the local retailer establish a more substantial branding presence in the community than would otherwise be possible.

The manufacturers want the local companies to spend the co-op money because it helps the manufacturer's brand image too. It's a shame, billions in co-op advertising dollars go unspent every year. All it takes is some training and attention to detail to find extra revenue for you and your Radio station.

Finally, co-op advertising can lend an air of legitimacy to your local customer. Small companies that can link their name with that of a nationally recognized product or service will benefit if the co-op brand already has strong user loyalty.

Accruals and Participation

In general, there are two basic requirements in any co-op advertising program.

The local company must first qualify for co-op advertising funds. Qualification depends on the amount of product purchased. The local company **accrues** advertising funds based on what they buy **and** how much they buy from the manufacturer. The more inventory the local business buys from the manufacturer, the more co-op advertising funds the local company will accrue.

Then the local business must advertise the manufacturer's product following the manufacturer's advertising rules and guidelines to qualify for reimbursement of the advertising costs. The manufacturer's guidelines often specify what the commercial should say and which media qualify for reimbursement.

The Toro Company has co-op advertising for the Toro Walk, Riding and LCE products. LCE stands for Landscape Contractor Equipment. The accrual period runs from November 1, 2018, through October 31, 2019.

Toro offers an escalating accrual scale. The more the local Toro dealer buys, the higher the accrual rate.

Look at Table 1. If the local dealer's inventory purchases of Toro Walk, Riding and LCE products is between $25,000 and $149,999, the local dealer would qualify for a 1% accrual and a 50% manufacturer's participation in the cost of the advertising.

If the local dealer bought $100,000 of qualifying products, they would earn $1,000 in co-op advertising funds. Toro would help pay for 50% of the advertising cost. To use the full amount of advertising co-op funds available, the local dealer would need to buy $2,000 in qualifying advertising. At 50% participation, Toro would pay for half of the $2,000 advertising, the $1,000 that the dealer accrued during the period. If the dealer bought $3,000 in advertising, Toro would still only pay $1,000 even though the participation rate is 50% because the local dealer only accrued $1,000 in co-op advertising funds.

Purchases	Accrual %	Participation
$25,000 - $149,999	1%	50%
$150,000 - $299,999	3%	50%
$300,000 - $449,999	4%	55%
$450,000 - $599,999	5%	60%
$600,000 +	6%	70%

TABLE 1

From Table 1, if the local dealer bought $500,000 in qualifying products in the accrual period, they would qualify for a 5% accrual rate and a 60% manufacturer's participation in the cost of the advertising. The more the local dealer buys from Toro, the faster their accrual grows, and Toro agrees to pay a more significant percentage of the advertising costs. The accelerating scale incentivizes the local dealer to buy more products from Toro. They get more advertising support from Toro.

Form of Reimbursement

If the local dealer buys $2,000 in qualifying advertising from your Radio station, your company is going to send the local Toro dealer a bill for $2,000. It is the local dealer's responsibility to send your company a check for $2,000 when they get the bill.

It is then up to the local dealer to submit the bill for the advertising to Toro with the required paperwork within 60 days of the invoice date. If the local dealer doesn't submit the paperwork in time, they may not get the reimbursement.

Reimbursement will come in the form of a credit memo to the local dealer's account with Toro. They won't get a check for $1,000. They will get $1,000 toward future purchases from Toro.

If you are working with a local business that has experience using their co-op funds, they will already be accustomed to working with these rules. However, if you jump in and try to sell with co-op without doing your training and homework, you could naively misinform a new prospect that their supplier will help **pay** for the advertising and they will likely get the wrong idea and expect their supplier to pay the Radio station directly for the advertising.

Advertising Specifications

Advertising submitted to the manufacturer for participation must meet the guidelines established in the co-op plan. You should always make sure the commercial you are preparing for your customer meets those guidelines. You can obtain the instructions directly from the manufacturer's co-op advertising representative.

For Toro dealers, they can download commercials or scripts created by Toro from the dealer portal. If the local dealer wants to create their Radio commercial, Toro must be the only product mentioned, and there must be at least one product feature or benefit.

Claim Requirements

When you create a sales order at the Radio station for one of your customers who is going to use co-op advertising, you must fill out the sales order accurately by checking the appropriate boxes indicating the order will using co-op. This way, your traffic and billing department will know the advertiser is using co-op advertising, and they will automatically produce the proper paperwork at billing time.

They will create a **notarized affidavit of performance** which includes a notarized copy of the invoice with the specific dates and air times of all the commercials and a notarized transcript of the actual script.

Your advertiser will take the notarized affidavit of performance and attach it to the completed Toro claim form and then send it to the co-op claims department at Toro and wait for a credit to their account.

If you fail to accurately indicate on your sales order that the customer is using co-op advertising, your customer won't get the proper billing at the end of the month. You will need to ask your office staff to redo the invoice to include the affidavit of performance. Your office staff will need to stop doing their work and spend extra time producing the affidavit for your customer. It's not an easy matter to correct, and they won't be happy with you. Your failure to do your paperwork correctly could cause your advertiser a delay in processing their co-op claim form, and they could miss the deadline and not receive their credit. Now your office staff AND your customer is unhappy with you.

Special Co-Op Funds

Sometimes, the factory rep or the regional sales manager is pushing the dealer network to buy more inventory or buy a specific line of products. As an incentive, they may have special co-op money not listed in the co-op files. Getting to know distributor reps helps you learn what their agenda is for your market. If they have more than one dealer in your territory, they may be interested in a unique advertising program involving the dealer network. You could get an introduction to new customers this way.

Sometimes your customer can go to the distributor and ask for extra help. Remember the cardinal rule of selling; **"If you don't ask, you don't get."**

Co-Op Advertising and the Small Retailer

The smaller retailer may not be buying enough inventory from any given supplier to accrue large sums of co-op advertising funds. Don't get discouraged. Check every product line your customer carries. You may need to write one order for ten commercials for one product line and another order for 15 commercials for another product line. Three or four of these small orders all running at the same time sounds like a big advertising order to your audience.

The Dealer Group

The professional Radio advertising salesperson identifies all the different people in the **co-op chain of command**, from the manufacturer's co-op administrators to the regional sales representatives. They all have an interest in spending the co-op funds. They may want to have all their retailers in your market advertise at the same time. They may create a **dealer-group** to spend the co-op money.

The manufacturer, or the distributor, depending on who forms the dealer group, will buy the advertising directly from you at the Radio station. They will be paying 100% of the advertising cost. They will use a standard commercial but reserve the last 15 seconds to list the local retailers who are participating in the co-op dealer group. They may say they want to *tag* **the commercial** with the retailer's name and address.

You will still need to indicate on your sales order that a contract is a co-op contract so your traffic and billing department will create the proper billing paperwork. In a dealer group advertisement, the manufacturer or distributor may want to know which retailer tags ran at which time. Just make sure you indicate that in your sales order paperwork. It wouldn't hurt to personally visit your traffic department to give them a heads up and ask for specific instructions.

The biggest downfall in co-op advertising comes when the paperwork is improperly submitted. It causes your co-workers extra work, and it could prevent you from getting paid.

Co-Op Fraud

There is a history of abuse in co-op advertising. Unscrupulous business owners **and** Radio stations would submit fraudulent co-op claim forms to manufacturers for advertising that didn't qualify. Any attempt to manipulate the Radio station's billing information to deceive a third party is a fraud.

That is why the station notarizes the paperwork certifying that the commercial ran on the dates and times specified. Even with these safeguards in place, you may encounter a business owner who may ask you to do something that you shouldn't.

Your Radio station's management team will spot any attempt to circumvent standard co-op rules immediately and stop you from making a grave mistake. If you commit co-op fraud, you and the Radio station could face the potential of both civil and criminal liability. The Radio station could face fines and even license forfeiture at the Federal Communications Commission, **and you could go to jail**.

Summary

In this chapter on Co-op Advertising, we covered the following topics:

- Co-op advertising is a system where manufacturers and distributors establish reimbursement plans to help a local company pay for a portion or sometimes, all their advertising costs.
- Co-op advertising helps your customer's advertising budget go farther.
- Co-op advertising lends credibility to your advertiser's image.
- Co-op funds are accrued based on what and how much your customer buys.
- To qualify, your local customer must follow the manufacturer's rules.
- Your local advertiser is responsible for paying the advertising bill. It is their responsibility to present their advertising bill to the manufacturer for their participation.
- Co-op reimbursement is most often not a check to the advertiser but a credit on their bill.
- There can be special co-op funds available at the regional sales manager's level.
- A small business may need to place several small orders to make their co-op advertising meaningful.

"Marketing is no longer about the stuff that you make, but about the stories you tell." – *Seth Godin*, Bestselling author. (1960 -

12

Building Your Presentation

The goal of the customized presentation meeting is to answer the prospect's questions, and concerns that you learned about during your Customer Needs Assessment interview. You want to use your presentation to show your prospect how you can help them accomplish the goals they identified in the interview. The presentation can also help the prospect gain a better appreciation for Radio advertising.

The quality of your sales presentation depends on the amount of preparation you invest in the effort. One of the most common mistakes a salesperson will make is to use a generic presentation that doesn't speak directly to your prospect's needs and desires. Your presentation is the best chance you will have to show your prospect how you and your Radio station can help solve their problems.

To be sure, over time, you will find that you use many of your key value propositions from one presentation to the next, but the **presentation must show your prospect how those value propositions are going to work for them to solve their problems**.

We recommend that you download the latest copy of the *Why Radio?* presentation from the Radio Advertising Bureau (www.rab.com). They keep it updated with up-to-date presentation statistics, and the slides are colorful and professionally prepared. This download will save you time and effort.

For example, if your prospect is concerned about Radio's ability to drive in-store traffic, you can use the slides from the RAB to help illustrate how your Radio station can help the prospect drive in-store traffic.

The RAB also maintains a sample presentation format on their website. It corresponds to the sample RAB Customer Needs Assessment questions. Both are valuable downloads that can help you create an informative and compelling presentation.

Method of Presentation

Too many people get bogged down, trying to determine what kind of presentation they should make. The most common presentation software is PowerPoint, but you can use Google Slides, Microsoft Word, Google Docs, any word processor, or even a typewriter if you can still find one. Our point is that it is **the content of your presentation that should take precedence**, not the software you use to create the pages.

We don't recommend using laptops or tablets to display your presentation in front of the prospect. These devices can cause a distraction. If you have a new device, your prospect may be more interested in the features of your machine than they are in what you came to discuss. The prospect can quickly become distracted before you even begin your presentation. Besides, you run the risk of mechanical or software issues interrupting your presentation. Then there is the question of the size of your device. Small portable devices come with small mobile screens making it challenging to see what you're trying to communicate.

Something as basic as the 25" X 30" Post-it® Flip Chart Easel can work for a presentation. They come in plain white, white with a light blue grid and yellow lined rule like a note pad. Of course, you will have to hand-write each page of the presentation and draw your graphics, but with different colored markers, your presentation will be unique and attention-getting.

If you want to make a dramatic entrance and differentiate yourself from all the rest, you could even take your slides to Office Depot or Office Max and have them printed in a large format and mounted on a piece of foam board. When you walk into the prospect's office with large foam boards of presentation materials, it quickly gets their attention, and they want to hear what you have to say.

If you are going to present to a group, then an investment in a laptop, projector, and screen might be warranted. Don't neglect the screen. If you can't project on a flat white wall, you need a projection screen. Projecting on to a colored wall or a wall with a textured wall covering will jeopardize the fidelity of the projector's image on the wall, and it will be distracting for your prospects.

You will need to have a device for audio playback of the commercial you are going to write and record for your prospect. Your phone or tablet can playback a recording of the commercial, but the speaker is small and doesn't provide much fidelity. A small investment in some Bluetooth speakers can enhance the playback of your commercial and impress the prospect.

The Flip Chart Notebook

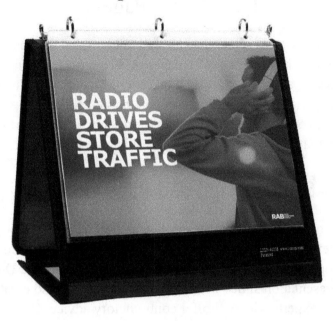

FIGURE 6

FIGURE 7

Our best recommendation is a flip chart notebook like the Lion Insta-Cover Ring Binder Easel, 3/4 Inches Ring, 1 Binder Easel (40008) available on Amazon. The notebook can hold up to 40 pages. The flip chart book gives you an edge in your presentation. The prospect can look at the presentation slide on their side of the flip chart notebook (Figure 6).

While at the same time, you can have your notes on your side of the notebook (Figure 7). This view helps you stay on track throughout the presentation. You won't be fumbling for the right words or lose your train of thought.

How Many Pages?

You will undoubtedly meet someone who will tell you that the best presentations are only "X" number of pages long. They might say 20 pages or 30 pages. It doesn't matter. Your presentation is going to take as many pages as it takes to tell your story. It all depends on what your story is, and that depends on the information you learned about in your Customer Needs Assessment. In any case, you will need to know your presentation by heart just in case. If you know your presentation material well, you should be able to deliver it with zero pages.

Slide Design and Page Content

With the advent of presentation software such as PowerPoint or Google Slides, many salespeople use these new software tools like word processors to create sales documents instead of using the more appropriate application like Microsoft Word or Google Docs. This choice has led to the problem of presentation slides with too much text. It has also created a cottage industry of so-called presentation experts who will offer contradictory advice. Our goal is to base our best recommendation on the latest brain science in learning, and just some plain common sense.

PowerPoint and Google Slides are presentation applications. Microsoft Word or Google Docs are sales document applications.

Salespeople have developed a bad habit of writing their sales proposals in a sales presentation application and then treating it like it was a sales document that should have been written in a word processor. The final document doesn't make a good sales presentation, nor does it make a good sales proposal. As a sales presentation, it has too much text on each page. As a sales document, it is printed in landscape mode, not portrait mode, and may not have enough information to tell the complete story.

Additional evidence that there is a difference in a word processor application and a presentation application is that both Microsoft PowerPoint and Google Slides include a **notes** component for each slide. This feature is a space attached to each slide for **the presenter's notes**, the script that goes with that slide (Figure 8). You can then print each slide on a page with an image of the slide in miniature and the slide notes below.

If you are now in the habit of creating presentations and just sending them to a long distant prospect, consider using the notes feature. Your presentation will look better and be more meaningful.

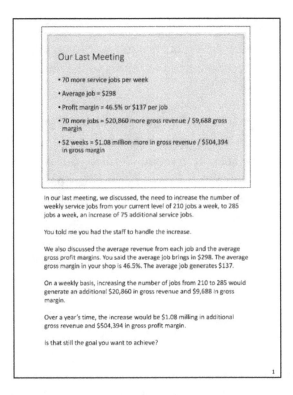

FIGURE 8

A sales presentation requires a narrator, you, for it to make any sense. Given a properly crafted sales presentation, the recipient shouldn't be able to determine the exact point of the presentation without the narrator's help. A sales document doesn't require a narrator because it includes a complete and detailed account of the proposal so the document can stand on its merit. It should be more comfortable for a recipient to understand a sales document more than a sales presentation. Believe it or not, there is a science behind the need to differentiate a sales presentation from a sales document.

An effective presentation is an exercise in visual storytelling. You are the storyteller. You are going to tell your prospect a story about how you and your Radio station can help the prospect achieve the goals, or overcome the challenges agreed upon in your Customer Needs Assessment interview. The slides in the presentation are there to add visual emphasis to your story. The words coming out of your mouth take precedence over the slides. **Your presentation slides should be light on words and strong on visual images**.

Adding too much text to a presentation slide is the biggest mistake the unprepared and poorly trained salesperson can make when creating a presentation slide. When you show the prospect a page with a paragraph of text and then start talking about the paragraph of text, **you shut down the brain's capacity for learning**. Neuroscientists have discovered that the brain processes visual and audio input separately. When the brain receives the same information simultaneously, both visually and audibly, the brain is forced to shut one or the other out and process one source of input.

You can prove this to yourself. Can you think of a time when you needed to read something important, and you asked the others around you to be quiet for a moment? Perhaps you were looking at a map for directions, and the others in the car were offering their suggestions.

When you ask your prospect to read a slide and listen to you at the same time, you are causing an information collision in the prospect's brain, and **you are inhibiting your prospect's ability to learn** how your proposal can help them. Neither your slide nor what you are saying about the slide can penetrate the prospect's limbic system, the pathway to the brain's central processing unit where decisions are made, and memories are stored. Your presentation material is all jammed up at the brain's central processing unit, forcing the brain to select one or the other. Rather than tell you to be quiet while they read the slide, your prospect just sits there, patiently acting like they are listening. When you finish, they say, "Thanks but no thanks." They didn't hear a word you said.

The words coming out of your mouth, the story you are telling the prospect is the primary delivery system for the information you want the prospect to consider. **It is the eye contact you make, the facial expressions you have and the enthusiasm you show while telling your story, that sells the prospect on your idea**. The slides in your presentation are designed to add visual emphasis to your story. The slides are the secondary delivery system. The two must work in harmony if you want your proposal information to reach the working memory of your prospect.

Here is an example of a typical presentation slide with too much text (Figure 9). The information is correct and factual, but this slide is better suited for your side of the flip chart notebook as your script for the slide. This page would make a good script for a slide, but it contains too much text for your prospect to process and retain easily. If you are essentially saying the same thing that's on the slide, you're going to create a mental traffic jam for your prospect. They will find it hard to process what you want them to learn from the slide.

> **Our Last Meeting**
>
> - In our last meeting we discussed the need to increase the number of weekly service jobs from your current level of 60% capacity to 80% capacity because you were already staffed up to handle 80% capacity. Maximum capacity is about 350 jobs a week. You're averaging about 210 jobs a week and you want to get that up to about 285 jobs a week. You also told me that the average service job was $298 and after parts and labor the gross profit margin was approximately $137 or 46.5%.
>
> - Seventy additional jobs each week is an additional $20,860 in gross revenue. At the 46.5% profit margin that's $9,688 in additional gross profit for the week.
>
> - Multiply that out for the 52 weeks in a year and that's an additional $1.08 million in gross revenue and $504,394 in gross profit margins.

FIGURE 9

The critical points on this slide are blended in with all the words you plan to say about this slide, giving them no special recognition. They don't stand out. It is difficult for the prospect to see that you have clearly outlined the goal of increasing the number of service jobs by 70 jobs per week. The impressive numbers, the increase in gross revenues and gross margin, are hidden in the paragraph. They don't pop out as you tell the story of your last meeting.

Also, the paragraph font size is 14-point. That is going to make it difficult for your prospect to read it from across the table from where you are sitting.

A much better approach is described in the second example (Figure 10). The key points are highlighted as bullet points. The items listed here are compatible with the words that you plan to speak as you tell your sales story.

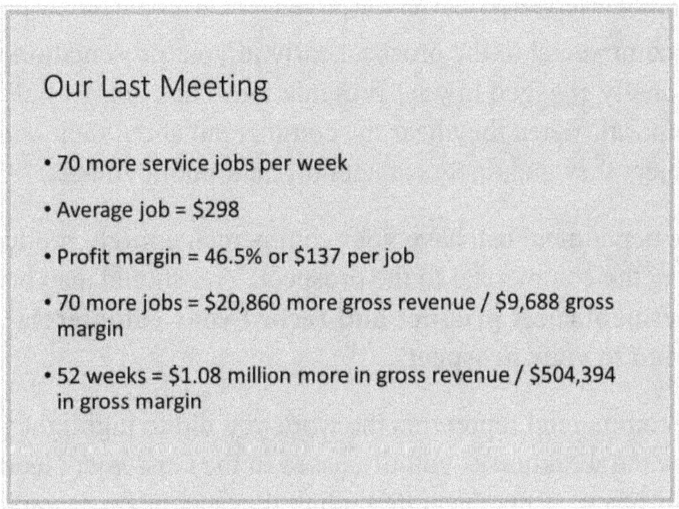

Our Last Meeting

- 70 more service jobs per week
- Average job = $298
- Profit margin = 46.5% or $137 per job
- 70 more jobs = $20,860 more gross revenue / $9,688 gross margin
- 52 weeks = $1.08 million more in gross revenue / $504,394 in gross margin

FIGURE 10

The prospect hears you recount the story of your last meeting and the recap of the critical points. As you tell the story behind this slide, each bullet point stands out and reminds the prospect of the essential reasons the two of you are meeting. You have a plan to accomplish these goals.

Refer to the slides in the RAB's *Why Radio?* presentation to see how a professional uses images, bullet points, and color to create an eye-catching slide.

Key Sections

The professional sales presentation is organized and to the point. The presentation is your story about how you and your company can help the prospect with their goals or challenges.

A Review of the Customer Needs Assessment Interview

The beginning of your presentation should be a review from the Customer Needs Assessment interview.

- A review of the goals or challenges agreed upon in the previous meeting with a focus on the gross margin questions.
- A **nail down**. "Are these still the issues we want to work on?"
- A review of the prospect's current advertising efforts and their perception of each, especially if they don't have a favorable view of Radio advertising.
- A **nail down**. "Has anything changed since our last meeting?"

The Commercial

Presenting the commercial to the prospect early in your presentation is a powerful way to get the prospect emotionally engaged in your presentation. The commercial is the most tangible component of your proposal. When they hear the commercial about their company, they become engaged in the one subject they genuinely care about, their public image.

If your creative department can have your commercial entirely produced and recorded, you will plan on playing the commercial to the prospect. You should also bring the printed script. **If your creative department can't produce and record your commercial, you can just read the commercial out loud to your prospect**.

Reviewing the commercial represents the work you did to highlight your prospect's strengths and overcome the weaknesses you discussed in the Customer Needs Assessment interview. When your prospect hears the commercial, they can begin to understand how your proposal will solve their marketing needs.

Presenting the commercial early in the presentation allows you to gauge the level of interest your prospect has in your proposal. You also can try a **soft closing question** by asking the prospect, "Could we run a commercial like that?" Even if the prospect takes issue with the commercial, you can ask, "What should we change?" Stopping at that point in the presentation and rewriting the script with the prospect's suggestions helps build buy-in. Their commitment to your idea is growing as they become engaged in the process of creating their commercial. The more conversation about the commercial message you have, the more engaged the prospect becomes in your proposal.

Media Strengths, Weaknesses and Adding Radio

Many times, when you encounter resistance, or the prospect tells you "No," there is a strong likelihood that what they mean is they don't yet **k-*NO*-w** enough to say "Yes." Given the study of human nature, it is improbable that you can ever change someone's mind. They are heavily invested in their current decision. Nobody wants to admit they made a wrong decision.

The truth of the matter is that **the prospect could make a new decision when presented with new information.**

One of the most important tools offered by the Radio Advertising Bureau is the information on competitive media. The RAB provides an extensive online library of detailed descriptions of all the most widely used advertising media. **Keep in mind that all advertising works**, they all can deliver a message to the public. Each medium has its strengths and weaknesses, even Radio.

If your prospect is using other media and has doubts about what Radio can do for them, your primary research destination should be the RAB's online *Competitive Media* section. You will find compelling evidence that by adding your Radio station to an existing advertising effort, your prospect can dramatically improve the reach and frequency of their current advertising efforts.

The Advertising Schedule

When describing the advertising schedule in your proposal, you have an opportunity to use a graphic instead of just words to explain where the commercials will broadcast on your Radio station.

When a TV advertiser buys TV advertising, they tend to buy a show like the 6:00 P.M. news or even more specific the sports report within the 6:00 P.M. news. When a prospect advertises in the newspaper, they often specify in which section they want their ad to appear. Both the newspaper and television station charge extra for specified placement.

The Schedule

• 35 60-second spots each week
• Commercials are evenly scheduled in all dayparts

FIGURE 11

The advertiser takes comfort knowing when and where their commercials will appear. You should take advantage of their need for a sense of security and illustrate in a graphic form when and where their commercials will broadcast on your Radio station.

If you are proposing a feature sponsorship that runs every day at the same time, your job is more straightforward than describing a schedule of commercials that are placed throughout the week. That's why a graphic description can help the prospect feel comfortable about their ad placement.

The description of the advertising plan illustrated in Figure 11 is not a graphic illustration. It is just words detailing how many commercials are in the proposal. **Please note, the poorly chosen words** *spots* **and** *dayparts.* Those are Radio terms. You need to use the word commercial and the word time slot instead to make it easier for your prospect to understand your proposal.

Rid your vocabulary of those words.

This illustration is an example of a presentation slide using a graphic depiction of the advertising schedule (Figure 12). Each day and time slot is labeled on the graphic, and we use the indicator of *1X* to represent one commercial in that specific time slot.

We have **replaced the word spots with commercials**, and **the word dayparts with time slots**. Please also note, the first time slot of the day is midnight to 6:00 A.M., not 6:00 A.M. to 10:00 A.M.

The Schedule

• 35 60-second commercials each week

• Commercials are evenly scheduled in all time slots

	Mon	Tue	Wed	Thu	Fri	Sat	Sun
12m-6a	1X	1X	1X	1X	1X	1X	1X
6a-10a	1X	1X	1X	1X	1X	1X	1X
10a-3p	1X	1X	1X	1X	1X	1X	1X
3p-7p	1X	1X	1X	1X	1X	1X	1X
7p-12m	1X	1X	1X	1X	1X	1X	1X

FIGURE 12

If your advertising proposal is less than a 52-week annual schedule, you should use a graphic to describe the specific weeks where the prospect's commercials will appear. Using the Radio Advertising Bureau's broadcast month calendar with a yellow highlighter is an easy and effective way to illustrate the coverage of your proposal.

The Reach and Frequency of the Proposal

If your Radio station subscribes to a rating service, you should provide a description of the reach and the frequency of your proposed advertising schedule. **Reach is how many people**

will hear the prospect's commercial. Frequency is how many times the average listener will hear the commercial. Be sure to use the feature for accumulated reach and accumulated frequency. **That is a calculation of the reach and frequency across the entire schedule, not just one week.**

The accumulated reach and frequency is one of Radio's most significant strengths! Reach, and frequency accumulate over time. This fact is compelling evidence for proposing a consistent advertising proposal. That's why the rating software has this function built right in. It takes some extra time for you to input the specific weeks for the entire schedule, but your reach and frequency numbers will be much more persuasive.

The Estimated Return on Investment

No presentation is complete without an estimated Return on Investment. The keyword is **estimated** return on investment. When you take the numbers necessary for your prospect to reach their goals or overcome their problems, and compare that to the reach and frequency of your proposed schedule, you will most likely find that only a small portion of the people who will be exposed to the prospects commercial need respond for the campaign to be a success. This sets you up for another trial close, "Don't you think it's possible with this great commercial we can get that many people to respond? Would you like to give it a try?"

You will learn how to calculate an estimated Return on Investment in the next chapter.

Summary

In this chapter on Building Your Presentation, we covered the following topics:

- The goal of the customized presentation is to use the presentation meeting to answer the prospect's questions, and concerns that you learned about during your Customer Needs Assessment interview.
- Download the latest copy of the *Why Radio?* presentation from the Radio Advertising Bureau.
- Using laptops or tablets to display your presentation in front of the prospect is not recommended. These devices can cause a distraction.
- You want to use your presentation to show your prospect just how you can help them accomplish the goals they identified in the interview.
- Your presentation is going to take as many pages as it takes to tell your story. It all depends on what your story is, and that depends on the information you learned about in your Customer Needs Assessment.
- The critical sections of a professional presentation:
  - o Review of the Customer Needs Assessment interview.
  - o Demonstrate the commercial.
  - o Discuss the strengths and weaknesses of the media involved.
  - o Demonstrate the benefits of adding Radio advertising.

- o   A graphical description of the advertising schedule.
- o   A reach and frequency estimate.
- o   The estimated return on investment.

"Nowadays, people know the price of everything and the value of nothing." – *Oscar Wilde*, Irish poet, and playwright. (1854 – 1900)

13

Return on Investment

The definition of a Return on Investment (ROI) is the gain or loss generated on an investment relative to the amount of money invested. ROI is usually expressed as a percentage.

For example, you buy some stock in a company for $1,000. One year later, you sell that same stock for $1,200. You get your $1,000 initial investment back, plus an additional $200. You made a 20% profit or a 20% ROI. Return on investment is usually directly related to the amount of risk involved. Treasury Bills issued by the U.S. Government are considered relatively risk free. In 2019, 10-year Treasury Bills were paying approximately 2.5% interest, or a 2.5% ROI, provided you are willing to invest your money with the U.S. Government for the next ten years.

On the other hand, a high-yield, high-risk security can pay a higher ROI, provided you are willing to risk losing some or all your original investment. The ROI is almost always directly related to the amount of risk the investor is willing to take. High risk can mean high returns or possibly a significant loss.

Advertising is not an Investment

Advertising is technically not an investment. It is a business expense. In accounting, the money spent on advertising is an expense on the income statement, sometimes called the Profit and Loss statement or the P&L. Investments, like a building, vehicles, or manufacturing equipment, are recorded as assets on the balance sheet. You won't find advertising on a balance sheet. So, don't make the mistake of telling your prospect that, "Advertising isn't an expense, it's an investment!" It simply isn't true.

That doesn't stop business owners from trying to measure an ROI on their advertising expense. It's only natural to hold every penny you spend accountable to the bottom line. If you spend money on advertising, you want to see that you get something back in return. This desire for accountability, or instant gratification, is what has driven the popularity of digital advertising. However, instead of measuring the ROI in terms of increased gross sales, too many business owners have become consumed with their cost-per-click (CPC) or cost-per-view (CPV) and other metrics and not on the overall increase in sales.

On their Q4 Earnings Call in 2017, the world's largest advertiser, Proctor & Gamble, revealed they had cut up to $200 million from their digital advertising spending in just six months because of bots, brand safety concerns, and ineffective ads.[31] The consumer products giant indicated they had moved those advertising funds to Radio and TV, which offer much more audience reach and improvements to the company's e-commerce efforts.

Six months later, Proctor & Gamble reported their most robust quarterly growth rate in five years.[32]

That is the accurate measure of a Return on Investment, year over year revenue growth. It must be year-over-year to take into consideration a host of external factors over which you and the business owner have no control.

Advertising is not an investment. Advertising is an expense. Advertising spreads the business owner's message around to thousands of people. **Consistent advertising builds awareness with thousands of people**. Brand awareness can sometimes be considered an asset. You might find it labeled **Good Will** on a balance sheet.

Mindshare Equals Market Share

The primary goal of advertising is to make consumers think of one brand over the brand's competitors. You can measure consumer awareness of different brands. **Mindshare** is a marketing term that describes the amount of consumer awareness of a company, brand, or product. Mindshare is a precursor to market share. The customer must know about the company, brand, or product before they can make a purchase. You can tell your prospect, **"They gotta know you before they need you."**

It is possible to have some negative mindshare in the market, especially if there has been a serious event involving the company, brand, or product. Poorly crafted and annoying advertising can also contribute to negative mindshare. Researchers can also measure **heart share**, the amount of positive or negative mindshare.

---

[31] Adweek *When Proctor & Gamble Cut $200 Million in Digital Ad Spend* (March 1, 2018)
[32] Wall Street Journal *P&G Posts Strongest Sales Growth in Five Years* (October 12, 2018)

While advertising is technically an expense on the income statement, growing the mindshare and positive heart share of your prospect's business will ultimately lead to market share growth.

Example ROI

In our example interview from the chapter on the Customer Needs Assessment, we used an auto service center as a prospect. In addition to other issues we identified, the interview revealed that the shop is running at 60% capacity when it is staffed to handle 80% capacity.

The service manager said that they are equipped to do 350 jobs a week, they are currently at 60% utilization or 210 service jobs a week. She said she would like to get to 80% utilization or an additional 70 service jobs a week.

We are using the 2018 Dealer Profile from the National Automobile Dealers Association for our example numbers. You can find monthly updates at www.nada.org every month. These numbers are for the average dealership. That includes dealerships from the largest cities to the smallest towns in America.

According to the NADA, the average dealership did 18,544 service orders in 2018. The average order was $298. The average gross profit margin was 46.5%. So, the dealership made $137 on the average service job. The average dealer did $6.9 million in service and part sales in 2018.

Your prospect wants to grow from 210 jobs a week to 280 jobs a week. Seventy additional jobs, at $298 per job, is an additional $20,860 per week in service and parts revenue. At the 46.5% profit margin, that's an additional $9,699 in gross profit for the week. Multiply those figures out by 52 weeks, and you're talking about trying to increase gross sales in the service department by $1.08 million and the gross profits by $504,394.

If you are working with a free-standing service center without a dealership, the overall gross numbers may be much smaller, but the average service order and the average profit margins should be about the same across the automotive service category. Some online resources suggest that the profit margins in a free-standing service center are between 50 and 60 percent, slightly more than the service center in a dealership. Regardless of the size of your customer, you want to devote a substantial amount of energy to determine the numbers.

Just for the sake of discussion, cut our example in half. Your prospective service center can do 175 service jobs a week instead of 350. They want to grow from 105 service jobs a week to 140 per week. You are still talking about increasing gross sales of more than $10,000 a week and gross profit margins of $5,000. In one year, that is $520,000 in gross sales and $250,000 in gross profit.

The Math of Return on Investment

To calculate the prospect's possible return on investment, you take the cost of your weekly advertising schedule, in this example, we will use a $2,000 weekly advertising schedule in our calculations. If the $2,000 advertising campaign reaches enough people enough times to cause 70 people to bring their car in for service, the additional gross revenue generated is $20,866.

Deduct the cost of the advertising from the additional gross revenue to determine the net revenue growth. Divide the net revenue growth by the cost of the advertising and multiply it by 100.

Additional Gross Revenue	$20,866
Advertising Costs	-$2,000
	========
Net Increase in Revenue	$18,866
Return on Investment	943%

Table 2

Your prospect may want to only calculate the return on investment on the gross profit margin gain. Do the math again on the gross profit margin of $9,699. It is still an impressive ROI

Additional Gross Margin	$9,699
Advertising Costs	-$2,000
	========
Net Increase in Margin	$7,699
Return on Investment	384%

Table 3

If you want to get even more granular, in our example, the average gross margin is $137 per customer. For $2,000 in advertising, you only need 14 new customers to come in per week to break even on the advertising. Each new customer, after that, represents a 6% return on investment.

Keep in mind that advertising builds awareness. The more your prospect advertises, the more people will hear the message. You need to set expectations that in the beginning, the response may fall short of 70 new customers a week. But with consistency, the results will grow and grow.

No presentation is complete without an estimated Return on Investment. The keyword is **estimated** return on investment. When you compare the numbers necessary for your prospect to reach their goals or overcome their problems, to the reach and frequency of your proposed schedule, you will most likely find that only a small portion of the people who will be exposed to the prospect's commercial need respond for the campaign to be a success.

Presenting an estimated return on investment sets you up for another trial close, "Don't you think it's possible with this great commercial we can get that many people to respond? Would you like to give it a try?"

Summary

In this chapter on Return on Investment, we covered the following topics:

- The definition of a Return on Investment (ROI) is the gain or loss generated on an investment relative to the amount of money invested. ROI is usually expressed as a percentage.
- Advertising is technically not an investment. It is a business expense. In accounting, the money spent on advertising is an expense on the income statement, sometimes called the Profit and Loss statement or the P&L. Advertising builds awareness and goodwill, which can be assets.
- **Mindshare** is a marketing term that describes the amount of consumer awareness of a company, brand, or product. Mindshare is a precursor to market share. The customer must know about the company, brand, or product before they can make a purchase. You can tell your prospect, **"They gotta know you before they need you."**

"Good advertising does not just circulate information. It penetrates the public mind with desire and belief." – *Leo Burnett*, Founder, *Leo Burnet Company, Inc.* (1891 – 1971)

14

Developing the Advertising Schedule

In Radio sales, increasing your knowledge is the most effective way to begin adding value because the added benefit is unique to you. Companies can duplicate products and manufacturing processes, but it is tough to replicate the individual who adds their exceptional value to the transaction.

Successful advertising depends on learning how to effectively schedule your client's commercials in such a way to ensure the schedule has a balance of both reach and frequency. **One of the leading causes of dissatisfaction among advertisers is poor scheduling techniques used by many salespeople that puts the client's reach AND frequency out of balance**.

To serve your customer's best interests, you must propose advertising schedules which provide a balanced reach and frequency that they can afford to maintain over the long term, not just for a few weeks. **One of the first traps that might victimize any advertising salesperson is letting the business test your advertising for a few weeks, and if it works, then they'll sign up for a consistent schedule.** Another trap is allowing your prospect to give you a few hundred dollars to see what you can do with it. In both cases, it is evident that an in-depth Customer Needs Assessment interview was not completed.

The cost of an advertising plan is based mainly on the amount of reach and the amount of frequency the schedule delivers. In some media, there are additional production costs like the cost of the billboard paper or the cost of the direct mail piece. Beyond that, the price boils down to reach and frequency.

Advertising is a lot like physical exercise. If you want to begin a new workout, at first, it is hard. If you choose jogging, the first day you may be able to run only a few tenths of a mile. But if you stick with it, each day you'll be able to run just a bit further. Same with strength conditioning. On your first day, you may be able to lift only 50 pounds. You may be able to do only a couple of reps. But if you stick with it, you'll be able to add weight and reps. In both examples, running and strength conditioning, the key to success is to pick something and stick with it.

If a prospect tells you that they tried Radio advertising once and it didn't work, that's like saying you tried exercise once and it didn't work. The problem word in both sentences is *once*. You can't go jogging *once* and get in shape. You can't go lift weights *once* and expect to increase your strength.

This is important to understand and teach your clients, so they will understand why some advertising plans cost less or cost more than what you are proposing. Upon close examination, you will find that either the reach or the frequency of the other proposal is different than what you are offering.

Therefore, it is so essential to understand the strengths and weaknesses of all the media options available to your prospect. Each one offers a different ability to deliver both reach and frequency. The Competitive Media Report maintained by the Radio Advertising Bureau at www.rab.com is the best resource for up-to-date competitive information on all of the major media choices.

Direct mail, individual direct mail not an envelope of coupons, has targeted reach, but because of the high cost of printing and postage, direct mail often has a frequency of one or two across an entire year.

Billboards have a reach of those consumers who pass by the board but not consumers in other parts of town. The frequency of the board is limited to the frequency of those commuters who routinely pass that location.

Social media offers targeted reach, sometimes large, sometimes small, but with a limited frequency depending on how many times your ad is served to the target audience.

When it comes to Radio scheduling, we must understand what our radio station can provide in the way of reach and frequency. There are two primary scheduling techniques, Call to Action scheduling and Branding Scheduling.

Call to Action Advertising

Call to Action is a marketing term used extensively in advertising and selling. It refers to any advertising designed to prompt an immediate response or encourage a quick sale. Call to Action advertising can also apply to the use of words or phrases that can be incorporated into sales scripts, advertising messages, or web pages that encourage consumers to take prompt action.

Phrases like "Call now and mention Rock 103" or "Enter promo code rock103" are examples of Call to Action advertising. Other examples could include "Hurry, sale ends Saturday" or "Limited to the next 50 callers."

The business owner's desire for instant and measurable results from their advertising or the need for immediate cash flow drives much of Call to Action advertising.

Call to Action advertising is not for every business. Imagine you are standing on a stage in front of 1,000 people with a Call to Action advertising message for a company. How many of the 1,000 people are likely to respond to your message?

Can you imagine a plumber using Call to Action advertising to promote a discount on plumbing repairs? It doesn't matter how great the offer if you don't have a plumbing problem, you probably won't call. And since the message included some encouragement to act now before the offer expires, your brain subconsciously says, "**I don't need to save that information for later**" and it is quickly forgotten.

Call to Action advertising is designed to encourage a consumer to make a purchase quickly. A car dealer advertises a big sale on new cars. It probably won't influence those consumers who have a relatively new vehicle with which they are already satisfied. A sale on appliances, carpet, or home improvement won't mean much to people who live in an apartment. Except for food products and other necessary consumables, not everyone is in the market for a specific product at the same time. The number of potential new customers is limited to those with an immediate need and the financial resources to take action.

Call to Action advertising requires more money than most of your local prospects are willing to spend. The advertiser must buy enough advertising across enough different media to reach as many people as possible, just to reach those few consumers who are in the right place at the right time, to take advantage of the Call to Action offer. The advertiser needs to buy Radio, TV, cable, newspaper, outdoor, digital, and even direct mail to reach as many potential customers as possible. The advertiser must cast a wide net across the entire population of the market to find enough new customers to generate a profitable Return on Investment.

An actual Call to Action advertising schedule on your Radio station would require at least one commercial each hour, 24 hours a day for many weeks in a row. If your station policy allows two commercials from the same advertiser, then you should run two commercials each hour, 24 hours a day, week after week. That's how the prospect can reach all your listeners with their offer.

If you are working with a prospect who thinks they want to advertise a Call to Action offer on just one of your Radio stations for a few weeks, STOP! You run the risk of committing **Marketing Malpractice** if you follow through and allow them to buy a small, short-term schedule that **fits their budget** with a Call to Action message. The results probably won't meet their expectations.

Think about it this way; would you respond to the advertiser's message yourself? Does the offer motivate you to make an immediate purchase? If you wouldn't respond to the Call to Action advertising message, chances are there are thousands of other people just like you, listening to your Radio station who won't respond either.

The truth behind most Call to Action advertising is it is often used as a matter of last resort. The business is usually in an overstocked condition, and they need to move a lot of inventory quickly. Not only do they increase their overhead with massive spending on advertising, but they also lower their profit margins by reducing the sale price. It's a matter of cash flow and not profit margins. Many times, the business must liquidate the inventory at any cost, sometimes at a loss just to pay bills and keep their creditors at bay.

Branding Advertising

Successful Branding Advertising is not about how much money your client spends. It is more about how long your client spends what they can afford to spend month after month after month after month. Branding Advertising is more in sync with the psychology of consumer behavior because the goal of Branding Advertising is to be known before you are needed. That way, when a consumer has a triggering event, they already know that your client can help them.

Branding Advertising can easily have a lower monthly cost because the success is based on consistency, not immediacy. Call to Action advertising has a substantial monthly cost because the emphasis is on the here-and-now, not on the future. Branding Advertising grows in reach and frequency every month; the longer your client follows your advice. The Call to Action customer is starting over from zero every time they do a Call to Action campaign because it is all sale based, time-dependent, the consumer must act by a specific date and time, and that doesn't lead to a place in the consumer's long term memory.

Instead of urging consumers to respond immediately because of an offer, usually a discount price, Branding Advertising is more about reminding the consumer about the next time they need a product or service. Branding Advertising is designed to encourage consumers to shop with the advertiser based on specific characteristics of the advertiser that resonates with the consumers instead of just a low price.

Think of the business categories you need when you least expect it, a tow truck, a locksmith, a body shop or a plumber, for example. When you need their services, **you need their services right away!** A compelling Branding Advertising message is memorable. It lives in long term memory because the consumer has a positive impression about that business before they need that business.

The future of online search will not involve typing on a computer or typing on a keypad. The future of search is the spoken word. Whether the consumer says, "Alexa, call ABC Plumbing," or they search for "Plumbers near me," the goal of Branding Advertising is to be that name that comes to mind first or stands out in a crowd, based on a previously formed positive impression. When the business owner's business name comes to mind first, **they have achieved Top of Mind Awareness.** They are on **the top rung of the Ladder of Importance**. They have **mindshare, which leads to market share.**

In all advertising, **the cost of the advertising is frequently driven by the amount of reach and frequency the advertiser can achieve with their advertising schedule**. If the advertiser has a large budget, they can achieve a large amount of reach and frequency. If they have a modest budget, they can achieve a modest amount of reach and frequency. But there is nothing wrong with that because with consistency, **on Radio, both reach and frequency accumulate over time.**

In other words, the more consistently an advertiser deploys their Branding message, the number of people exposed to the message will grow. The consumers who have already been exposed to the message will hear it time and time again, but only with consistency. Over time, your listeners will begin to believe that they hear that advertiser's message all the time, but that is just the result of the accumulated impressions in the listener's mind.

With Branding Advertising, the size of the advertising budget dictates the speed at which the audience exposure grows. With a larger budget, the Branding message can reach more people more quickly because the advertiser has more commercials. They can reach the total audience sooner than the smaller budget advertiser. They will also build more frequency with the audience in the same time period.

But even with a smaller budget, the advertising campaign will also reach the total audience in due time **because reach and frequency accumulate over time**. But both require a commitment to consistency.

The Standard Broadcast Calendar

The Gregorian calendar is the calendar used most in the world. It is named after Pope Gregory XIII who introduced it in October 1582. It has twelve months of 28 to 31 days each. Months don't always start and end on the same day every year. Some months may begin on a Tuesday while others might begin on a Friday.

In advertising, we use what is called a **broadcast calendar**. The broadcast calendar is a standardized calendar used primarily for the planning and purchase of radio and television programs and advertising. Every week in the broadcast calendar starts on a Monday and ends on a Sunday, and every month has either four or five such weeks. Broadcast calendar months have either 28 or 35 days. See the example of a broadcast calendar from the Radio Advertising Bureau in Appendix E. An updated version is freely available online at www.rab.com.

The first day of the broadcast calendar month is always the first day after the last Sunday of the month. That means if the last Sunday of the month is the 27th, the first day of a broadcast calendar month will be the 28th day on the Gregorian calendar. This difference can be confusing at first, but you can train your brain to see advertising in a weekly format.

Why would the advertising business come up with a different kind of calendar for developing advertising schedules?

The broadcast calendar closely matches certain specialized financial calendars, such as the **4-4-5 calendar**. This dedicated calendar is used for managing accounting periods in business and is a standard calendar structure for many industries such as retail and manufacturing. The 4-4-5 calendar allows a company to compare a period to the same period in the prior year or use week by week data comparisons. Its primary advantage over a regular calendar is that the end date of the period is always the same day of the week, which is useful for shift or manufacturing planning as every period is the same length.

So, the advertising industry developed similar calendars so that advertising schedules and billing statements would closely mirror the business accounting policies of the advertiser.

There are 52 weeks in a year. There are 13 weeks in a quarter. Advertising schedules are built on the unit of a week at a time, not a month at a time. **The week always starts on Monday. The week always ends on Sunday**.

Time Slots vs. Day Parts

Which do you think is easier for a businessperson to understand, the word **time slot** or the word **daypart**? Go with the safe choice, **time slot**. Brain science tells you that when confusion begins, learning stops. You don't want to inhibit teaching your prospect how you can help them by using too many industry **buzz-words**.

There are five major time slots throughout the day; midnight to 6:00 a.m., 6:00 a.m. to 10:00 a.m., 10:00 a.m. to 3:00 p.m., 3:00 p.m. to 7:00 p.m. to 12:00 midnight. Over a week, there are thirty-five different time slots (Figure 13).

The day begins at midnight, not 6:00 a.m. Your Radio station scheduling and billing software treat the day that way in your business records. You need to start thinking that way in your schedule planning. Stay away from calling it the *overnight* time slot, especially in our 24-hour, 7-day a week world we live in today. **We live in a mobile society** where everyone drives. So, midnight to 6:00 a.m. is night drive time. There is a morning drive, mid-day drive, afternoon drive, evening drive, and weekend drive time.

The Schedule – 168 Commercials

	Mon	Tue	Wed	Thu	Fri	Sat	Sun
12m-6a	6X	6X	6X	6X	6X	6X	6X
6a-10a	4X	4X	4X	4X	4X	4X	4X
10a-3p	5X	5X	5X	5X	5X	5X	5X
3p-7p	4X	4X	4X	4X	4X	4X	4X
7p-12m	5X	5X	5X	5X	5X	5X	5X

FIGURE 13

Building **Top of Mind Awareness** is all about concentrating an advertiser's branding message to reach the total audience of your Radio station. **There are 168 hours in a week**. An advertising schedule of 168 commercials, one in every hour during the week, is a concentration across the entire week (Figure 13).

Own a Week Schedule – 35 Commercials

	Mon	Tue	Wed	Thu	Fri	Sat	Sun
12m-6a	1X	1X	1X	1X	1X	1X	1X
6a-10a	1X	1X	1X	1X	1X	1X	1X
10a-3p	1X	1X	1X	1X	1X	1X	1X
3p-7p	1X	1X	1X	1X	1X	1X	1X
7p-12m	1X	1X	1X	1X	1X	1X	1X

FIGURE 14

Thirty-five commercials in a week, one in every time slot, is a practical concentration across the week for most advertising budgets you will encounter. This type of advertising schedule targets every time slot of every day with the advertiser's branding message. This type of blanket coverage across a week has been called; **owning the week** (Figure 14).

Own a Day Schedule – 1 per hour

	Mon	Tue	Wed	Thu	Fri	Sat	Sun
12m-6a	6X						6X
6a-10a	4X						4X
10a-3p	5X						5X
3p-7p	4X						4X
7p-12m	5X						5X

FIGURE 15

Some Radio schedules are designed to **own a day**, running one commercial every hour for 24 hours a day on a specific day or days of the week (Figure 15). This scheduling technique has proven effective for the weight loss category as people who overindulge on the weekends, fret about it on Monday and Tuesday. It is also a useful technique in the food category if a restaurant is trying to promote dining specials on a specific day of the week, consistently, week after week.

Own a Time Slot Schedule – 1 per hour

	Mon	Tue	Wed	Thu	Fri	Sat	Sun
12m-6a							
6a-10a							
10a-3p							
3p-7p	4X	4X	4X	4X	4X	4X	4X
7p-12m							

FIGURE 16

You can even take the **own a week** and **own a day concept** and create an **own a time slot schedule** with one or two commercials every hour, four hours a day, seven days a week (Figure 16).

The advertising schedule to **own a week** goes from a shotgun blast with many commercials covering all the time slots over the entire week, to a rifle shot covering a single time slot every day.

For an advertiser on a very tight budget, perhaps the **feature sponsorship** is most appropriate. Instead of four commercials, one in every hour of the time slot, the advertiser sponsors a **feature** like the *7:00 a.m. newscast* or the *George Strait Straight at Eight*. Even though the advertising schedule is limited in the number of commercials, the listeners associate the commercials with the **programming element** that the programming department uses to attract a larger listening audience. The advertiser's commercial is right in the middle of something different; it is set apart from the other commercials helping the advertiser stand out and get noticed.

When an advertiser sponsors a programming element that the listeners like and enjoy, the advertiser's business name becomes associated in the listener's mind with the affection the listener has for the programming element. Listeners understand that Radio is an advertiser-sponsored medium. Without the commercials, the listeners wouldn't have free access to their favorite music and programming. They appreciate the sponsors for supporting their favorite Radio station.

A good strategy for a small advertiser is to buy a feature in the morning and one in the afternoon every day, catching listeners as they drive to work and then back home again.

Pricing Structure

The only source of revenue in a Radio station comes from the sale of advertising time on the air, or on your stream or display space in your digital products. Radio stations do not receive any government support to stay on the air. **The sales of advertising is the only source of revenue**.

Advertising prices are based on the number of people listening in any given time slot. The *Morning Drive* from 6:00 a.m. to 10:00 a.m. on most Radio stations, generally has the largest audience and consequently, the highest prices for commercials. The night drive time from 12:00 midnight to 6:00 a.m. often has a smaller audience, so the price for commercials is usually less.

When comparing the different prices between Radio stations and other media choices, the difference always comes down to the amount of **reach** and the amount of **frequency** that the medium can provide.

Within a time slot, say 6:00 a.m. to 10:00 a.m., a Radio station may charge a premium, an extra charge, if the advertiser wants to narrow the time slot down to 7:00 a.m. to 8:00 a.m.

Rotators

A **rotator** is a name given to a commercial schedule that can run anytime over many time slots, midnight to midnight, for example. Rotators often come with a slightly lower price because the Radio station has the flexibility to schedule the rotator commercials last after all the higher-priced commercials are scheduled in their time slots.

Rotators are often requested by advertising agencies to get your station **on the buy** or to meet the advertiser's **target cost-per-point**. Many advertising salespeople have fallen into this trap and regularly offer rotators to make a sale.

We enthusiastically discourage the use of rotators because they will inevitably lead to a misunderstanding between you and your customer and you will always lose.

The higher the price of the commercial, the greater control the customer has on the placement of the commercial. The lower the price of the commercial, the greater control the Radio station has on the placement of the commercial.

Because rotators usually cost less than drive time commercials, the rotators get scheduled last. Rotators get any time left over. The problem is one of expectations. Theoretically, rotators purchased to rotate between midnight and midnight, could all run between 1:00 a.m. and 3:00 a.m. The customer expects some of those rotators to run in the daytime drive time slots. When they get their bill and see that they didn't receive many commercials in the daytime time slots, they are unhappy.

Another common rotator is 6:00 a.m. to 10:00 p.m. Once again, the advertiser expects their rotators to fall evenly throughout the day. But because the rotator has a lower price, it has a lower priority. It will be scheduled last. All the commercials could end up between 7:00 p.m. and 10:00 p.m.

It is our opinion that many salespeople also use rotators to save time when writing up a sales order. Instead of creating five separate line-items, one for each of the time slots, the salesperson enters one line-item with a broad time slot. That sales order is your instruction to your scheduling office that the commercials can run anytime within that time slot. Take the time to increase the accuracy and detail of your sales order by being specific about the time slots requested.

If you want to avoid confusion and customer problems, don't sell rotators.

Accumulated Reach & Frequency

Regardless of whether the plan is to own a week, a day, a time slot or a feature sponsorship, it will only work, **it will only build Top of Mind Awareness if the advertiser commits to be consistent, week after week, month after month**. That's why the First Key to Advertising Success is consistency.

Advertising reach, the number of different people who will hear your prospect's commercial, and advertising frequency, the number of times each consumer hears your prospect's commercial, grow over time. When your prospect follows your advice to be consistent, their advertising message will eventually reach enough of your audience, enough times, to start making a meaningful and profitable difference at the advertiser's cash register.

If your Radio station subscribes to a rating service, you need to learn how to calculate the accumulated reach and the accumulated frequency of your proposed schedule. The accumulated reach and frequency will be an imposing number.

This example is a real-world example of a local Radio station in a small midwestern town, population 150,000; it is using rating research from the leading audience measurement company. Using the **Own a Week** schedule of thirty-five commercials each week, one in each time slot on every day, that schedule will be heard by 25,400 different people approximately three times in one week.

However, if the prospect commits to running the same **Own a Week** schedule every week for fifty-two straight weeks, **the accumulated reach grows to 76,600 different people** who heard the message over forty different times.

Frequency is defined as the **average number of times a person is exposed to the radio schedule**. Over a year, your schedule has over 1,000 commercials. That means that some of your station's listeners will hear the commercial hundreds of times.

When you persuade your prospect to commit to the First Key of Advertising Success, **consistency**, their advertising reach, and frequency grows and grows to the point of market saturation. Then, when a consumer has a **triggering event**, your prospect's brand name has **top-of-mind awareness** and is going to be the brand name selected.

If you want to sell more long-term advertising schedules, then you need to stop using short term data.

Summary

In this chapter on Developing the Advertising Schedule, we covered the following topics:

- In Radio sales, increasing your knowledge is the most effective way to begin adding value because the added benefit is unique to you. Companies can duplicate products and manufacturing processes, but it is tough to replicate the individual who adds their exceptional value to the transaction.
- Call to Action is a marketing term used extensively in advertising and selling. It refers to any advertising designed to prompt an immediate response or encourage a quick sale.

- The broadcast calendar closely matches certain specialized financial calendars, such as the **4-4-5 calendar**. The 4-4-5 calendar allows a company to compare a period to the same period in the prior year or use week by week data comparisons.
- Which do you think is easier for a businessperson to understand, the word **time slot** or the word **daypart**? Go with the safe choice, **time slot**. Brain science tells you that when confusion begins, learning stops. You don't want to inhibit teaching your prospect how you can help them by using too many industry **buzz-words**.
- A **rotator** is a name given to a commercial schedule that can run anytime over many time slots, midnight to midnight, for example. Rotators often come with a slightly lower price because the Radio station has the flexibility to schedule the rotator commercials last after all the higher-priced commercials are scheduled in their time slots.
- Advertising reach, the number of different people who will hear your prospect's commercial, and advertising frequency, the number of times each consumer hears your prospect's commercial, grow over time.

"Creativity may well be the last legal unfair competitive advantage we can take to run over the competition." – *Dave Trott*, Award-winning copywriter. (1947 -

15

Writing the Creative Message

To be a good copywriter, you must learn to work **with** the psychology of the consumer, not against it. You must first understand why people buy things and why they buy them **when** they buy them. If you don't consider this critical science in your scriptwriting efforts, your commercial will likely prove to be ineffective.

Consumers are motivated from within, not from external sources. Any decision to buy a product or a service begins as a conscious, or, many times, an unconscious need or a desire. That need or desire, that thought is what we call the **felt need**. The felt need is something that the consumer is thinking about throughout the day **and** night.

You must also learn how consumers decide to act out on the felt need. As you study the research and the brain science involved, you will come to realize that having a sale or offering a discount is not one of the primary considerations in the process.

Maslow's Hierarchy of Needs

In his 1943 paper *A Theory of Human Motivation*, Abraham Maslow proposed that the motivation for action is an unfulfilled need. Maslow's research suggests that humans seek to satisfy their needs and desires in a specific hierarchy. Maslow contends that people must fulfill their most basic needs first before they can go forward and fulfill the more sophisticated needs.

Level One – Physiological Needs

A human's physiological needs take the highest priority. You need be able to breathe, have plenty of water and food, and have healthy bodily functions.

Level Two – Safety Needs

People need to feel secure in their life. They are concerned about the safety and security of their families, their property, and their future.

Level Three – Social Needs

People need to have a network of friends and social connections. Loneliness can lead to social anxiety and depression. Loneliness often leads to severe physical illness and possibly even heart disease.

Level Four – Self Esteem

We have a need to feel good about ourselves; we need to have self-respect. We need people who we can look up to in life. Respecting role models and leaders is something Maslow identified as part of our need for esteem.

Level Five – Self Actualization

At the pinnacle of Maslow's Hierarchy of Needs is the need for self-actualization, the instinctual need of humans to make the most of their unique abilities and to strive to be the best they can be. In short, self-actualization is reaching one's fullest potential.

How is this relevant to advertising? Start observing the advertising you are exposed to through the lens of Maslow's Hierarchy of Needs, and you'll see the word **you** and **your** throughout.

Pharmaceutical advertising is the sixth-largest advertising category. Examples: "When **you** have COPD, it can be hard to breathe," "Chantix can help **you** quit smoking," "When **you're** depressed, Cymbalta can help."

Consider the proliferation of advertising for home security systems, insurance, and financial services. Examples: "Can **your** doorbell do that?" "Are **you** in good hands?" "If **you** don't like their answer, ask again at Schwab."

Human beings have a natural need to be involved in emotionally based relationships. Whether those relationships come from large or small social groups or one-on-one relationships, people need to love and be loved by others. Examples: "**You** don't have to be lonely at Farmers Only Dot Com."

The National Car Rental advertising campaign script appeals to the need for esteem with the script: "**You** are a business pro, executor of efficiency; **you** can spot an amateur from a mile away, and **you** rent from National."

Advertising for higher education, degree completion programs, and technical colleges appeal to the instinctual need for self-actualization. The United States Army created a very compelling message using the appeal to this instinctual need for self-actualization with the *Be All That **You** Can Be, In the Army* campaign.

When you understand the psychology of consumer behavior, you begin to realize that you are not just selling a product, you are selling the idea of the product, the image of the product, and the result of the product. In your commercial, you are trying to tell the consumer how your advertiser can fulfill one or more of the needs in the listener's hierarchy.

As you observe advertising through the lens of Maslow's Hierarchy of Needs, you'll see it can be the *Copywriter's Playbook.*

The Four Key Elements

Imagine you can put your advertiser on a large stage with one thousand people in the audience and they have a chance to tell them all about their business and give them a reason why they should come and shop with them.

What would your client say? Oh, and another thing. Their time is limited. In this example, they have sixty seconds.

We have a great selection and low prices. We're locally owned and operated. We've been in business for 35 years. We service what we sell. Our phone number is, Find us on Facebook.

While those may be the first things that come to your customer's mind, modern research tells us **those are the last things that come to the customer's mind**.

Your client is telling the audience about their company. The story is from the owner's point of view. The audience is waiting to hear, "What's in it for me?"

To help you create a better message for your client, here are the *Four Key Elements of an Emotionally Engaging Commercial*.

First, even though they are on a large stage in front of the audience ready to speak, the people in the audience may not be paying any attention to them. They might be looking at their phone, talking to the person next to them, or reading the program. If the first few words out of your client's mouth, don't grab their attention, they probably won't hear the rest of the story.

Second, the first few words of the commercial must engage the audience about something on **their** mind, something that **they need or want**, something that **they need to resolve**. This

something can be called a **felt need**. You can learn much about consumer behavior by investigating the *Instant Background Report* for your prospect's business category at the Radio Advertising Bureau's website. The report details who buys, what they buy, when they buy, and why they buy. This understanding can prove to be very helpful when writing your commercial.

Emotion is what drives a person to action. Every decision is driven by the need to protect or promote our self-interests. For your commercial to be effective, you must get to the **felt need** early in your commercial.

Engaging messages need an **easy on-ramp**, that is, accessible, quick, and immediate for the listener. Consumers will allow approximately 3 seconds for any one detail or part of the script to register an emotional response that they can relate to; otherwise, they will tune out the commercial.

It's essential, then, to always keep in mind the 3-second rule making sure that everything in the script can be absorbed, reflected, and responded to quickly. It is vital to keep the message as simple as possible with a single core idea to bring the commercial to life and make things happen around it.

With modern technology and the latest developments in brain science, we have learned the word **you,** is an attention-getting word. Now, we don't recommend starting your commercial with "Hey You! I want to talk to you!" But the beginning of your commercial, the very first line in your commercial must accomplish that very thing, grab their attention. You have about three seconds to grab the attention of the customer on an emotional level, or you've lost them altogether.

Liberty Mutual Insurance makes effective use of the word **you** and getting to **the felt need** quickly in their advertising. Here are a couple of examples.

"You've totaled your brand-new car. Nobody is hurt. But there will still be pain. It comes when your insurance company says they'll only pay three-quarters of what it takes to replace it. What are you supposed to do, drive three-quarters of a car?"

"Your sixteen-year-old daughter studies day and night for her driver's test. Secretly inside you hope she wouldn't pass. The thought of your baby girl driving around all by herself was, you just weren't ready. But she did pass because she's your baby girl. But now you're proud. A bundle of nerves proud."

The beginning of the commercial utilizes actors and the rest of the commercial uses an announcer and some onscreen graphics explaining the third component in an emotionally engaging commercial, **the action step, switch to Liberty Mutual**.

To be effective, every advertisement should include these four creative elements:

1. The single most important word to the consumer: *You*. The most important word isn't *sale* or *discount* or even *free*. The most important word to the consumer is the word you.

2. The **felt need of the consumer**. The felt need is something that the consumer feels strongly about. They think about it whenever the subject comes up. It is something that they want or need but have yet to act.

A good advertisement combines the first two creative elements early. For example:

"**You** love your home. But **you hate your bathroom**. It's small, it's cold, and it's old- fashioned. You want a new bathroom."

This first part of the advertisement contains the most important word, **you**, three times. And many of us can identify with the felt need for a larger, warmer, more modern bathroom.

3. The **Call to Action**. This essential element describes what the consumer needs to do to address their felt need.

"Call the bathroom remodeling experts, ABC Bathrooms. They can make your bathroom dreams come true right before your very eyes."

4. **Return on Investment**. This element tells the consumer what they'll get when they call or, more importantly, how their life will be better after calling ABC Bathrooms.

"Before you know it, you will be relaxing in your larger, warmer, more modern bathroom."

Oh yes, the fourth key element, **"the bathroom you've always dreamed about."** That's the ribbon that ties all the elements up into a great, emotionally engaging commercial.

- You
- The Felt Need
- The Action Step
- Life Ever After

As an advertising sales professional, you can learn how to write emotionally engaging commercials that sell. All you need to do is to try to learn. You will build stronger relationships with your clients; close more long-term business, and **you will make more money**.

Finally, a well-produced commercial will use sound effects, an announcer and voice actors that will add polish and professionalism. All too often, a small business owner will want to play a role in the writing and producing of the commercial. But it's important to realize that good commercials are written from the perspective of the consumer, not the small business owner.

The consumers see the business from the outside in, with a **what's in it for me** attitude at the forefront of their thoughts. In contrast, the small business owner sees their business from the inside, looking out and focuses on the features the business offers. For a business feature to have any meaning for the consumer, the commercial must translate that business feature into a benefit for the consumer.

Marketing slogans like "We're family-owned," "We're local," and "We have good prices," on their own, without articulating a direct consumer benefit, don't do much to motivate the savvy consumer in this competitive age. None of those features articulate any benefits for the consumer.

Instead, slogans like "The next time you have a backed-up drain, call ABC Plumbing where there is never an extra charge for service on nights or weekends" will have better results. This slogan differentiates you from the competition with the feature that you do not charge extra for nights or weekends.

Some might ask how ABC can afford not to charge extra on nights and weekends. With that kind of a positioning statement, **ABC could charge a little bit more all the time**.

Once a compelling creative message is crafted to your advertiser's liking, put it on the air, and just let it run and run. Frequent changes in the commercial message can sharply reduce campaign effectiveness. About the time the advertiser grows tired of hearing their commercial message is just about the time when the consumers are just starting to take notice.

Finally, **don't call your commercial a spot**. I know, everybody calls the commercial a spot. But a spot is a stain on your beautiful new shirt. Many times, a spot will ruin a beautiful blouse or a new tie.

You are writing and selling commercials. One of Radio's biggest challenges is, Radio is not considered a primary advertising medium. For many years, Radio was considered a medium to fill in spots, or openings, in a larger media plan. Buying Radio advertising used to be called spot placement advertising, to fill in the spots between TV, newspaper and other media. Calling your commercial a spot only perpetuates this second-class perception of Radio advertising. **On Madison Avenue in New York City, the big creative advertising agencies do not use the word spot to describe their work, and neither should you.**

Your creative commercials are works of creative writing, and you should always speak of them with respect because it is the commercial that your customer will most identify with in your business relationship.

Summary

In this chapter on Writing the Creative Message, we covered the following topics:

- To be a good copywriter, you must learn to work **with** the psychology of the consumer, not against it. You must first understand why people buy things and why they buy them **when** they buy them.

- In his 1943 paper *A Theory of Human Motivation*, Abraham Maslow proposed that the motivation for action is an unfulfilled need. Maslow's research suggests that humans seek to satisfy their needs and desires in a specific hierarchy.
- There are Four Key Elements every script must include; the word you, the felt need, the call to action step, and the ROI.
- Engaging messages need an *easy on-ramp*, that is, accessible, quick, and immediate for the listener. Consumers will allow approximately 3 seconds for any one detail or part of the script to register an emotional response that they can relate to; otherwise, they will tune out the commercial.
- Marketing slogans like "We're family-owned," "We're local," and "We have good prices," on their own, without articulating a direct consumer benefit, don't do much to motivate the savvy consumer in this competitive age. None of those features articulate any benefits for the consumer.
- **Don't call your commercial a spot.**

"People who know what they are talking about don't need PowerPoint." –
Steve Jobs, Entrepreneur. (1955 – 2011)

16

Presenting Your Proposal

Experience demonstrates that the well prepared, well-informed salesperson is the exception, rather than the rule. Since you have decided to make Radio advertising sales your profession, through your training, you want to be the best informed and best-trained salesperson the prospect ever sees.

A well-prepared presentation isn't something your prospect is going to see every day. **When you make a professionally prepared presentation, you contribute to the perception that you are well prepared, well informed, and most of all, professional.**

Pre-Presentation Check List

Let's review some of the basics of making a professional presentation.

- Practice beforehand.
- Show up on time.
- Dress professionally, make sure your shoes are shined.
- Have your materials ready.
- Have your commercial ready to play.
- Have the agreement ready to sign.

Presentation Attitude

Before you make any sales presentation, you must be in a positive mental state. You must feel positive that you have developed the perfect solution to the prospect's needs. Selling is the transference of feelings. **For your prospect to feel good about your proposal, you need to feel good about your plan.** You must be confident that your proposal will do exactly what you believe it will do. This air of confidence will go a long way in shaping the perceptions your prospect holds about your proposal.

Positive emotions and feelings are contagious. Behavioral scientist Elaine Hatfield refers to this contagion as *"Emotional cognition*, the notion that people tend to catch other's emotions."[33] When people encounter someone showing intense emotion, like happiness or sadness, it evokes that same emotion in them. In the sales process, you could have all the critical points covered with excellent supporting evidence, but if the prospect doesn't sense strong emotion from you, they won't feel right about making the decision, you will be at a loss. With the correct mental attitude, with a sense of confidence that your idea is the best choice your prospect can make, your prospect will feel the effect of your confidence, and this will add to their understanding that they are making the right decision.

Professional Appearance

There is much debate about dress codes in business today. Some people encourage a more relaxed approach to professional dress than others. Some people think that if they are overdressed, they appear to be too formal. Some men believe that nobody in town wears a tie. In many cases, the real problem is the salesperson has not invested any money in a set of clothing for their profession of selling. Some don't have business clothing. Sometimes their business clothes are painfully out of date. Styles change.

You must invest in some professional-looking business clothes on an ongoing basis. Most people new to the profession of selling don't have much extra income to invest in a new wardrobe, so start with one new piece at a time. Make the sacrifice and buy at least one new piece of business attire for each new presentation. It could be a new scarf or a new tie, a new blouse or a new shirt or maybe a new pair of shoes or a belt.

Shop around for bargains. In my case, I have some very nice suits, slacks, and shirts that cost me some money from a high-end retailer that I wear on more formal occasions. Then I have some very nice looking, inexpensive suites that I bought at a discount store. They look nice enough for everyday wear. I try to take good care of both so they will last a long time.

---

[33] Elain Hatfield, John T. Cacioppo and Richard L. Rapson, *Emotional Contagion* (Cambridge University Press, 1994), 79.

Little by little, you'll start to remake your image into a sharp-looking selling professional. Above all else, please make sure your clothes are clean and well pressed and your shoes are shined.

If you smoke, quit. But if you can't stop, at least avoid smoking long enough before your presentation so you can air out and be sure to use a breath mint. Make sure your hands are washed, your fingernails are clean, and your hair is in place.

When it comes to facial hair, it works for some men who have enough facial hair, but for those of us who don't, a stubble look just looks like we are too lazy to shave.

If you devote some time and money to your grooming and professional appearance, you will look better, you will feel better, you will feel more confident, and **that will help you close more sales**.

Voice Inflection

One of the most profound steps you can take to become a successful sales professional is to devote yourself to learning how to use your voice more effectively. The power of voice inflection is hugely influential in the professional selling process. Scientific evidence tells us that the way you speak your words is one of the primary ways you can effectively convey the meaning of your presentation. In addition to providing factual evidence that your idea will help the prospect, **the way you deliver those facts, the emotion in your voice, will help the prospect feel good about those facts**.

According to an article in *Biological Psychology*, your brain gives more precedence to nonverbal speech sounds expressing emotions than to words expressing the same emotion.[34] Consequently, when you use your voice inflection, you are influencing the prospect on an emotional level and assisting them in mentally processing what you are saying.[35]

With your cell phone or tablet, you can use the built-in voice recorder to practice using your voice inflection to improve your sales presentations. You probably already use your device to listen to podcasts or audiobooks, so why not start listening to yourself.

I can hear you now; "Spike, I don't like how I sound when I record myself." Well, I've got news for you, that's exactly how you sound to me and your prospect! So, you need to get comfortable with the sound of your voice, just the same way your prospect hears your voice.

You must start using the voice recorder on your device for the training and development of your voice and your sales procedures so you can say what you mean to say even more

---

[34] M.D. Pell, K. Rothermich, P. Liu, S. Paulmann, S. Sethi, and S. Rigoulot, *Preferential Decoding of Emotion from Human Non-Linguistic Vocalizations Versus Speech Prosody*, Biological Psychology 111 (October 2015): 14-25

[35] Kathering I. Miller, *Compassionate Communication in the Worklace: Exploring Processes of Noticing, Connecting and Responding*, Journal of Applied Communication Research 35, no. 3 (August 2007): 223-245

effectively. Not only should you record your presentation and your sales talk, but you should also record how you handle objections, stalls, and closing the sale.

At first, you're going to feel a little embarrassed. You need to get over those feelings and start listening to what you are saying. It is far better for you to be embarrassed in your practice session than in front of a real prospect. When you listen to yourself, you're going to find that you say a lot of things that you don't need to say. You're just adding a bunch of words that don't help you in the selling process. That's why when preparing your preparation, you prepare your script and put it on the opposite page of your flipchart notebook.

That way, the prospect sees the presentation slide on their side of the flipchart, and you see and can read your script on your side.

Second, you may notice the absence of voice inflection because you probably present in a monotone delivery. One of the most powerful skills you can learn that will increase your sales is the skill of using your voice in the presentation.

Social psychologists Roland Newmann and Fritz Strack illustrated the impact of voice inflection in one of their experiments. They took two different groups of people. One group heard the speaker deliver the speech in a monotone style. The second group listened to the same speaker, give the same speech, but this time delivered in an upbeat manner with voice inflection. The group that heard the upbeat presentation reported they felt more optimistic about the subject matter than the group who listened to the monotone version.[36]

Record yourself delivering your presentation to one of your coworkers. If you feel too intimidated at first, practice recording yourself alone, **but**, then record yourself practicing with your coworker.

Setting Up Your Presentation

After you meet the prospect and exchange some pleasantries, it is time to get down to the reason for the meeting; you are there to demonstrate that you have developed a plan to help the prospect with their challenges and goals.

You need to be in a private place like a personal office where the prospect won't be interrupted during your meeting. If something has changed since you made the appointment and the prospect is working the sales counter at the same time that you are trying to explain your idea, you should probably ask the prospect if you can reschedule at a better time when you can have some privacy, perhaps before the store opens.

Ask permission to begin the presentation.

---

[36] Roland Newmann and Fritz Strack, Mood Contagion: *The Automatic Transfer of Mood Between Persons*, Journal of Personality and Social Psychology 79 (2000): 211-213

"I've been looking forward to this meeting. Is this a good time to get started?"

Ask if you can set up your flipchart notebook and Bluetooth speaker.

"May I set up my flipchart and speaker here on your desk or should we sit over at your table?"

If you're going to use a speaker to play the commercial, make sure you have rehearsed how to use your equipment, and the commercial is easy to find on your phone or playback device.

Involve the Prospect Early

Generally, in selling, getting the prospect involved in the presentation early is a crucial building block that dramatically increases the closing ratio of the sales presentation. When you go to buy a new car, the first thing the car salesperson wants to do is get you into a vehicle for a test drive. The odds of selling the car increase exponentially if they can get you to take a test drive.

Product sampling is another way to get the prospect involved in the presentation process. Sampling appeals to most consumers. Two-thirds of consumers say they will try the product sample that is offered. Fifty-eight percent of consumers plan to buy a product they sampled, and more than a quarter will switch from one brand to the sample brand.[37]

In Radio advertising sales, the best way to get your prospect involved in the process early is through the emotionally engaging Radio script you have written for the prospect. At the beginning of your presentation, use the power of a strong belief statement to introduce the commercial to your prospect.

"Let me play (or read) your Radio commercial I wrote for you. I believe this is a strong commercial for you because we used the latest scriptwriting techniques proven to influence listener behavior and drive audience response, which in turn generates more sales."

Play the commercial for the prospect. When it is over, look the prospect in the eye and ask, **"Could we run a commercial like that for you?"** Not only do you involve the prospect in your presentation early, but you are also attempting a trial close. If the prospect agrees to the commercial, you are on your way to a sale. If the prospect doesn't like the commercial, ask them how they would like to change it. Have your script ready, note the changes the prospect would like, clear your throat and read back the new script and try again; **"Is that better, could we run that commercial for you?"**

---

[37] Arbitron Product Sampling Study, Arbitron & Edison Media Research 2008

When you receive a positive indication about the commercial, you can use another strong belief statement, "Great, this commercial is going to do you a great job because the plan I have for you checks off all of the concerns you said you had. May I show you?"

The Customer Needs Assessment Review

Once the prospect gives you an initial approval for the commercial, you want to start your presentation where you left off, at the end of the Customer Needs Assessment interview.

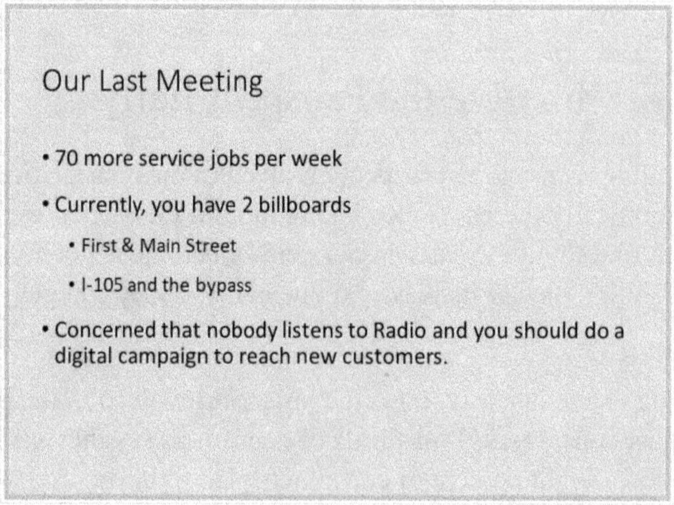

Our Last Meeting

- 70 more service jobs per week
- Currently, you have 2 billboards
  - First & Main Street
  - I-105 and the bypass
- Concerned that nobody listens to Radio and you should do a digital campaign to reach new customers.

FIGURE 17

This example page (Figure 17) would be the page in your flipchart notebook that the prospect will see. On your side of the flipchart notebook, you see your script for that page (Figure 18).

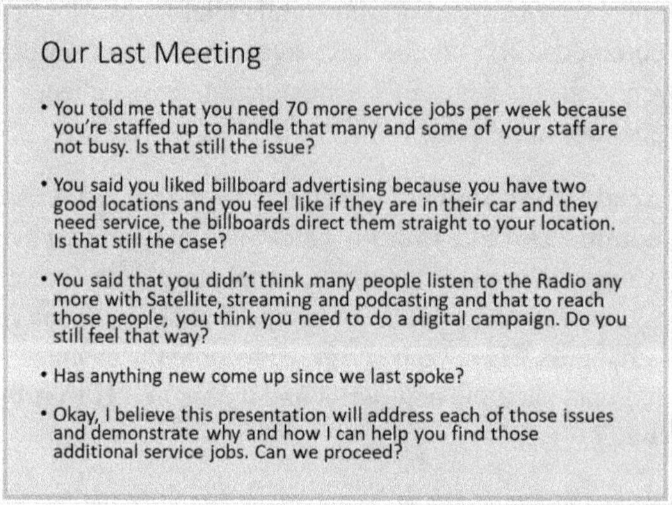

Our Last Meeting

- You told me that you need 70 more service jobs per week because you're staffed up to handle that many and some of your staff are not busy. Is that still the issue?

- You said you liked billboard advertising because you have two good locations and you feel like if they are in their car and they need service, the billboards direct them straight to your location. Is that still the case?

- You said that you didn't think many people listen to the Radio any more with Satellite, streaming and podcasting and that to reach those people, you think you need to do a digital campaign. Do you still feel that way?

- Has anything new come up since we last spoke?

- Okay, I believe this presentation will address each of those issues and demonstrate why and how I can help you find those additional service jobs. Can we proceed?

FIGURE 18

Notice how your slide (Figure 18), the slide you see while the customer is looking at the bullet point slide on the other side of your flipchart notebook (Figure 17), has the words you plan to say when showing the prospect their slide. There are even confirmation questions included after each bullet point to ensure that you're on point with the prospect's concerns. You even ask if anything else has popped up since you last spoke.

Before you leave this slide, plan to make another strong belief statement and then ask if the prospect is ready to proceed. It is written directly on your notes page.

The Fact Bridge Benefit

As you deliver your presentation, you are going to present some factual research to substantiate your proposal and persuade the prospect to agree. Facts can be boring things. They can even be controversial if they run counter to what the prospect already believes. Consequently, it is essential that you remember what you learned about voice inflection. Learning proper voice inflection techniques and practicing those techniques when presenting can add emotion to a factual statement and make it easier for the brain to interpret.

You must learn to take these impressive facts about Radio advertising and build a **Fact-Bridge-Benefit** statement. It is a fact that more people listen to AM & FM Radio than any other medium. The bridge is just a word like *so* or, **therefore**. The benefit is what the lead wants to know, **"What's in it for me?"**

FACT: "More people listen to AM & FM Radio than any other media."

BRIDGE: "So…"

BENEFIT: "Your commercial can be heard by more people."

Then comes the **nail down**. The nail down is a tactic to keep the conversation on track. The nail down is, **"You do want more customers to know about you, don't you?"**

In the Customer Needs Assessment interview, our sample prospect said they didn't think very many people listen to AM or FM Radio anymore. That is one of the perceptions you want to address in the presentation.

The Radio Advertising Bureau website (www.rab.com) is always your first stop for powerfully persuasive sales materials. The must-have tool is the *Why Radio?* slide deck. The RAB updates this slide presentation regularly, so the information is current.

Even though the slide deck is in the PowerPoint format, you can easily open the file in Google Slides, which is a free app with your Gmail account.

There are several impressive slides with eye-catching artwork that you can lift right out of the *Why Radio?* presentation and insert it into your custom presentation for your prospect.

We want to illustrate how many people listen to AM & FM Radio in our presentation, so we pick this slide in Figure 19.

That is the slide that your prospect will see when you use your flipchart notebook. On your side of the flipchart notebook, you see your notes page, the page with the script you want to follow for this fact (Figure 20).

> One of the things you told me was that you didn't think many people listen to AM & FM Radio any more because of satellite Radio and streaming, is that correct?
>
> Take a look at this figure here.
>
> According to the very latest research from the Nielsen Company, you've heard of them, they are the worlds largest consumer research company, they do the TV ratings, Nielsen says in their latest study from March 2019, that 249.7 million different people listen to AM or FM Radio every week! That's more than TV or even Facebook. That number is up over six million listeners since 2015. Radio's audience is growing.
>
> So, when you advertise your business on Radio, you are using the medium with the largest possible audience, that's important, right?

FIGURE 20

Your script for this slide begins with the first concern the prospect has: they believe that Radio listenership is down due to other new technology. You pause and then ask if that is still a concern. Then you direct the prospect's attention to the fact that 249.7 million people listen to AM & FM Radio every week!

If you do some additional research, you'll find that 249.7 million people is more than watch broadcast TV or cable, and more than use Facebook[38] in the United States. According to the Pew Research Center, only 69% of Americans use Facebook.[39]

The study goes on to say;

> "The shares of adults who say they use Facebook, Pinterest, LinkedIn, and Twitter are each largely the same as in 2016."

So, social media is mostly showing flat or little growth, while Radio is showing strong growth in listenership. Radio's audience has increased from 243 million people in 2015 to 249.7 million people in 2019.[40]

Those are the facts in the Fact Bridge Benefit. The bridge is just a word. In our script, we use the word **so** to bridge to the benefit.

> "So, when you advertise your business on Radio, you are using the medium with the largest possible audience."

We don't use the word reach because that is a Radio term, and we know from brain science that learning stops the moment confusion begins. You don't want to confuse the prospect with a Radio term when **the word audience is a better, more descriptive, and easier to understand**.

Next comes the **Nail Down**. The nail down is an easy question to answer that will help tie the fact and the benefit together in the prospect's mind to help persuade them to make a new decision about Radio's audience size. **The nail down is, "That's important, right?"**

At this point in the conversation, your voice inflection training comes into play. By training your voice to moderate at different paces and levels, the nail down would sound like this;

> "That's important, (pause), right?" (softly)

Then you pause slightly to get acknowledgment from the prospect before moving on to the next slide, the slide to address the prospect's concerns.

The RAB *Why Radio?* presentation has additional slides that help demonstrate the strength of Radio when compared to other media choices. You can pick and choose which slides make the best case for your presentation. The RAB provides so much useful information in the *Why Radio?* Presentation, it is a **must-have** tool.

---

[38] Nielsen Total Audience Report Q3 2018

[39] Pew Research Center survey conducted Jan. 8 to Feb. 7, 2019.

[40] Nielsen Audio, RADAR 123, December 2014 (Persons 12+, Monday-Sunday 24-Hour Cume Estimates)

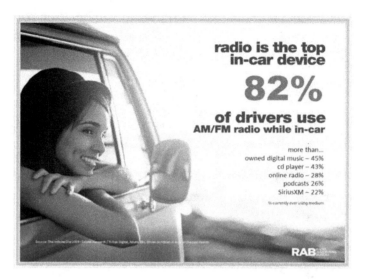

FIGURE 21

In our sample presentation, the prospect is an auto service center who believes his billboards reach people in their cars. Once again, you should go back to the RAB website for more information from the *Why Radio?* presentation for details about in-car listening. Here is a slide that illustrates that Radio is the top in-car device.[41] You can copy the RAB slide into your presentation (Figure 21).

There is no better way to advertiser to the automotive service category than on Radio because the consumers are using the product at the very moment they hear your commercial. If something is wrong with their car, and they hear your commercial, they make the connection that you can help them.

The AM & FM Radio remains the top in-car device, used by 82% of drivers while in the car. That's according to Edison Research and Triton Digital and their 2019 *Infinite Dial Survey*.

Satellite Radio was at the bottom of the list. Sirius XM reported to Wall Street that as of September 30, 2018, they had approximately 33.7 million subscribers, 28.5 million were paid and 5.2 million were promotional subscribers.

Radio has 249.7 million listeners and satellite has 33.7 subscribers, that's a big difference, right?

Sirius XM Holdings Inc. Form 10-Q 10/23/18

FIGURE 22

In your flipchart notebook, you have your notes for the slide, with the *fact-bridge-benefit-nail down* ready for you to deliver (Figure 22).

---

[41] Infinite Dial 2019 – Edison Research / Triton Digital, Adults 18+ driven or ridden in a car in the past month.

The subscriber information about Sirius / XM radio is not found on the RAB website. That information comes from the company's annual report they are required by law to file with the Securities and Exchange Commission. They must report their subscriber information accurately under penalty of law, so they don't exaggerate. It's easy to find this information on any publicly traded company. Just go to the CNBC website (www.cnbc.com), enter the name of the company you are researching and then **go to the *financials* tab**.

Next, you want to address the prospect's advertising on his two billboards. Keep in mind that **all advertising *works***. So, you don't want to bash other media. It's unprofessional, and it shows that you lack confidence in your product.

When you talk down other media, especially the one your prospect is currently using, you are telling your prospect they made a poor decision. You immediately put the prospect into a defensive posture where they feel compelled to defend that decision. You're not going to be very successful in selling Radio advertising when you do that.

All media have their strengths and weaknesses; even Radio has weaknesses. The real selling professional will research the media choices under consideration and develop a proposal that illustrates how an additional media choice can build on the reach and frequency of the existing media choice, in this case, billboards.

The RAB website (www.rab.com) has a detailed database on other media choices. Each media section has media facts, advantages, disadvantages, plus Radio and a glossary of terms.

There is also a nice feature called *Create a Profile*. This feature allows you to select from all the information that you want, and the website creates a nice downloadable file you can use without retyping all the information. You can easily cut and paste the information you want to use. That can save you some time when preparing your presentation.

The example prospect is advertising on billboards. The prospect has two billboards on the two busiest intersections in town. Chances are those are the most expensive billboards in town. You must also consider that your prospect may be proud of those two billboards and the fact that your prospect has the billboards and his competitors don't. You can be sure the billboard salesperson reminds him of that at renewal time. The prospect probably refers to them as "his billboards."

So, you need to propose a plan to add Radio to his current billboard advertising if you want to have a chance at earning some of the business. That's where the *Other Media* section of the RAB website can be so helpful.

Billboards reach consumers when they are in their cars. Radio reaches consumers when they are in their vehicles. When people are in their car or truck, they are aware of what their vehicle needs in the way of service or repairs because they are living with those needs every time they drive. When they see a billboard or hear a commercial about automotive services, the advertiser is reaching the consumer at the best possible moment. That's the premise for adding your Radio advertising proposal to the current billboard advertising campaign.

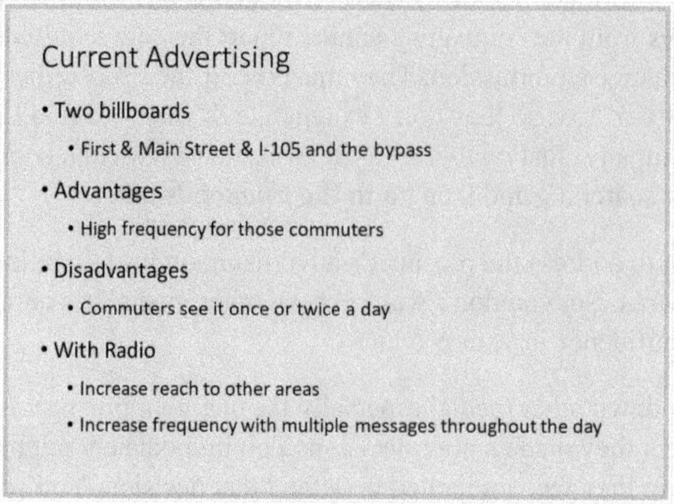

FIGURE 23

On the presentation slide for current advertising, you list a brief description of the existing advertising; in this case, you list the locations of the two billboards (Figure 23). Next, you follow that with some of the advantages of billboard advertising. We have selected the **high-frequency** advantage. People who commute along that route will see the billboard every day they commute or drive past that intersection. But what about consumers who don't travel that route? That's where Radio can help.

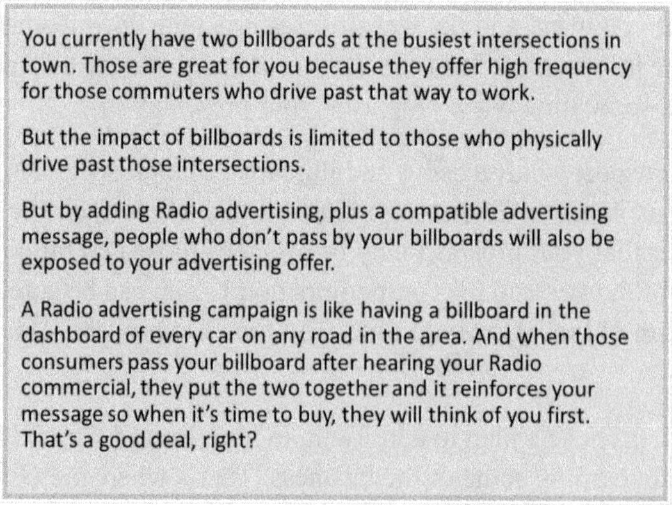

FIGURE 24

The script on your page in the flip chart notebook has the *fact-bridge-benefit-nail down* written out so you can stay on point (Figure 24).

The Advertising Schedule

So far, the prospect likes the commercial and indicated that you could run that commercial. By using the **fact-bridge-benefit-nail down** technique, the prospect has acknowledged that AM & FM Radio listenership is 249.7 million people, more than they perceived and that Radio is still the dominant in-car choice for entertainment.

Now you are going to show the prospect how your proposal will help them increase the number of service jobs each week with your suggested advertising schedule.

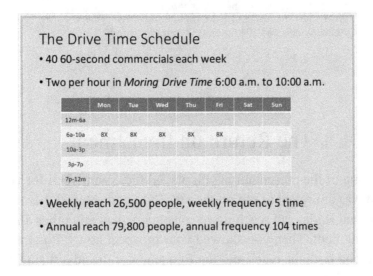

FIGURE 25

Our example prospect is an auto service center with staff on hand to handle 70 more service jobs a week. That means that they can accommodate customers without an appointment. You propose to write a commercial thats offers same-day openings and a ride to work when a customer drops off their vehicle. You are proposing to run two commercials per hour in the morning drive time slot between 6:00 a.m. and 10:00 a.m.

Your flip chart page could look something like Figure 25. The page details the number of commercials per week, in this case, forty commercials. You indicate the commercials are 60-seconds in length. You specify two commercials per hour, a total of eight commercials each morning. Finally, you include the weekly and the annual reach and frequency estimates.

We didn't include the price of the advertising schedule yet because we want to set up the estimated Return on Investment first.

Your slide, the one that you read from on your side of your flipchart notebooks is illustrated in Figure 26.

Here is the advertising schedule I worked up for you. Since you currently have the staff and time to offer immediate service, I propose we advertise immediate service openings that very day during the morning drive time. As our listeners are on their way to work, they will hear your advertising message. If there is something wrong with their car, they will hear your message of immediate openings and that you will give them a ride to work.

If they are running short of time and can't stop by the first day they hear it, your commercial will tell them to call and schedule an appointment for the next day.

The first week your commercials are on the air, Nielsen estimates that 26,500 people will hear your commercial approximately five times. Over the next 52 weeks, those numbers will grow to 79,800 people and 104 times. Isn't that impressive?

FIGURE 26

The Return on Investment

At the beginning of the presentation, you played the commercial for your prospect, and they indicated that it was approved to run on the air. Then you showed them that the Radio audience is growing, and Radio can reach more consumers than any other dominant medium and received an acknowledgment. Then you showed your prospect how billboards and Radio advertising could expand both the reach and the frequency of the advertising efforts. Now it's time to demonstrate the Return on Investment.

Estimated Return on Investment

- Goal – 70 additional service jobs
    - $20,860 increase in gross revenue
    - $9,688 in gross profit margin

- Advertising Schedule
    - Heard by 26,500 consumers approximately 5 times
    - Only .002% need to respond to reach your goal

FIGURE 27

Figure 27 represents the image on the slide your prospect will see on their side of the flipchart notebook, just bullet points.

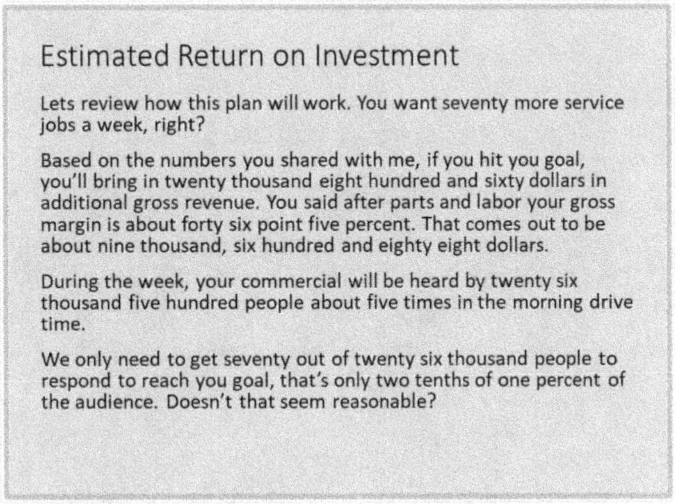

Estimated Return on Investment

Lets review how this plan will work. You want seventy more service jobs a week, right?

Based on the numbers you shared with me, if you hit you goal, you'll bring in twenty thousand eight hundred and sixty dollars in additional gross revenue. You said after parts and labor your gross margin is about forty six point five percent. That comes out to be about nine thousand, six hundred and eighty eight dollars.

During the week, your commercial will be heard by twenty six thousand five hundred people about five times in the morning drive time.

We only need to get seventy out of twenty six thousand people to respond to reach you goal, that's only two tenths of one percent of the audience. Doesn't that seem reasonable?

FIGURE 28

Figure 28 is an example of the slide that will be on your side of the flip chart notebook. Before we go much further, **notice how the numbers are typed out as words**. This slide will help you deliver the presentation more smoothly. You won't get tripped up dealing with the numbers when it really counts. This is also the time to use your voice inflection and clearly articulate the numbers. Be sure to slow down and add some emphasis.

For example, when you read the number of people who will hear the commercial, don't just quickly say twenty-six thousand five hundred. Say it with some flair. Use your *voice inflection*. "Your commercial will be heard by **twenty-six thousand,** (slight pause) **six hundred,** (another slight pause) **and fifty people,** (another pause) approximate **five times** in the morning drive time." When you get to the end of your script for this page, don't forget the **nail down, "Doesn't that seem impressive?"**

Now it is time to reveal the cost of your proposal. You turn the page (Figure 29) and reveal the price to be just eighteen hundred. Not one thousand eight hundred dollars. Just say eighteen hundred. You want to use the words **thousands** and **dollars** when describing the economic value for the advertiser but not when describing your price.

Below the price is an example of the Return on Investment calculation. On one page, you disclose the price of the advertising plan, but you also demonstrate the plan goals of increasing the number of service jobs and the resulting revenue, gross and net margin increases. This represents a way to show your prospect, "What's in it for them."

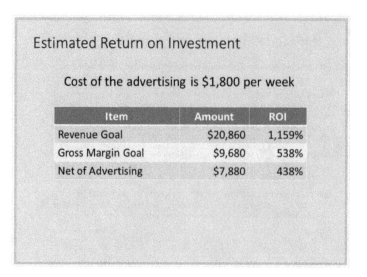

FIGURE 29

But when you describe the value the advertiser receives, you can say, "You can increase your service sales by twenty thousand, eight hundred and sixty dollars. That is a one thousand one hundred and fifty-nine percent return on your investment."

Estimated Return on Investment

The weekly cost of the advertising is eighteen hundred. If we get seventy out of the twenty six thousand five hundred people who hear your commercial to bring in their vehicles for service, we'll reach these goals. That's only two tenths of one percent of the people who hear the commercial!

The gross sales increase of twenty thousand, eight hundred and sixty dollars would be an eleven to one increase or a one thousand one hundred fifty nine percent return on investment.

The gross profit margin increase of nine thousand six hundred and eighty eight dollars would be a five to one increase or a five hundred and thirty eight percent return on investment.

The increase in gross profit after deducting the cost of the advertising is seven thousand eight hundred and eighty dollars. That's is a four to one increase or a four hundred and thirty eight percent return on investment.

All of this is possible if we get just two tenths of one percent of the people who will hear your commercial to bring their vehicle for service.

Isn't that what you want to do?

FIGURE 30

Don't forget the *nail down*. Say it with voice inflection. Say it slowly and somewhat softly, "Isn't that what you want?"

Summary

In this chapter on Presenting Your Proposal, we covered the following topics:

- Experience demonstrates that the well-prepared, well-informed salesperson is the exception, rather than the rule. Since you have decided to make Radio advertising sales your profession, through your training, you want to be the best-informed and best-trained salesperson the prospect ever sees.
- Create and follow a pre-presentation checklist.
- Before you make any sales presentation, you must be in a positive mental state. You must feel positive that you have developed the perfect solution to the prospect's needs. Selling is the transference of feelings. **For your prospect to feel good about your proposal, you need to feel good about your plan.**
- The power of voice inflection is hugely influential in the professional selling process. Scientific evidence tells us that the way you speak your words is one of the primary ways you can effectively convey the meaning of your presentation.
- You should deliver your presentation in a private area where you won't be interrupted. Make sure you have rehearsed how to use your equipment, and you can easily find the commercial on your phone or playback device.
- Present your sample commercial early in the meeting for their approval.
- The Fact-Bridge-Benefit is a presentation technique to secure on-going agreement to the critical portions of your presentation.
- The Advertising Schedule is a graphic depiction of on which days and at which times the commercials will broadcast. You avoid using the word **spot** and **daypart** in favor of **commercial** and **time slot**.
- No presentation is complete without an **Estimated Return on Investment**.

"I have never worked a day in my life without selling. If I believe in something, I sell it, and I sell it hard." - *Estée Lauder*, Founder *Estée Lauder Companies*. (1906 – 2004)

17

Reaching Agreement

Closing the sale, or reaching an agreement, is usually defined as the moment you ask your prospect to make the decision to sign the agreement to purchase your advertising proposal. Asking for the order is just another step in the professional sales process. Following the professional sales process, positions you to close the sale.

Statistics vary, but most sales are made after more than one attempt to close the sale. According to the marketing website *MarketingDonut*, 92% of salespeople give up before the fourth attempt to close the sale. On the other hand, 80% of prospects say "No," at least four times before they say "Yes."[42]

Another startling statistic comes from Zig Ziglar. He claims that 63% of all salespeople fail to ask for the order at all![43]

The close tends to receive much of the time and attention in sales training. Closing the sale is the glamor stage of the selling process. But, closing the sale won't be possible if you don't have a prospect in the first place, so prospecting is also essential. Each step in the sales process leads to the close.

You can't close something that hasn't been opened. Most leads tend to be close-minded when approached by a salesperson. They don't want to be **sold**. As you become proficient in the professional sales process, you may find that closing the sale is easier than finding someone willing to buy, the prospecting phase of the process.

---

[42] 2019 MarketingDonut
[43] Ziglar, Zig. *Secrets of Closing the Sale* (Revell 2004) 109

It is nearly impossible to close a sale if you haven't completed a thorough **Customer Needs Assessment**. You need to do an in-depth Customer Needs Assessment interview that uncovers a mutually agreed-upon problem or need the prospect wants to solve.

You will find it difficult to close the sale if you haven't prepared a meaningful presentation to illustrate the value your advertising will provide.

You will find it almost impossible to sell Radio advertising if you don't learn how to write emotionally engaging commercials and include your suggested commercial for the prospect in every sales presentation.

Closing the sale is simply one part of the overall sales process, so don't expect to close many deals if you don't follow the sales process. According to the TAS Group and the Dealmaker Index, salespeople who follow a well-defined sales process are 33% more likely to be high performers and close more sales than salespeople who just meander through their day **hoping** to make a sale.[44]

If you jumped ahead in this book to this section hoping to fast track your way to closing the sale with some slick closing lines, STOP! Go back and follow through on learning the sales process. You won't find any one-liners or tricky ways to make a sale. According to the book *Spin Selling*, slick closing techniques may increase the chances of making a sale with low-priced products. With expensive products or services, they reduce the chance of making a sale[45].

Slick closing techniques are ineffective or have a negative effect when:

- The sale is large, involving high-value goods.
- The customer is sophisticated: for example, a professional buyer.
- There is a continuing post-sale relationship with the customer.[46]

Those are the characteristics of a professional radio advertising customer.

If you and your prospect have worked together following the sales process, asking for the sale, reaching an agreement, should be the natural culmination of your efforts.

Zig Ziglar tells us The First Key of Closing is the *Key of Positive Projection*. "Your business is never either good or bad – *out there*. Your business is either good or bad *between your own two ears*. In your mind, you should have made the sale before you even talk to the prospect."[47] That's why we role-play in advertising sales. That's why we record ourselves as we practice our presentation.

When it is time to close the sale, it doesn't have to be a big deal if you have laid the proper groundwork. The close might be as simple as "Would you like to get started next

---

[44] TAS Group, Dealmaker Index Study 2011
[45] Rackham, Neil. *Spin Selling* (McGraw Hill 1988) 33
[46] Rackham, Neil. *Spin Selling* (McGraw Hill 1988) 40-41
[47] Ziglar, Zig. *Secrets of Closing the Sale* (Revell 2004) 341

Monday?"

With that being said, the best closing techniques probably won't work until you build the foundation for a win-win agreement between you and your prospect.

Dealing with Stalls and Objections.

Very few prospects will **self-close**, so you, as the salesperson will need to initiate the **closing discussion,** the conversation that leads to an agreement to buy. As we discussed at the beginning of this chapter, many sales are lost simply because the salesperson is fearful of rejection. Countless additional deals are lost because the salesperson doesn't follow through with a second or a third attempt to close the sale.

If you try to close a sale and the prospect says "No," your first reaction should be to realize that **the prospect is saying they don't know, k-NO-w enough yet to say "Yes**." You have left some questions or concerns unanswered. If you ask the right questions and listen carefully to the answers and respond accordingly, you can turn that initial "No" into a reliable "Yes."

Don't be afraid to follow through and ask your prospect for more information. Ask your prospect why they are saying "No" to your proposal. This won't be so difficult if your proposal has been built on the foundation of a thorough Customer Needs Assessment that uncovered agreed upon needs the prospect wants to satisfy. Your response could be something like "Why are you hesitant to proceed? What did I miss?" Make sure the question is open-ended. You want the prospect to volunteer what is on their mind.

One of the reasons you ask trial closing questions during the presentation itself is to establish reference points for your proposal. If your prospect can't offer a specific reason for their hesitancy, you can refer to the trial closing questions as you probe for the real reason the prospect is hesitating.

I don't know if it will work.

Since advertising is an intangible product, one of the most common reasons your prospect will be hesitant to agree to your proposal will be their fear that the advertising just won't work. They are afraid they won't see a return on their advertising investment. They are worried they won't see any sales growth from the advertising.

Chances are your prospect has purchased advertising in the past from other advertising salespeople. **They tried advertising once, and it didn't work.** Business owners tend to be impatient when they are spending their hard-earned money, so it's only natural, they will be looking for instant gratification from their advertising expenditures.

The leading cause of this fear of advertising failure is other poorly trained salespeople who have come before you with empty promises or slick promotions that fed the prospect's desire for a quick fix to their business problems.

Therefore, during the sales presentation, **it is so important not to skimp on explaining how advertising affects the consumer's behavior and how advertising influences the buying cycle.** Save yourself the grief of lost sales and **always devote part of your presentation to demonstrating how advertising *works*.**

Advertising is a significant expense for most companies, and your prospect wants to know what they are getting for their money. There is going to be a period at the beginning of the advertising campaign where they will have doubts about their decision. That's why you must build the foundation that **advertising is building market awareness or mindshare** in the beginning and that **mindshare will become market share** as consumers travel through their buying cycle for your prospect's products.

Advertising helps the prospect develop a new self-image; they see themselves in a new way. **When the prospect hears their commercial, they hear their name**, and that will stimulate a positive emotion. The commercial is telling their story about their company.

If the prospect is unsure whether your proposal will work, replay the commercial and ask them, "That's a great commercial. Don't you think your commercial will work? Don't you think the commercial will bring in the 70 additional customers you need each week?" Then stop. **Don't say a word.** You asked the question. Now, wait for the response.

You just played the prospect's commercial. You've just asked them if they think it will work. It's going to be difficult for them to say that it won't work. The prospect will most likely agree that it's an excellent commercial and then you can say something like "Of course it's a great commercial. The sooner you say 'Yes,' the sooner we can start running it on the air, sign here and we can get started."

If you have identified a problem the business owner wants to solve, if you have identified how badly they want to solve the issue, if you have laid out how your plan will solve the problem, your closing question could be, **"If you don't do this plan, what are you going to do?"** You can't ask a question like that if you don't follow the sales process.

You will undoubtedly encounter some objections you didn't plan for in developing your presentation. Remember that the objections you will likely encounter, tend to be consistent from one prospect to the next, so bear in mind, **you can develop a skill set** for dealing with the most common objections.

We're not going to cover all the possible stalls and objections you will encounter in your sales profession. There are many great books that explore the full range of different stalls and objections prospects may use. **Instead, we are going to focus on learning a system for dealing with stalls and objections that you can use in virtually any sales encounter.**

The basic formula for dealing with a stall or an objection is this: 1) acknowledge, 2) respond, 3) continue.

When you first hear the stall or objection, acknowledge what the prospect is saying to you. Hear the prospect out. Don't jump to a response before the prospect has finished. It is always a good idea to restate the stall or objection as a question to the prospect to ensure you understood them correctly. When you restate the stall or objection as a question to the prospect, use your voice inflection. "You don't think the advertising will work?"

Be sure to ask the prospect if that is the only question preventing them from saying yes to your proposal. "I'll be happy to answer that issue but before I do, are there any other reasons that would prevent you from moving forward with our proposal?"

Another approach could be, "If I can answer your concern to your satisfaction, would you be in a position to say 'Yes' to our proposal?"

Once you determine what the prospect needs to proceed, you respond to the stall or objection politely and skillfully based on your sales training and preparation. You provide the information the prospect is asking for, and you follow up with a confirmation question like, "Is that the answer you were looking for?"

When the prospect confirms they are satisfied with your response, then you continue with your closing question, "Great, if you just sign right here, we can get started."

If you don't ask your prospect if that is the only issue preventing them from approving the sale, you run the risk of falling into a trap where the prospect isn't really sold, but they are hesitant to tell you "No." In selling, when a prospect wants to end the sales conversation, and they don't want to use the word "No," and they don't want to appear to be rude or hurt your feelings, they come up with what they think is a reasonable-sounding excuse. As the well-trained salesperson, you should recognize this avoidance tactic and respond accordingly.

Learning to recognize avoidance tactics will significantly improve your overall closing ratio and help you make more money. When you realize that your prospect is stalling, you want to summon the courage to deal with the stall head-on. You can't succumb to the stall yourself. You will find yourself endlessly waiting on prospects who want to tell you "No" but are avoiding doing so.

Indeed, there isn't a hard rule for determining if your prospect is trying to put you off or if they have a real question, with which you can help them. You will have to use your training and your common sense to make up your mind. But remember, holding out hope that a real "No" is somehow tomorrow's "Yes" will waste your valuable time that you could use prospecting for your next customer.

Too many good salespeople who have trouble dealing with objections, end up with a long list of prospects that are **pending**, meaning that the actual contract signing is in the works. As a sales manager, when one of my salespeople tells me that a presentation is **pending**, I like to ask them, "What is the close **de-pending** on?" If the answer involves some form of waiting on the prospect to take the next step, that is a good indication that you have a prospect who is stalling you.

In sales, you are not in the waiting business. **You are in the taking action business.** You make things happen. You help prospects decide to either say "Yes" or to say "No" by assisting them through the process of making that decision.

Objections seem like stumbling blocks, but the prospect is just asking for more information. Objections don't always sound like a request for more information, but with training and practice you'll be able to recognize the objection as part of the overall sales process, and you are getting one step closer to making the sale.

We know from experience that there are a handful of stalls and objections that you will hear consistently so, with a little training and practice, you can develop effective ways to either respond to the stall and close the sale or move on without doubts or regrets.

When you first encounter a stall or an objection, you should immediately begin to ask some questions to isolate the objection. You want to determine if the stated stall or objection is the only issue holding the prospect back from deciding on your proposal. When you hear the stall or objection, simply ask the prospect if that is the only issue holding up their decision.

"I hear what you're saying, and I'm glad you brought that up. Before we talk about that, is that the only concern you have with our proposal?"

"That's a good point. Is that the only issue you have before moving forward with our proposal?"

I need to think about it.

One of the most common stalls you will hear is this; "Ok, give me time to think about it, and I'll get back to you." Perhaps you have heard this stall before. It comes in many forms;

"I want to sleep on it."

"Leave your information, and I'll get back to you."

"Come back next week, and we'll let you know."

Business prospects use this type of stall because it is very effective. They expect you to be just like every other salesperson who sheepishly agrees and leaves.

Are they really going to think it over? The minute you walk out the door, their attention will return to their other pressing priorities. They will forget all about your proposal and before you know it, days, maybe even weeks have gone by, and when you return for a follow-up meeting, they're not going to admit they didn't think about it. Instead, they're going to tell you something like,

> "Yes, we thought about your proposal, we gave it careful consideration, but we're not going to do it right now. We'll keep your proposal on file and if anything changes, we'll get back to you."

Remember, **you are not in the waiting business**. But you're not a pushy rude salesperson either. You are a thoughtful professional, so you need a tactful way to respond to this stall.

The best way to respond to any objection or stall is, begin with respect for the prospect and respect for the prospect's need to feel secure in whatever decision you are asking them to make. Here is an example of how you might respond.

> "I understand what you're saying. I'm happy you want to think about this decision because that tells me you are interested in my proposal. I assume you don't want to make a bad decision, is that right?"

Now, you must wait for an answer. You just asked a question. You just asked the prospect if it is reasonable for you to assume that they are interested in your proposal, but they want to be sure they are about to make a good decision, even if the decision is to say "No" to your proposal. So, wait for an answer.

> "I appreciate your need to make an informed decision. From everything I read, most experts agree that the best time to make an important decision is when you have all the necessary information right in front of you when that information is fresh in your mind. Could we spend a few minutes thinking about this decision together, to make certain you reach the best decision for you, which is what you want, isn't it?"

Again, you must wait for an answer. "Yes," is an answer. "No" is an answer. But, "Let me think about it," is not an answer. That is a stall.

If your prospect agrees to think it over with you, you need a plan for guiding the thinking process. You could begin with something like this;

> "Would you help me out by letting me know what you need to think over, is it the integrity of my Radio station or my company?"

Even though that is two questions, there is no comma between the first question and the second. Therefore, you need to ask the question with the emphasis on "Is it the integrity of my Radio station or my company?" Otherwise, they may take back control of the conversation and bring up something you are not prepared for.

> "Is there something wrong with the commercial?"

"No, the commercial sounds great."

"Is it the estimated ROI of two new customers a month too aggressive?"

"No, 70 new customers a week seems possible."

You want to ask questions that walk through the different benefits of your presentation because that will cause them to reconfirm your previous trial closes and get them to tell you how good your proposal is. They are in effect, reselling themselves on your proposal.

Finally, you get to the money question.

"Is it the amount of the monthly advertising investment for the advertising campaign?"

"Yes, it's the money."

Not surprisingly, money is the issue. Despite the reasonable ROI that you propose and their acknowledgment that it is doable, the money is still holding them back. If you get a positive response to everything except the price, perhaps this approach may help.

"I hear what you're saying. Price is important. But tell me, which is worse, paying a bit more than you want, or not spending as much as you should?"

Then be quiet. Be patient. Wait for the answer.

When you first hear the "I need to think about it," objection, you can't just jump in and ask if it's the money. You must first build the foundation; the consensus that everything else about your proposal is acceptable. You need to make sure the only issue is the money.

The formula for responding to a stall or an objection is always a respectful question; respectful because you want to continue the relationship even if you don't make a sale, and a question to learn more. You may discover that something has come up that prevents the prospect from agreeing to your proposal. If that happens, you need to identify this new situation and plan accordingly.

I can get it cheaper.

Another common objection you will hear is, "I can get it cheaper from the other Radio station." That's probably true, and you should tell your prospect it's probably true.

Remember your training from the previous chapter on *Developing the Advertising Schedule*? Only products of similar quality will have similar pricing unless someone has made a grave pricing error. In Radio advertising, the elements that can affect price are the number of commercials, the amount of reach and frequency, or the placement of the commercials. If the price from another Radio station is less than your price, you will be able to trace the difference to a shortcoming in one or perhaps all those areas.

You may see a brand name lawnmower on sale at a big-box retailer for less money than a similar lawnmower at the local authorized dealer. Many manufacturers make similar looking products, one for the authorized local dealer and another, less expensive model for the big-box retailers. Visually, they may appear the same, but during the manufacturing process, lesser grade materials are used to save money on the discount item. The thickness of the metal used for the mower deck is less and subject to damage or rust more quickly. Perhaps the engine is from a different manufacturer and has less power. Or maybe the mower deck is an inch smaller.

Why is a seemingly similar product available at a lower cost? Consider the law of the Iron Triangle.

Something quick and high quality is never cheap.

Something quick and cheap is never high quality.

Something of high quality and low cost is never quick.

There are market forces that heavily influence the price or quality of every product available. Products of similar quality will have similar pricing. You can't get the same product for less money from another vendor unless the other vendor has made a pricing mistake in their offer.

In Radio advertising, if there is a difference in price between two Radio proposals, there must be a difference in the number of commercials, the length of the commercial (30 or 60-seconds), the reach, and frequency of the schedule, or the time of day the commercial will be on the air. Ask your prospect if they have a copy of the proposal from the other Radio station so you can make a direct comparison. You can't point out these differences without impugning the reputation of the other Radio station.

In the world of Radio advertising sales, the sample commercial can provide you with the emotional tipping point to close the deal. While Radio stations can have similar audience size and demographics, there is only one you. You make the difference when all other considerations appear similar. The Radio script you write is your creative work product. Your personal interest in helping the prospect solve their problems is unique to you. All things being somewhat equal, even with a lower price from a competitor, **you make the difference in the final analysis.**

Even if your prospect doesn't bring up your low-cost competitor in the presentation process, once the sale is made, you can advise your new customer that some of the first people to call after the first commercials run on your station will be other advertising vendors. Tell your new customer the other media will be calling for an appointment because they listen to your Radio station for new prospects. Tell your new customer that if the other advertising proposal is similar in strategy and technique to your proposal, you will help them place that advertising if they wish to add another media station to their plans. This presents you as a consultant, a resource, not just a salesperson.

I Want to Try it for a Month.

"I want to try it for a month." The root cause of this objection from your prospect is their fear of spending their advertising money with you and not seeing new customers from the advertising. As we discussed earlier, this is a common fear for prospects, but you can alleviate this fear by clearly demonstrating how advertising works.

Every proposal you make needs to demonstrate the Four Keys to Advertising Success®, 1) consistency, 2) reach, 3) frequency, and 4) an emotionally engaging message. Research clearly illustrates that unsatisfied advertisers are missing one, if not more, of the Four Keys. Because people are impatient by nature, the most common missing component is the commitment to a consistent plan.

If you have followed every step in the professional sales process, and your prospect still insists on **testing** the advertising for a month before making a longer-term commitment, you must recognize that **you have failed to show them how advertising works**. You must recognize that if you proceed and sell the prospect **a test schedule**, you are about to contribute to the legacy of poor selling that has plagued the profession of Radio advertising sales from the very beginning. **Your prospect will just be the next business to tell the next Radio advertising salesperson, "I tried Radio advertising once, and it didn't work."**

Advertising is not a quick fix. It might work once or twice, but the third time when it doesn't deliver, your new customer will assume that they have tapped out your audience for all it has, and they won't feel compelled to advertise with you anymore.

That's why learning about the Four Keys to Advertising Success® is so essential. You must understand concepts like the *decision journey* or the *path to purchase* and be skilled enough to remind your prospect of how the process works. Testing an advertising campaign for a few weeks will stimulate new customer interest. But, if the prospect's commercial disappears from the airwaves, all your prospect did was stimulate new business for their competitors.

"When you tell me you want to test this before you make a commitment, what I think I hear you are saying is you want to be sure you are making a wise business decision that is going to pay off, am I right?"

Wait for the answer.

"I understand, nobody wants to make a costly advertising mistake. But starting and stopping your commercials after a few weeks will only help your competitors more than it helps you! Lots of people will hear your commercial when it first comes on. Some will decide to begin their path to purchase for your product. As that new customer does their research and moves closer to a buying decision, they begin to pay more attention to advertising and research. If you pull your commercial off the air, that new customer might hear your competitor's advertising and end up going to them instead of you. You'll lose the sale. That's exactly why you need your commercial out there consistently month after month, so those new customers come to you first! After all, isn't that what you really want?"

If you follow the selling process and don't take short cuts, reaching an agreement at the end of the presentation should be a matter of asking the prospect if your proposal meets with their satisfaction. If the answer is yes, then the next question should be, "Would you like to get started on Monday?"

If you don't follow a sales process, closing the sale is going to be more difficult because you haven't walked your prospect through the necessary thought process they need for making an important decision about their business. Remember the statistics from the TAS Group and the Dealmaker Index; **salespeople who follow a well-defined sales process are 33% more likely to be high performers and close more sales**.

Closing the sale is just one part of a professional selling process. It is not the end of the selling process either; it's only one part. Closing the sale is part of a complete package of skills the professional salesperson develops through study, practice, and application. But you must also have a high level of belief in your ability to help your customer get the results they expect.

For many businesspeople, Radio advertising is an intangible product. This perception adds a degree of difficulty to the sales process because your customer can't take delivery of a physical product when they agree to your plan. Your belief and enthusiasm for your proposal will help persuade the prospect that they are making the right decision.

Closing the sale leads to servicing the customer. In the next chapter on customer service, you will learn essential techniques to help your new customer get the most out of their decision to buy advertising from you.

Go for the "No"

In their book, *Go for No!*, authors Andrea Waltz and Richard Fenton argue for *"No" Goals* as opposed for **success goals**. "Rather than setting goals for the number of yes's you are planning to get each week, you set goals for the number of no's you're going to collect."[48] Their point is you will power beyond your success goals instead of stopping when you reach your success goals. If you stop at your success goal, you are essentially taking yourself out of the game when you are doing well and should keep going.

When you analyze your selling career, you'll find that the statistics are in your favor when you begin to **understand that a "No" today is much better than the "No" tomorrow.**

The advantage you gain from learning how to recognize a stall is a better command over your time and your resources. The "No" you get today frees you up to move on to the next

---

[48] Fenton, Richard. Waltz, Waltz. *Go for No!* (Accelerated Performance Training; 4th edition (March 13, 2019)

SPIKE SANTEE

closing attempt with that prospect, or you can move on to another selling opportunity.

Summary

In this chapter on Reaching Agreement, we covered the following topics:

- According to the marketing website *MarketingDonut*, 92% of salespeople give up before the fourth attempt to close the sale, and 80% of prospects say "No," at least four times before they say "Yes."
- Zig Ziglar claims that 63% of all salespeople fail to ask for the order at all!
- It is nearly impossible to close a sale if you haven't completed a thorough **Customer Needs Assessment**.
- According to the TAS Group and the Dealmaker Index, salespeople who follow a well-defined sales process are 33% more likely to be high performers and close more sales.
- When the prospect says "No," your first reaction should be to realize that **the prospect is saying they don't know, k-NO-w enough yet to say yes**.
- Reaching an agreement is the result of a good sales process. Leave out a step in the process and reaching agreement becomes difficult if not impossible.
- During the sales presentation, **it is so important not to skimp on explaining how advertising affects the consumer's behavior and how advertising influences the buying cycle.**
- There are no magic closing lines. Don't take shortcuts in your presentation.
- There is a system for dealing with objections and stalls. The basic formula for dealing with a stall or an objection is this: 1) acknowledge, 2) respond, 3) continue.
- Learn the system, and you won't get stumped.

Page 202

"Value the relationship more than the quota." *Jeffrey Gitomer*, Author and sales trainer. (1946 -

18

Customer Service

After you work so hard to earn a new customer, don't blow the new relationship with poor customer service. Poor customer service is a big problem in business today. According to a report from NewVoiceMedia, poor customer service is costing American business over $75 billion a year.[49]

In the Radio advertising business, the first few weeks after your new customer begins to advertise on your Radio station, are the most critical to establishing a continuous business relationship. In those first few weeks, your new customer's expectations are high. They want to see some new customers from their advertising. Even though they acknowledge that advertising success is based on consistency, they will have a hard time resisting the need for instant gratification. It is during this initial period of the advertising plan when you should be in regular contact with your new customer.

In the beginning, the new customer is excited about the new advertising plan. But as the weeks pass, it's possible for the new customer to become somewhat disappointed, even if things are going as planned. It usually happens after the first advertising bill arrives. Your new customer will make a mental profit and loss statement as they write the check. We call this the *Zone of Doubt and Blame*. They start to wonder if the advertising plan is going to work as you proposed.

In the report from NewVoiceMedia, eighty-six percent of the customers surveyed said that even after poor customer service, if there were an emotional connection with a customer service agent, they would be willing to continue to do business with that company. **In the Radio**

---

[49] NewVoiceMedia (A Vonage Company) 2018 *Serial Switchers* Report

advertising business, that customer service agent is you! Don't wait for your new customer to complain, or worse yet, cancel without telling you why. Build up that emotional connection early and reinforce it often, so you hold on to that new customer year after year.

That positive emotional connection your new customer feels for you has many benefits. The NewVoiceMedia study indicates that if companies provide good customer service, 66% of their customers would be more loyal, 65% would be willing to recommend the company to others, and 48% would spend more money.

It's not enough just to provide good customer service. Your competitors will try just as hard as you to provide good customer service. It is essential to emotionally connect with your new customer. It is that personal connection you build with your new customer that will create loyalty. **Satisfied customers aren't the same as loyal customers. Satisfaction is a rating. Loyalty is an emotion.**

The level of the customer service you provide will have far-reaching consequences. According to the report *Quantifying the Business Impact of Customer Service* from Dimensional Research, 76% of customers who received poor customer service shared their experience with others.[50] But on the flip side, so do satisfied customers. Seventy-four percent of satisfied customers shared their experiences with others. However, unsatisfied customers are more likely to post a bad review or comment through social media.

One of the contributing factors to customer dissatisfaction is the use of technology in customer service. When your customer wants customer service, they don't want to live chat, correspond through email or text; 76% said they want to talk to you on the phone or in-person, and they don't want to wait.

Among the top reasons a customer may want to cancel with you:

- Your new customer doesn't feel appreciated. Nobody sends a Thank You card.
- They don't see you after the sale is made.
- They only hear from the billing office.
- When they do contact you, you don't respond, or you don't respond quickly.
- You just email or text. You don't call or stop by.
- They only see you for the contract renewal.

Providing Top-Quality Customer Service

Thank You Notes

Handwritten ***thank-you notes*** are not just a thing of the past. While you might not see many these days, the cards you do send will mean more than you'd ever think. Handwritten notes are a powerful way to send a message to a customer to thank them for doing business with you.

---

[50] Quantifying the Business Impact of Customer Service – Dimensional Research December 2018

They don't take that long to write, and you will stand out amongst other vendors because of the five extra minutes you took to write the note.

Most people underestimate the emotional impact of mailing a thank-you note rather than sending an email or text. According to scientific research, expressing gratitude improves well-being for both you and your new customer.

According to the study *Undervaluing Gratitude* from the Booth School of Business at the University of Chicago[51], most note senders significantly underestimated how surprised recipients would be about the sender's gratitude.

Sending a hand-written Thank You Note doesn't take up that much time. In lab experiments, Dr. Kumar observed that it took most people less than five minutes to write the notes. Just five minutes to make another person feel **ecstatic**! That's doesn't seem like much to ask if you want to build an emotional relationship with your new customer.

In our instant world we live in these days, the idea of finding an actual pen, writing a genuine note, finding a stamp and a mailbox, somehow seems too challenging to do. We do what's easy and convenient for us; we send an email or a quick text. Knowing the research behind the pitfalls of poor service and the benefits of excellent service, doesn't it seem like a good investment to spend five minutes writing a thank-you note knowing that a happy customer is more likely to buy more and recommend you to others?

In an LA Times article *Your 3-step plan to writing the perfect 'Thank You' note,* Lizzie Post, the great-great-granddaughter of Emily Post — breaks down three critical ingredients for handwritten notes of appreciation.

Step 1: Start with an opener or greeting: "It was so lovely to see you at Thanksgiving this year!"

Step 2: Thank them for the specific item given and tell them how you have already used the gift, or plan to: "Thank you for the lovely bowl. It is the perfect fall color for my dining room table, and I can't wait to enjoy it all season long."

Step 3: Then, add a closing. It's nice to include a wish for the future, but not obligatory: for example, "I look forward to visiting in the New Year and hope that you enjoy the holidays."

In your world as the Radio advertising professional, you would make appropriate edits for each thank-you note you would send.

By taking the time to write a handwritten thank-you note, your customer service will be a notch above your competition. Everyone sends surveys and emails these days. Only a small percentage of salespeople take the time to write a thank-you note. Getting into the habit of

---

[51] Undervaluing Gratitude: Expressers Misunderstand the Consequences of Showing Appreciation 2018 – Amit Kumar and Nicholas Epley, Booth School of Business, University of Chicago

sending a thank-you note will help you build that emotional connection with your customers that the research says will help you create a successful career in Radio advertising sales.

Regular In-Person Contact

One of the most special relationships I made in this business is with Terry Burford. He is one of the nicest people you would ever want to meet, and he is a remarkable salesperson. Terry was the first Radio salesperson to sell over $1 million in advertising in a year in Wichita Kansas. This accomplishment occurred before consolidation when he just had one AM and one FM Radio station to sell. By any standard, it was an impressive accomplishment.

When I tell other salespeople about Terry, they jump to the conclusion that Terry must have had all the biggest accounts on the Radio station. But they would be wrong; Terry didn't want to rely too heavily on large accounts. No, Terry had over 100 active accounts on the air every month. You can do the math, that's a lot of average size accounts on the air at any given time.

People assume that with that many accounts, Terry probably didn't have time enough to service them all properly. Again, they would be wrong. Terry made it a point to see all his customers in person at least once each month. A majority of his 100 clients saw Terry twice a month and some even more if necessary.

When I would go on sales calls with Terry, I couldn't help but notice how much his customers looked forward to seeing Terry walk through their door. For sure, many of his client contacts were brief "Hi, how are you" meetings, just to check-in. But it was the fact that Terry was there on a regular and frequent basis that helped Terry build such an impressive book of business.

As you read this, if you start thinking you'll never find the time to see that many customers regularly, here is one more thing to consider, Terry had only half a day to do his selling work. He was the afternoon DJ on the radio every day, too!

Become a Referral Machine

When you get a new customer, share the news! Be sure to tell your friends and family about your new customer. Someone might be in the market for what your customer offers.

As you develop your customer list, you'll become familiar with each customer's non-advertising needs. Helping them solve a non-advertising need by referring them to another one of your business clients for help is a double play in customer service!

Share information about your new customer in your social media, but only if you have been cultivating a responsible and professional social media identity.

Do Business with Your Customers

If it is appropriate, you should try and do some of your business with your new customer. Some salespeople don't like this suggestion because if something goes wrong with their purchase, they don't want to be in a position where they need to go to their new advertiser and ask that the issue be made right.

But this is when you need to put on your consultant's hat and look at this issue as more than just a customer service issue with only you. If you are having a customer service issue, are there other customers out there who are being treated in a similar way? Is this a customer service issue that could negate all the good advertising you and your Radio station are providing? If your experience is not an isolated incident, you probably need to work up the courage to examine the issue as a consultant and not a customer.

Much of your value as a consultant lies in your viewpoint as a customer of the business. However, having the courage to speak to your advertiser as a consultant and tell your client what nobody else has the courage to say can be very stressful. You don't want to lose your new customer. On the other hand, if you don't bring the issue to their attention, they risk alienating more of their customers. They may even end up blaming your advertising for the lack of sales growth.

Approaching your customer as a consultant and not as a salesperson is scary, but it could become the defining moment that helps to establish a long-term relationship based on your willingness to tell the advertiser the truth.

Tune-Up Presentation

After the first three months of your new customer's advertising campaign, things are either going well, or they're not going well. In either case, it's time for the Tune-Up Presentation!

The Tune-Up Presentation is a quarterly meeting with your new advertiser to review and update the advertising campaign you created for them. During the presentation process, you told the prospect that you would be conducting a quarterly Tune-Up Presentation as a part of your regular service work.

The Tune-Up Presentation uses many of the same slides used in the original sales presentation, especially the pages about the customer's plans and expectations. These pages serve as your reference point for discussing the campaign's progress. This is another reminder of why it is so important to do a thorough Customer Needs Assessment, sales presentation, emotionally engaging commercial, and an estimated return on investment.

If the advertiser's campaign isn't going as planned, perhaps you overlooked a critical component necessary for your new customer's advertising success. If the campaign is going well, maybe the same information will help persuade your customer to add another one of your Radio stations to the plan.

Summary

In this chapter on Customer Service, we covered the following topics:

- Poor customer service is costing American business over $75 billion a year.
- Eighty-six percent of the customers surveyed said that even after poor customer service if there were an emotional connection with a customer service agent, they would be willing to continue to do business with that company.
- According to research at the Booth School of Business at the University of Chicago, most note senders significantly underestimated how surprised recipients are when they receive a thank-you card.
- Going to see your customers in person on a regular basis builds strong relationships that last for years.
- Try to do business with your customers whenever it is practical to do so.
- You can help your new customer by referring new leads to them.
- Schedule a Tune-Up Presentation once a quarter.

"Often when you think you're at the end of something, you're at the beginning of something else." - *Fred Rogers*, TV personality. (1928 – 2003)

19

Digital Advertising Products

With the advent of the Internet, Radio stations have many new ways to bring buyers and sellers together. Your Radio station's listeners are the buyers, and your advertisers are the sellers. In addition to Radio commercials broadcast over the air, Radio stations attract those same listeners to your Radio station's website and mobile app. By adding one of your Radio station's digital products to a broadcast advertising campaign, your advertiser can achieve greater reach and increase the frequency with your audience.

As a professional Radio advertising salesperson, digital advertising represents a way for you to increase your sales revenue and ultimately, your commissions.

Why Sell Digital Marketing?

Borrell Associates, Inc., an advertising tracking firm, reports that more than 85% of Radio advertisers are buying some form of digital advertising and 75% are buying Radio and digital advertising together.[52] The study surveyed over 10,000 Radio stations and 1,300 local advertisers. According to the report, the average Radio station cluster sold over $1 million in digital advertising. There is nothing but growth in the forecast. Digital advertising revenue represents approximately 10% of the average Radio station's overall revenue.

The Borrell Associates, Inc. report indicates that **79% of Radio advertisers surveyed said they buy the Radio station's digital advertising product when offered**. However, only 57% say their Radio salespeople have offered them a digital product.

---

[52] Borrell Associates, Inc. *Benchmarking Local Radio Stations' Online Revenues 2018*

Seventy-two percent of the local businesses in the survey reported that they see digital advertising proposals from your competitors, the newspaper, the yellow pages, TV, and cable advertising salespeople. If you don't learn how to sell your Radio station's digital products, your Radio advertising customers will end up buying digital advertising from your competitor.

In our very first chapter in this training, we challenged you to determine your mindset and become a person with a growth mindset. **Learning how to sell your Radio station's digital products requires you to have a growth mindset because you need to be willing to learn everything you can about your station's digital product line**. The challenge of learning how to sell digital is a test for people who say they have a growth mindset when they really don't. If they have a fixed mindset, they will find many reasons not to learn how to sell your station's digital products.

Even with such compelling evidence, we still encounter Radio salespeople who refuse to embrace the value of selling their Radio station's digital advertising products. They make up all sorts of excuses to avoid taking the steps of self-improvement to learn about their new product line. They have a fixed mindset.

The report's conclusion confirms our anecdotal evidence from working with thousands of Radio salespeople. The authors of the report state, "There's something wrong. The vast majority (82%) of (radio) station managers told us that only 1 in 3 of their radio customers are buying digital advertising from them. Yet 85% of the 1,500 radio advertisers we surveyed said they're buying some sort of digital media. Radio often has the same digital offerings as print and TV competitors. So, the problem may be in the sales pitch."

You will do better when you avoid people with a fixed mindset and learn how to sell your Radio station's digital products. You will be well rewarded for your efforts.

The menu of digital advertising products a Radio station may offer will vary from one company to the next. In our training, we will introduce you to the basics of digital advertising products offered by most Radio stations. Your Radio station may have a different offering than we teach in this training. Don't limit your learning to just what we include in this course. **A person with a growth mindset believes "they can't learn less."**

Radio and Digital Advertising Combined

Radio advertising is a **mass reach medium**. Ninety-two percent of Americans listen to either an AM or an FM Radio station every week. No other medium can make that claim. Radio advertising can reach more people more frequently for less money than any other medium. When an advertiser buys Radio advertising, they are paying to reach as many different people as possible, a very sound marketing objective because you never know where your next customer will come from.

Digital advertising is a **targeted reach medium.** The digital advertiser pays to reach a targeted group of people based on sociographic and geographic criteria. Many digital advertising products can measure how many of the target audience **interacted** with the advertising message. Many advertisers find this tracking ability attractive. It helps them feel better about spending their money if they know people are seeing or hearing their advertising. However, this ability to track audience interaction has caused some advertisers to lose track of the real bottom line, are their sales growing because of their advertising?

In recent years, many advertisers are beginning to realize that digital advertising metrics don't always equal sales growth. One of the most dramatic examples is the world's largest advertiser, Proctor & Gamble. P&G was one of these companies that invested heavily in digital advertising, cutting back on traditional advertising like Radio, Television, and print. In 2017, P&G had second thoughts after five years of lackluster sales growth. They publicly questioned the effectiveness of their digital advertising by cutting their digital advertising budget and demanding more accountability from their digital advertising vendors.

At the same time, P&G reinvested in Radio and Television advertising and saw their sales grow by more than 7% year over year. P&G was so happy with the change in the direction of their sales, P&G became the fifth largest Radio advertiser in 2018. John Fix, a marketing executive at P&G, told attendees to the 2017 Radio Conference, *"[P&G and] other CPG giants have grown frustrated by narrow digital-ad targeting. P&G wants to speak to everyone, not a narrow target. P&G wants to reach as much of America as it can, once a week."*

As a Radio advertising professional, you have the advantage of selling a mass reach medium like Radio advertising along with a targeted reach medium like digital. You can offer the best of two worlds.

You may encounter a local company who has invested heavily in digital advertising at the expense of reach media like Radio. But through your suite of digital products, you can introduce them to your Radio station's audience. You offer something more than other digital providers; your audience is loyal to your Radio station. Your audience listens to your Radio station because they like and enjoy using your product. That same affection applies to their use of your digital products. In short, because your listeners like your Radio station, they trust what your DJs say to them. They trust the messenger, so they trust the message, your customer's advertising, regardless if it is on the air or over the Internet.

But just like P&G, local companies who invested heavily in digital at the expense of reach media will also become frustrated by the lack of reach, and you'll see them return to using more Radio advertising in the future.

As a professional Radio advertising salesperson with professional digital selling skills, you are ready for the future!

Digital Advertising Basics

Almost every Radio station in America has a website. Listeners visit the site for news and information about the Radio station. Radio stations encourage their listeners to visit their website or use the station app to gain access to content not available on the air.

If your Radio station has an app for your listeners, the app is a program written for a tablet or smartphone to access your Radio station's web content. It may not bear any resemblance to your Radio station's website. The app may be designed for more comfortable use and visibility on the smaller screen.

If your station has a website and an app, you will have digital advertising to sell on the site and a different set of digital advertising to sell on the app.

The Display Ad

A display ad is like a print ad in a magazine or newspaper. The display ad is designed to be visually appealing to encourage the viewer to click on the ad and then go to the advertiser's website.

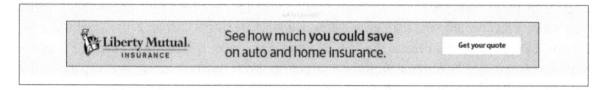

FIGURE 31

In digital advertising, a display ad is *served* to the website's visitors. Display ads are shown at the top of the web page as a banner ad, as seen in Figure 31 or in the side column next to the content, as seen in Figure 32.

FIGURE 32

Some display ads are served in the actual content interrupting the reader's line of sight, forcing the reader to read past the display ad to the next chapter, as seen in Figure 33.

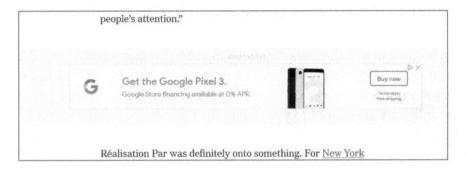

FIGURE 33

Display ads are sold in standard sizes for uniformity between websites. Display ads are measured in pixels. There are 96 pixels to the inch.

The Streaming Radio Commercial

Many Radio stations now **stream** the Radio broadcast over the Internet. Your audience can listen to your Radio station on their computers, tablets, smartphones, and now on Alexa and Google Home.

In most cases, when a Radio station streams the broadcast over the Internet, the studio computer system is set up **NOT** to stream the Radio commercials over the Internet on purpose. The Radio station wants to create an additional commercial inventory that you can sell to generate additional revenue.

If you are listening to the Radio at your desk, and at the same time you are streaming the Radio station on your computer, you would hear the same song and the same DJ talk at the same time. When the commercials come on the air, you would hear a commercial on the Radio and a different commercial on your computer. When the commercials end, the programming will again be the same; you hear the same song on both the Radio and the Internet.

For the advertiser to have a commercial on both the broadcast station and the Internet station, you will turn in two orders or instructions to duplicate the order on the Internet stream, for an extra charge.

Your one Radio station has two commercial logs or lists to follow. There is one list of commercials that will broadcast over the AM or FM airwaves and another list of commercials that will transmit over the Internet stream.

In some cases, a Radio station will sell **Internet-only streaming commercials**. Your listeners will hear these commercials on their computers and devices, but they won't hear the commercial on your AM or FM Radio station.

Commercial requirements for an Internet Radio commercial will be much the same as the requirements for your commercials on your AM or FM Radio station.

Email Marketing

Email marketing to a Radio station curated member list is more effective than buying an email list from an email marketing firm. Your Radio station email list is an **opt-in mailing list**. That means the subscribers to your email list **want to receive** the information your Radio station offers. Those people have subscribed to your email list because they like your Radio station. Remember, if they like your Radio station, they like the messenger, and consequently, they like the message.

Your email list may not be as big as a list your advertiser could buy from an email service, but the quality and the responsiveness of the subscribers on your list will be much higher because the list is curated around your Radio station. Your listeners are loyal to your Radio station, and they know that Radio is an advertiser-supported medium. They understand they need to do business with the advertisers who support their favorite Radio station. Your listeners will turn out for you if you ask them.

Adding an email marketing campaign to a Radio commercial campaign will increase the reach and the frequency of your customer's message with your audience.

Podcasting

The podcast is one of the fastest-growing digital products on the Internet today. The podcast is a digital recording that your audience can download and listen to on their computer, tablet, smartphone, and now on Alexa and Google Home. Listeners can download a podcast from your Radio station website or mobile app or their favorite podcasts source if your Radio station makes the podcasts available that way.

A podcast is a little Radio show all by itself. It could be a recording of segments from the DJ's show, or it could be original content not heard over the Radio. Podcasts are a great way of giving more time to a subject like an artist interview or an in-depth news story. Podcasts should not include music. Your Radio station's licensing agreement with ASCAP, BMI, and SESAC does not cover all the rights needed to include podcasting.[53] (On August 16, 2019, PodcastMusic.com announced plans for an online music clearinghouse for music in podcasts to begin in 2020. Check to ensure you have the proper music rights before including music in a podcast.)

A podcast can have a sponsor just like any other programming elements on your Radio station. When the podcast begins, there is an announcement indicating the podcast is sponsored by the advertiser. There can be a commercial in the podcast. And at the end of the podcast, there can be another sponsorship announcement. The exact format of your station's podcast is up to the programming department.

---

[53] https://www.broadcastlawblog.com/2018/11/articles/podcaster-sued-for-copyright-infringement-for-using-music-without-permission-remember-ascap-bmi-and-sesac-licenses-dont-cover-all-the-rights-needed-for-podcasting/

Other Digital Marketing Tools

We covered the most common forms of digital marketing services offered by Radio stations: the display ad on your website or station app, the streaming commercial on your Internet stream, email marketing to your Radio station's subscriber list, and podcasting. In the following sections, we will cover some of the more advanced digital marketing tools available.

Your Radio station may not offer these services. Many require hiring a third-party or hiring additional staff, and that means your station must pass those costs on to your advertiser. There is no right or wrong; it is just a business decision that your Radio station makes.

Find out what digital product your Radio station offers and use your **growth mindset** to learn everything you can so you can sell more advertising and, ultimately, earn higher commissions.

Ad Serving Technology

Ad serving is the technology and service that places advertisements on websites and mobile apps. It is common to hear a digital salesperson use the word *serve* to explain the placement and display of digital advertising.

If you are selling digital advertising on your Radio station's website, there is probably someone on your staff who is responsible for putting your customer's digital advertising online. Just like the production department records your customer's commercial and schedules it to broadcast on the air, someone in your Radio station creates the digital advertisement and programs it to be *served* to your audience.

If your Radio station sells advertising placement to local companies on other websites and mobile apps beside your station's, your Radio station might be using an **ad serving company**.

There are many ad serving companies offering their services to Radio stations and advertising agencies. They allow the Radio station or advertising agency to **white label** their services, so it looks like the Radio station is doing all the work when they are passing the job off to a third party for a fee.

Most of these third-party companies are using Google to provide ad serving services. Perhaps your Radio station has someone on staff who is trained to use the Google Ad Manager, so you don't need a third party for ad placement services.

Google is the biggest in the business, serving display ads on hundreds of thousands of websites and mobile apps. The Google Network reaches more than 80% of all internet users around the world in more than 30 languages and 100 countries. The Google Ad Network is divided into two significant areas: the Google Display Network and the Google Search Network, which we cover in Search Engine Marketing. The Google Ad Network is continuously evolving.

Perhaps you have heard of *DoubleClick for Publishers* or *Google Adwords*; those two have been combined into one tool called the *Google Ad Manager*.

Yahoo and Bing are numbers two and three in the ad serving business, and they can be bought together using the media.net tool. Media.net combines the Bing and Yahoo Ad networks so that you can advertise on both networks from one place.

ONE by AOL is a mobile advertising network that runs ads across nearly 50,000 mobile applications and websites. Customers have flexibility, and no minimum deposit. It is helpful for companies who want to reach customers on mobile devices and have a very small budget.

Ad serving companies offer the advertiser many socioeconomic and geographic targeting options for whom, when, and where their display ads will be served.

Social Media Advertising

Social Media Advertising is more than just paying to boost a post on Facebook. Social media sites offer a full range of ad placement services, just like Google offers for display ad placement on websites. The advertiser pays to reach potential customers outside of their existing fan base.

Just like ad serving companies, social media sites offer the advertiser many socioeconomic and geographic targeting options for whom, when, and where their display ads will be served.

OTT – Over the Top Video

The term over-the-top refers to any device or service used to stream digital content to a TV, computer, tablet, or a smartphone. OTT includes Roku, Chromecast, Amazon Fire Stick, and similar apps.

The Internet allows anyone to stream video content directly to consumers and bypass cable systems, broadcast, and satellite television providers who control the advertising time sold in television programming. OTT is big business with companies like Amazon Video, Netflix, and Hulu dominating the field.

Even small companies can take advantage of OTT. With low-cost equipment, easy to learn software and a little practice, an amateur can create professional-looking video content. Companies don't need a lot of computer power either. Websites like YouTube and Vimeo make hosting and streaming videos on the Internet very easy and affordable.

OTT creates two different ways to advertise on the Internet, creating and serving video content on the Internet or by placing your commercial in OTT video content.

Companies are no longer limited to the standard commercial lengths of 30 or 60-seconds. They can now create long-form videos of many minutes to demonstrate their products or offer how-to videos.

Easy access to video creation and distribution has allowed thousands of companies and individuals to launch their own YouTube channels attracting millions of viewers. Those channels that attract enough viewership can begin to earn money from YouTube by allowing YouTube to place ads at the beginning of their videos.

Advertisers can place their TV commercials into popular videos on the Internet in much the same way as they can place their display add on websites. You have seen this in action on YouTube, CNN.com, and other popular sites. You click on some video content you want to see, and you are served a video commercial before you see the desired content.

Since you are forced to view the commercial before you see the desired content, the ads are very short, or a button appears after a few seconds that allows you to skip the commercial and see the content.

Search Engine Marketing

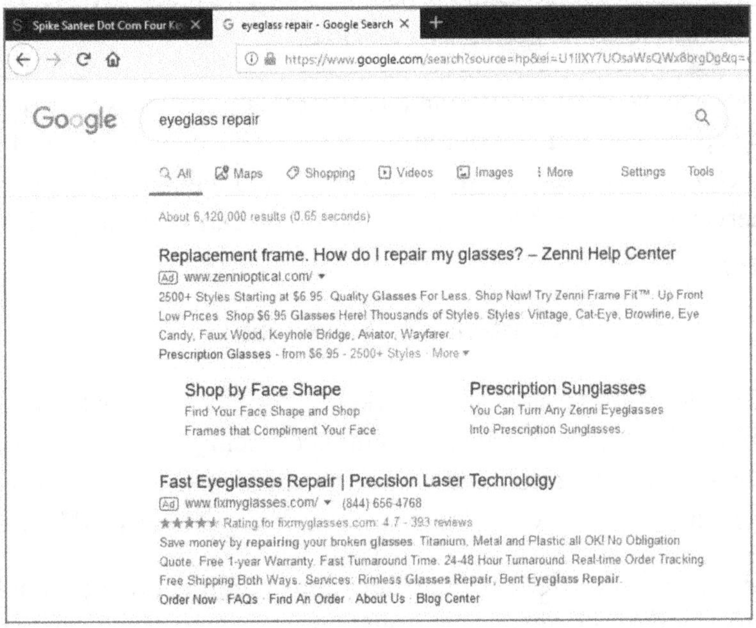

FIGURE 34

Companies listed at the top of Internet search results have paid the search engine to position their link at the top of the results page. The industry calls this search engine marketing. Those are the first couple of links that you see in Google Search that say sponsored or promoted. Paying for search engine marketing is an advantage over organic listings. Google has 95% of the market share when it comes to search engines.

An entire industry has sprung up to help companies take advantage of search engine marketing. Since Google won't reveal how their system works precisely, many companies offer their "expertise" for a fee.

At the heart of the search engine marketing at Google is a system of bidding for position. The more a company offers for a position, the higher the company's position will be. But search engine marketing companies have sprung up to help your competitor identify how much you are spending on search engine marketing, and they will try to outbid you. When you lose your top position, you will feel compelled to raise your bid, and the process goes back and forth all the while your cost for search engine marketing increases with every bid.

Behavioral Targeting - Retargeting

Have you ever searched on Amazon for a product that you wanted to buy, and then you start seeing display advertising for that very product on every website you visit? You may wonder if someone is watching your every move. When you see a display ad for the same product you recently searched for, that is two different kinds of digital marketing working together at the same time.

The first is display ads served to the consumer using ad placement services like Google. The second is called **behavioral targeting or retargeting**.

The advertiser who is using behavioral targeting places a pixel on their website or in their email campaign. This pixel will trigger your browser to store a cookie in your browsing history. Once the cookie is set, the advertiser can show display ads to that user elsewhere on the internet via the ad display services they purchase from Google. You can stop this tracking by clearing your browsing history.

Geofencing Advertising

Geofencing is a location-based digital marketing tool that lets marketers send messages to smartphone users in a defined geographic area. With geofencing, the advertiser can build a **virtual boundary** or a **virtual fence** around a location. Geofencing mobile ads will be **pushed** to a mobile device when the mobile device enters or leaves the **geofenced-off** area.

The geofence can be any size the advertiser wants, but it is often designed to reach the potential customer close to the advertiser's physical location. However, a lawyer looking for new clients might create three geofenced areas, one around the courthouse, another around the jail, and the third around the area hospital.

A fast-food chain might create a temporary geofence around a sporting event or large concert, inviting those people in attendance to visit the restaurant chain after the event for a late-night snack.

Geofencing is one of the options an advertiser can request when they are buying display advertising placement services from providers like Google.

While geofencing sounds like a good idea, to reach people with geofencing advertising on a mobile device, the user must be using an app or browsing the Internet at the time they enter the geofenced area. They must be able to see their device. If they are busy driving, they may miss the geofencing advertising before they leave the geofenced area.

Geofencing is not limited to mobile devices. Geofencing can target any device, including a computer, if the device has a GPS or other device location services enabled.

Geotargeting Advertising

Geotargeting is the practice of delivering ads to people that fit specific targeting criteria and are located within a defined geography. The difference with geotargeting is that it drills down on consumer criteria, such as demographics, behaviors, interests, and a person's location. Geotargeting can also exclude specific areas. This targeting tends to work better for a larger geographical area because the ads can be customized by demographics and keywords. Geotargeting advertising is an option offered by display advertising providers like Google.

Summary

In this chapter on Digital Advertising Products, we covered these topics:

- Borrell Associates, Inc., an advertising tracking firm, reports that more than 85% of Radio advertisers are buying some form of digital advertising and 75% are buying Radio and digital advertising together.
- The report indicates that **79% of Radio advertisers surveyed said they buy the Radio station's digital advertising product when offered**. However, only 57% say their Radio salespeople have offered them a digital product.
- As a Radio advertising professional, you have the advantage of selling a mass reach medium like Radio advertising along with a targeted reach medium like digital. You can offer the best of two worlds.
- An introduction to digital advertising products that most Radio stations offer.
- The benefits of combining Radio advertising and digital advertising.
- A description of the common third-party digital advertising products a Radio station might offer.

Appendix A – Goal Setting Worksheet

Month	Goal		Avg Order		No of Customers
1) _____ :	$ _____	÷	$ _____	=	_____
2) _____ :	$ _____	÷	$ _____	=	_____
3) _____ :	$ _____	÷	$ _____	=	_____
4) _____ :	$ _____	÷	$ _____	=	_____
5) _____ :	$ _____	÷	$ _____	=	_____
6) _____ :	$ _____	÷	$ _____	=	_____
7) _____ :	$ _____	÷	$ _____	=	_____
8) _____ :	$ _____	÷	$ _____	=	_____
9) _____ :	$ _____	÷	$ _____	=	_____
10) _____ :	$ _____	÷	$ _____	=	_____
11) _____ :	$ _____	÷	$ _____	=	_____
12) _____ :	$ _____	÷	$ _____	=	_____

Instructions:

Fill in the name of the upcoming month on your calendar in the first column labeled Month.

Ask your sales manager for your monthly goal for the next twelve months and enter those amounts in the column labeled Goal.

Ask your sales manager for the average order size on your station, enter that number in the formula. Divide your sales goal by the average order size to calculate a rough estimate of how many customers you need to have on the air each month to reach your sales goal.

Appendix B – Goal Setting Activity Planner

What is your monthly sales goal (or your GAP to goal)? _____

What is your (or the station's) average monthly sales order? _____

Calculate how many monthly orders you need to sell each month to reach your sales goal:
16,000 (goal) ÷ 1,000 (average order) = 16 (customers needed)

Write down how many accounts you need to sell each month: _____

What is your closing ratio? _____ %

Divide the number of accounts you need to sell each month by your closing ratio:
16 (accounts needed) ÷ .50 (50% closing ratio) = 32 (presentations required)

Write down how many proposals you need to present each month: _____

How many CNAs result in a sales presentation? _____ %

Divide the number of proposals needed each month by the ratio of CNAs that result in a presentation:
32 (presentations required) ÷ 50 (CNAs to proposal ratio) = 64 CNAs required

Write down how many CNAs you need to conduct each month: _____

How many prospecting calls result in a CNA appointment? _____ %

Divide the number of CNAs needed each month by the ratio of prospecting calls that result in a CNA:
64 (CNAs required) ÷ 50 (prospecting call to CNA ratio) = 128 (prospecting calls required)

Write down the number of prospecting calls you need to make each month: _____

There are approximately 21 business days each month, divide your numbers by 21 to determine the number of activities you need to accomplish each day: (Round up)

Sales required each month: *(20 ÷ 21 = 1 per day)* _____

Presentations required each month: *(40 ÷ 21 = 2 per day)* _____

CNAs required each month: *(80 ÷ 21 = 4 per day)* _____

Prospecting calls required each month: *(160 ÷ 21 = 8 per day)* _____

Appendix C – Basic Appointment Script

You have the prospect on the phone. You have just a few seconds to convey why you are calling and why it is important to the prospect. Make sure you **slow down** and speak clearly.

Just imagine that the prospect answered the phone by saying "Who are you and what do you want"?

You politely respond by saying;

> Good Morning Mr. Smith. My name is Spike Santee. I'm calling from Results Radio WXYZ. I was doing some research on your business, and I came up with an idea that could help you see more in-store customers, more website visits, and help you grow your email list.

Most business owners suspect that this is a sales call. It's not. **It's an appointment call**. You're telling the prospect that you're not trying to do business on this call. You are calling to set an appointment with them to show them an idea that could help them find some new customers and maybe save them some money at the same time.

Then imagine the business owner responds by saying, "Why would I want to see your idea"? You *follow up with;*

> *My idea doesn't require you to spend a lot of money or waste a lot of time. In ten to fifteen minutes, you can judge for yourself whether it might work for you. Would you let me come by next week and show you what it's all about?*

Here is the entire script from start to finish;

> Good Morning Mr. Smith. My name is Spike Santee. I'm calling from Results Radio WXYZ. I was doing some research on your business, and I came up with an idea that could help you see more in-store customers, more website visits, and help you grow your email list.

> My idea doesn't require you to spend a lot of money or waste a lot of time. In ten to fifteen minutes, you can judge for yourself whether it might work for you. Would you let me come by next week and show you what it's all about?

When the prospect agrees to the appointment, be sure to confirm their phone number and their email address. You will send the prospect an email confirmation with the date and time of your meeting.

Selling is the transfer of emotions. When someone agrees to attend the presentation, you're going to feel good, maybe even a little excited. Let the prospect know! You could say something like;

Excellent! Thank you. You'll really enjoy the information. I can't wait to meet you in person.

Then confirm the details one more time before hanging up the phone.

Immediately send them an email confirmation. Make sure the email goes through. If not, follow up with another phone call. YOU NEED THE EMAIL ADDRESS.

Appendix D – Stalls & Objections

The most important thing to remember about stalls and objections is that it is nothing personal. The most likely cause for a stall or an objection is that the prospect didn't understand why you were calling. Perhaps you talked too fast, or you got off the script. In any case, when you get a stall or an objection, you should follow this formula; Acknowledge, Respond and Continue.

In the simplest form, the response would be;

ACKNOWLEDGE: "I understand; that's why I'm calling."

RESPOND: "A lot of our customers found this was the answer they were looking for."

CONTINUE: "Could I stop by tomorrow and show you how it works?"

The **acknowledgment phrase** is to show you heard what they said. You know for a fact that people don't like spending their money on advertising. They have had a bad experience, or it didn't work out the way they planned. Whatever the reason, you must show that you understand what they are going through and are eager to show them a better way.

The **respond phrase** is customized to the objection they put forth. We have many personalized responses in this training manual.

The **continue phrase** is simply another ask for the appointment.

Just like other skills, learning how to deal with stalls and objections will take some time and practice. You must learn the formula of Acknowledge, Respond and Continue so well that you can respond appropriately at the moment and it doesn't sound like a canned response.

Is this about Radio advertising?

ACKNOWLEDGE: "I don't know yet. That's exactly why I'm calling."

RESPOND: "I'm calling to set an appointment to show you how we are helping other local companies see more in-store customers, more visitors to their websites, and more email subscribers. We might even be able to save you some money at the same time."

CONTINUE: "Could I come by tomorrow and show you how it works?"

Or,

ACKNOWLEDGE: "That's up to you. That's exactly why I'm calling."

RESPOND: "Well, I do work for the Radio station, that's right. But in recent years, we've become experts in digital advertising too. I just want to set an appointment to show you an idea that will help you see more in-store customers, increase visits to your website, and grow your email list. We might even save you some money at the same time."

CONTINUE: "Could I come by tomorrow and show you how it works?"

I'm not interested at this time.

ACKNOWLEDGE: "I understand, but that's exactly why I'm calling!"

RESPOND: "When someone says they are not interested; I find it's because they don't want to feel obligated or pressured to buy something right away. I don't work that way. I just want to set an appointment to show you how we can help you see more in-store customers, see more visits to your website, and grow your email list. We might even be able to save you some money at the same time."

CONTINUE: "Could I come by tomorrow and show you how it works?"

Or,

ACKNOWLEDGE: "I understand what you're saying. That's exactly why I'm calling!"

RESPOND: "When people say that to me, it makes me wonder what they're not interested in, **making money** or **saving money**. We can do both! I'm just calling to set an appointment to show you how we can help you see more in-store customers, see more visits to your website and grow your email list I promise you I won't pressure you to buy something that you don't want, don't need or can't afford, I promise that won't happen."

CONTINUE: "Could I come by tomorrow and show you how it works?"

Or,

ACKNOWLEDGE: "I understand. That's exactly why I'm calling!"

RESPOND: "What is it exactly that you're not interested in? I'm just calling to set an appointment to show you an idea that could help you get more customers in the store, more visits to your web site and more subscribers to your email list."

CONTINUE: "Could I come by tomorrow and show you how it works?"

Or,

ACKNOWLEDGE: "I understand. That's exactly why I'm calling!"

RESPOND: "That's why it only takes a few minutes to introduce you to how our company is helping local companies see more in-store customers, drive more people to their websites and increase your email subscribers. And we can probably save you some money at the same time."

CONTINUE: "Could I come by and show you how it works?"

Or,

ACKNOWLEDGE: "I understand. That's exactly why I'm calling!"

RESPOND: "I wouldn't be calling if I didn't think that I could help you see more in-store customers, more traffic to your web site and more email subscribers. I might even be able to save you some money."

CONTINUE: "Could I come by tomorrow and show you how it works for other businesses?"

Or,

ACKNOWLEDGE: "I understand. That's exactly why I'm calling!"

"**RESPOND:** "You might not be interested right now, so there won't be any pressure to buy anything. You'll be able to look at the material; see how we increase in-store traffic, increase website visitors and grow your email list, then when you need it, you'll at least know what is available."

CONTINUE: "Could I come by tomorrow and show you how it works?"

Could You Send Me Some Information?

ACKNOWLEDGE: "That's exactly why I'm calling!"

RESPOND: "I'd be happy to, but it might take longer to read it than it would for me to show it to you. We have a way of doing three things, drive more in-store traffic, increase website visitors, and grow your email list."

CONTINUE: "Could I come by tomorrow and show you how it works?"

Or,

ACKNOWLEDGE: "That's exactly why I'm calling."

RESPOND: "Since our way of building in-store traffic, increasing website visitors and growing your email list is new, people tell me it's easier to see how our plan works in-person when they can ask questions. If you have been wondering about social media and the Internet, this could really be helpful."

CONTINUE: "Could I come by tomorrow and show you how it works?"

Or,

ACKNOWLEDGE: "That's exactly why I'm calling."

RESPOND: "I would be happy to. What would you like to see?" (You will probably get a non-responsive response like, "Uh, I don't know, send it all over." That's when you know they are just trying to avoid an appointment.)

CONTINUE: "Could I bring it over tomorrow?"

NO, I don't think so.

ACKNOWLEDGE: "I understand. That's exactly why I'm calling!"

RESPOND: "Lots of people tell me 'No' at first because they think I'm just calling to sell them something. I'm just calling for an appointment to show you an idea that could help you find new in-store customers, more website visitors, and more email subscribers. We might even save you some money. Whether or not you ever spend any money with me is totally up to you."

CONTINUE: "Could I come by tomorrow and show you how it works?"

Give me a call Friday, and we'll set something up.

ACKNOWLEDGE: "That's exactly why I'm calling!"

RESPOND: "What time on Friday?"

CONTINUE: "Could I just come by at that time?"

Or,

ACKNOWLEDGE: "That's exactly why I'm calling!"

RESPOND: "I have my calendar right here do you have yours handy. Let's set something up now. I'll call back the day before to confirm. If something comes up, we'll reschedule."

CONTINUE: "Let's plan for Friday morning okay?"

Or,

ACKNOWLEDGE: "I can appreciate that you're a busy person."

RESPOND: "I won't waste your time. In 10 to 15 minutes you can see all about it."

CONTINUE: "What about early Friday morning at 8:30?"

Or,

ACKNOWLEDGE: "I understand."

RESPOND: "If you're busy right now and need to go, but please tell me,"

CONTINUE: "Will I be wasting my time if I try to call you back on Friday?"

Or,

ACKNOWLEDGE: "I understand."

RESPOND: "Are you just brushing me off because you don't like spending your money on advertising? If you are, that is exactly why we should meet. We only do business together if YOU say so."

CONTINUE: "May I stop by on Friday and show you how our plan works?"

I have more business than I know what to do with.

ACKNOWLEDGE: "That's exactly why I'm calling."

RESPOND: "People tell us our ideas help them squeeze out more profits and take more of that money home and put it in your own pocket."

CONTINUE: "Can I come by on Tuesday and show you how it works?"

How much does it cost?

ACKNOWLEDGE: "That's exactly why I'm calling."

RESPOND: "If it's not what you're looking for, it won't cost you a thing. Look at it this way; bad advertising is expensive no matter how little you pay. That's why we start by showing you how we bring more in-store customers, increase website visitors, and sign up more people to your email list. If you feel good about the plan, we can talk about the price at that time."

CONTINUE: "Would Wednesday work for you?"

Is this about advertising?

ACKNOWLEDGE: "Yes! That's why I'm calling."

RESPOND: "It's really about showing you how our company is helping other local companies find more in-store customers, more website visitors, and more email list subscribers. I want to show you how we do that. If, **and only if you** feel we may be able to help you, then we can discuss doing some business, Ok?"

CONTINUE: "Would it be okay to come over tomorrow?"

I don't use advertising.

ACKNOWLEDGE: "That's exactly why I'm calling!"

RESPOND: "I really just want to set an appointment to show you the way my company helps local companies see more in-store customers, more website visitors, and more email subscribers. In about 10 minutes you can see for yourself what it's all about."

CONTINUE: "Could I come by tomorrow and show you how it works?"

I don't use radio advertising.

ACKNOWLEDGE: "That's exactly why I'm calling."

RESPOND: "If you let me stop by, you can see what we're doing to help local business owners bring back their old customers, increase their repeat business and find new customers for the future. We have a new way of helping you see more in-store customers, more website visitors, and more email subscribers."

CONTINUE: "Could I come by on Tuesday and show you how it works?"

Or,

ACKNOWLEDGE: "I'm glad you told me that."

RESPOND: "We have many satisfied customers who will recommend our advertising services. That's because we help them see more in-store customers, more website visitors, and more email subscribers. If you let me come by, you will be able to learn more about why they work with my company."

CONTINUE: "Could I come by tomorrow and show you how it works?"

Or,

ACKNOWLEDGE: "That's exactly why I'm calling."

RESPOND: "When you see the material, you'll see that nine out of ten people listen to the Radio every week. You'll see that it is the most effective and affordable way to bring back your old customers, increase your repeat business, and find new customers in the future."

CONTINUE: "Could I come by Tuesday morning?"

I use the newspaper because it gets results.

ACKNOWLEDGE: "I understand. That's exactly why I'm calling!"

RESPOND: "I'm not asking you to stop using the newspaper; I'm simply trying to come over and show you how we help other newspaper advertisers see more in-store customers, more website visitors, and more email subscribers. If you look at the plan and don't think it can do anything for you, it won't cost you a thing."

CONTINUE: "Could I come by tomorrow and show you how it works?"

Or,

ACKNOWLEDGE: "That's exactly why I'm calling."

RESPOND: "Companies who add Radio to their newspaper advertising see more in-store traffic, more website visitors and more email subscribers."

CONTINUE: "Could I come by tomorrow and show you how it works?"

Or,

ACKNOWLEDGE: "That's exactly why I'm calling."

RESPOND: "If you could invest the exact same amount of time and money as you are now, but have it bring you more in-store customers, more website visitors and more email subscribers, that would be worth looking at, wouldn't it?"

CONTINUE: "Could I come by tomorrow and show you how it works?"

Or,

ACKNOWLEDGE: "That's exactly why I'm calling."

RESPOND: "We help newspaper advertisers see more in-store customers, more website visitors, and more email subscribers. If you just look, you'll be able to judge for yourself whether or not we can help you too."

CONTINUE: "Could I come by tomorrow and show you how it works?"

I tried Radio once, and it didn't work?

ACKNOWLEDGE: "That's exactly why I'm calling!"

RESPOND: "I want you to see what our company is doing to about that. A lot has changed. I'd like to show you The Four Keys to Advertising Success. You'll probably be able to see why your previous efforts didn't work out the way you planned. If you're not convinced that we can help, there is absolutely no obligation to spend any money."

CONTINUE: "Could I come by tomorrow and show you how it works?"

Or,

ACKNOWLEDGE: "I hear what you're saying, that makes my job a lot harder!"

RESPOND: "A lot of people out there have been burned by **marketing malpractice**. That's when the sales rep sells you some **BADvertising**. Our company is the leader in client education when it comes to good advertising techniques. We're in business today because we help our customers see more in-store customers, more website visitors, and more email subscribers?"

CONTINUE: "That's why I'm calling for an appointment. Could I come by tomorrow and show you how it works?"

Or,

ACKNOWLEDGE: "I understand. I'm sure there is a reason."

RESPOND: "Could you tell me please what that reason would be? (Then listen and say) Based on what you're telling me, I can address that very subject. But better yet, I can show what we're doing now, helping our clients see more in-store customers, more website visitors, and more email subscribers."

CONTINUE: "Could I come by tomorrow and show you how it works?"

Or,

ACKNOWLEDGE: "That's exactly why I'm calling."

RESPOND: "I can understand that you may have had a problem in the past. But a lot has changed recently, and I'd like to show you how we help our clients see more in-store customers, more website visitors, and more email subscribers. Our current clients use this information every day, and they renew with us over and over."

CONTINUE: "Could I come by tomorrow and show you how it works?"

Or,

ACKNOWLEDGE: "I'm glad to hear you say that, we're doing something about it."

RESPOND: "That's why I'm calling for an appointment. This is a low-risk way to see that Radio can help you see more in-store customers, more website visitors, and more email subscribers."

CONTINUE: "Can I come by tomorrow and show you how it works?"

Or,

ACKNOWLEDGE: "I can appreciate where you are coming from."

RESPOND: "If this 15-minute meeting could PROVE to you that this is a smart way to see more in-store customers, more website visitors and more email subscribers, wouldn't you like to know that?"

CONTINUE: "Could I come by tomorrow and show you how it works?"

I can't afford it.

ACKNOWLEDGE: "That's exactly why I'm calling!"

RESPOND: "**Bad advertising** is very expensive. That's why I want you to come by and show you what we're doing about it as a company. In just a few minutes, you can see for yourself how we help local companies see more in-store customers, more website visitors, and more email subscribers. If you don't like what you see, no problem. But if you do see something that you think might make a difference, then we can talk."

CONTINUE: "Could I come by tomorrow and show you how it works?"

Or,

ACKNOWLEDGE: "That's exactly why I'm calling!"

RESPOND: "We have a new plan that brings in more in-store customers, more website visitor, and more subscribers to your email list. I can probably save you some money at the same time."

CONTINUE: "When is a good time to come by and show it to you."

Or,

ACKNOWLEDGE: "That's exactly why I'm calling!"

RESPOND: "We're doing something about the high cost of advertising at the same time helping companies find more in-store customers, more website visitors, and more subscribers to your email list. Most people are glad they took the time to look at the ideas."

CONTINUE: "Could I come by this week?

Or,

ACKNOWLEDGE: "I understand exact completely. That's why I'm calling."

RESPOND: "I'm simply asking for an appointment so you can be the judge. If it's not exactly what you're looking for, there won't be any charge at all. And I can promise you, no high-pressure selling."

CONTINUE: "Could I come by this week?"

Or,

ACKNOWLEDGE: "I can appreciate that, but we haven't even discussed any prices."

RESPOND: "When you see our new program, you'll see we're the most affordable solution in town."

CONTINUE: "Could I come by on Tuesday?"

Or,

ACKNOWLEDGE: "That's exactly why I'm calling!"

RESPOND: "It doesn't cost anything to look at some new ideas. At least you'll know how we help other companies see more in-store customers, more website visitors, and more subscribers to their email list."

CONTINUE: "Could I come sometime this week?"

Or,

ACKNOWLEDGE: "That's exactly why I'm calling."

RESPOND: "Our new program is not an expense if it brings in more new business than what it costs. It doesn't cost anything to look a new idea does it?"

CONTINUE: "Could I come by this week and just show it to you?"

Or

ACKNOWLEDGE: "That's exactly why I'm calling!"

RESPOND: "If you look at the ideas and you determine that we can save you money, then the price shouldn't be a problem. A better Return on Investment, which I know our program can deliver, is certainly worth looking at."

CONTINUE: "Could I stop by tomorrow and show you how it works?"

What's This All About?

ACKNOWLEDGE: "I'm glad you asked."

RESPOND: "It's all about what our company is doing to help small businesses thrive in today's crowded market. Our new program will help you see more in-store customers, more website visitors, and more subscribers to your email list."

CONTINUE: "Could I come by tomorrow and show you how it works?"

Prospect No Longer There or No Contact Information

There is a possibility that when you call a business and ask for the contact person on your list, they may no longer work there. Here is a useful technique to keep the call on course. When they tell you the person no longer works there, you can say;

"Oh, that's exactly why I'm calling. I'm working on the Radio station invitation list to make sure it is accurate and up-to-date. May I get the name of the owner, please"?

You may want to follow up with;

"Are there any other VIPs that should be included on my list?"

You may get the names of some other key people within the organization that could be important to developing a profitable relationship with this new prospect.

Once you have collected the proper contact information, politely ask if you can speak with the prospect and invite them to the event using the basic invitation script.

This technique is also very useful when you have no contact information at all. Instead of calling and asking, "Who handles your advertising?" or "Who handles your marketing?" say;

"My name is Spike Santee. I'm working on the WXYZ station invitation list, and I notice we don't have anyone from your company represented on our station invitation list. May I get the name of the owner, please"?

Then follow up by asking;

"Are there any other VIPs that we should include?"

Work your way through the organizational chart of the business one or two levels deep.

The owner may be the person that answers the phone, and before they identify themselves, they may ask, "What do you invite people to?" You can respond by saying;

"The Radio station has many events throughout the year. Are you the owner? May I get your name, please"?

After you collect the contact information, you can then proceed to try and set an appointment using the basic script.

Appendix E – Broadcast Calendar

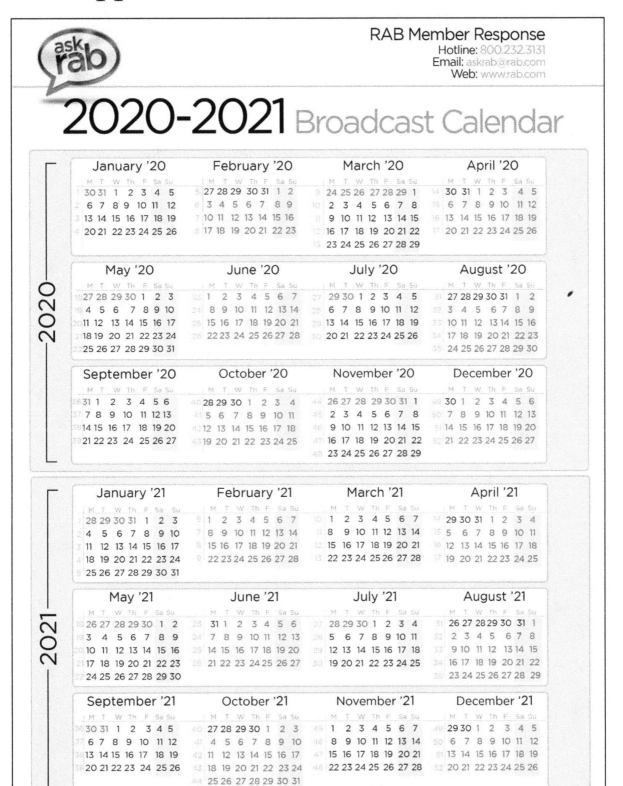

RAB Member Response
Hotline: 800.232.3131
Email: askrab@rab.com
Web: www.rab.com

2020-2021 Broadcast Calendar

2020

January '20

M	T	W	Th	F	Sa	Su
1 30	31	1	2	3	4	5
2 6	7	8	9	10	11	12
3 13	14	15	16	17	18	19
4 20	21	22	23	24	25	26

February '20

M	T	W	Th	F	Sa	Su
5 27	28	29	30	31	1	2
6 3	4	5	6	7	8	9
7 10	11	12	13	14	15	16
8 17	18	19	20	21	22	23

March '20

M	T	W	Th	F	Sa	Su
9 24	25	26	27	28	29	1
10 2	3	4	5	6	7	8
11 9	10	11	12	13	14	15
12 16	17	18	19	20	21	22
13 23	24	25	26	27	28	29

April '20

M	T	W	Th	F	Sa	Su
14 30	31	1	2	3	4	5
15 6	7	8	9	10	11	12
16 13	14	15	16	17	18	19
17 20	21	22	23	24	25	26

May '20

M	T	W	Th	F	Sa	Su
19 27	28	29	30	1	2	3
4	5	6	7	8	9	10
11	12	13	14	15	16	17
18	19	20	21	22	23	24
25	26	27	28	29	30	31

June '20

M	T	W	Th	F	Sa	Su
23 1	2	3	4	5	6	7
24 8	9	10	11	12	13	14
25 15	16	17	18	19	20	21
26 22	23	24	25	26	27	28

July '20

M	T	W	Th	F	Sa	Su
27 29	30	1	2	3	4	5
28 6	7	8	9	10	11	12
29 13	14	15	16	17	18	19
30 20	21	22	23	24	25	26

August '20

M	T	W	Th	F	Sa	Su
31 27	28	29	30	31	1	2
32 3	4	5	6	7	8	9
33 10	11	12	13	14	15	16
34 17	18	19	20	21	22	23
35 24	25	26	27	28	29	30

September '20

M	T	W	Th	F	Sa	Su
36 31	1	2	3	4	5	6
37 7	8	9	10	11	12	13
38 14	15	16	17	18	19	20
39 21	22	23	24	25	26	27

October '20

M	T	W	Th	F	Sa	Su
40 28	29	30	1	2	3	4
41 5	6	7	8	9	10	11
42 12	13	14	15	16	17	18
43 19	20	21	22	23	24	25

November '20

M	T	W	Th	F	Sa	Su
44 26	27	28	29	30	31	1
45 2	3	4	5	6	7	8
46 9	10	11	12	13	14	15
47 16	17	18	19	20	21	22
48 23	24	25	26	27	28	29

December '20

M	T	W	Th	F	Sa	Su
49 30	1	2	3	4	5	6
50 7	8	9	10	11	12	13
51 14	15	16	17	18	19	20
52 21	22	23	24	25	26	27

2021

January '21

M	T	W	Th	F	Sa	Su
1 28	29	30	31	1	2	3
2 4	5	6	7	8	9	10
3 11	12	13	14	15	16	17
4 18	19	20	21	22	23	24
5 25	26	27	28	29	30	31

February '21

M	T	W	Th	F	Sa	Su
6 1	2	3	4	5	6	7
7 8	9	10	11	12	13	14
8 15	16	17	18	19	20	21
9 22	23	24	25	26	27	28

March '21

M	T	W	Th	F	Sa	Su
10 1	2	3	4	5	6	7
11 8	9	10	11	12	13	14
12 15	16	17	18	19	20	21
13 22	23	24	25	26	27	28

April '21

M	T	W	Th	F	Sa	Su
14 29	30	31	1	2	3	4
15 5	6	7	8	9	10	11
16 12	13	14	15	16	17	18
17 19	20	21	22	23	24	25

May '21

M	T	W	Th	F	Sa	Su
18 26	27	28	29	30	1	2
19 3	4	5	6	7	8	9
20 10	11	12	13	14	15	16
21 17	18	19	20	21	22	23
22 24	25	26	27	28	29	30

June '21

M	T	W	Th	F	Sa	Su
23 31	1	2	3	4	5	6
24 7	8	9	10	11	12	13
25 14	15	16	17	18	19	20
26 21	22	23	24	25	26	27

July '21

M	T	W	Th	F	Sa	Su
27 28	29	30	1	2	3	4
28 5	6	7	8	9	10	11
29 12	13	14	15	16	17	18
30 19	20	21	22	23	24	25

August '21

M	T	W	Th	F	Sa	Su
31 26	27	28	29	30	31	1
32 2	3	4	5	6	7	8
33 9	10	11	12	13	14	15
34 16	17	18	19	20	21	22
35 23	24	25	26	27	28	29

September '21

M	T	W	Th	F	Sa	Su
36 30	31	1	2	3	4	5
37 6	7	8	9	10	11	12
38 13	14	15	16	17	18	19
39 20	21	22	23	24	25	26

October '21

M	T	W	Th	F	Sa	Su
40 27	28	29	30	1	2	3
41 4	5	6	7	8	9	10
42 11	12	13	14	15	16	17
43 18	19	20	21	22	23	24
44 25	26	27	28	29	30	31

November '21

M	T	W	Th	F	Sa	Su
45 1	2	3	4	5	6	7
46 8	9	10	11	12	13	14
47 15	16	17	18	19	20	21
48 22	23	24	25	26	27	28

December '21

M	T	W	Th	F	Sa	Su
49 29	30	1	2	3	4	5
50 6	7	8	9	10	11	12
51 13	14	15	16	17	18	19
52 20	21	22	23	24	25	26

Appendix F - Glossary of Digital Marketing Terms

Search Engine Marketing

CLICK-THROUGH RATE (CTR): The percentage of the people who saw a search result, ad, or e-mail, which then clicked through to your website. (clicks / impressions = CTR)

CONVERSION RATE: The percentage of the people who clicked through to a website who then took positive action, such as purchasing something or signing up for a newsletter.

COST PER ACQUISITION (CPA): Cost per Acquisition is a pricing model where companies are charged by advertising platforms only when leads, sales, or conversions are generated.

COST PER CLICK (CPC): The amount the advertiser pays on an advertising platform for each click.

COST PER THOUSAND IMPRESSIONS (CPM): The amount the advertiser pays on an advertising platform per thousand times people see your ad.

VIRAL MARKETING: Marketing where the audience is encouraged by companies to pass on their content to others for more exposure. Paying for traffic wouldn't be considered "Viral Marketing."

Search Engine Optimization Terms

BOUNCE RATE: The percentage of people who visit a website but leave without visiting any other page.

DOMAIN AUTHORITY: This is a scale from 1-100 that search engines use to determine how authoritative a company's website is — the higher the website's domain authority, the more Search Engines the website.

ENGAGEMENT RATE: This is how much users are interacting with a brand. How many comments did the site get on a post? How many shares did that blog receive? If search engines see that users are interacting with a website and social media channels, the brand will be viewed as a notable source in their industry, which is good for SEO.

IMPRESSION: A single display of a particular ad or search result on a web page.

KEYWORD: A keyword is a word or phrase that your audience uses to search for relevant topics on search engines.

KEYWORD STUFFING: This is the practice of using too many keywords in content in hopes of making it more visible on search engines. A website will be penalized by search engines for Keyword Stuffing.

LONG-TAIL KEYWORDS: The specific, three- or four-word phrases that potential customers use when searching for products or services. These are often easier and quicker to rank for in search engines and can account for the bulk of a website's traffic.

META TAG: Hidden bits of code on a website that help determine the various ways that a site appears within search engines, from supplying the "title" and "description" that appear in Google to telling search engines what kind of business it is and what products it offers.

ORGANIC TRAFFIC: This is traffic that is generated to your website, which is generated by a Search Engine. This could be traffic from Google, Yahoo, or Bing. It's also known as "Free" traffic.

SEARCH ENGINE RESULTS PAGE (SERP): Search Engine Results Page is the list of results provided by a search engine after a search query is made indicating how well a website ranks in the search.

Paid Media

AFFILIATE MARKETING: A strategy where businesses reward individual affiliates (people or organizations outside the company) for bringing in new customers or visitors through ads or content on the affiliate's website. Affiliates receive payments or product discounts based on the number of customers they generate.

BEHAVIORAL TARGETING: Serving advertising to people who should be receptive to the advertiser's message given past web behavior such as purchases, or websites visited.

DYNAMIC RETARGETING: Essentially, next-level retargeting—serving ads to users who have been to a website that contain images and information about the exact item they viewed.

EVENT TRACKING: Using Facebook's pixel implementation, you can track not just revenue and conversions, but a customer's journey every step of the way, including form fills, cart additions, and newsletter sign-ups, all in one place.

EXPANDED TEXT ADS: Google has recently allowed users to include an additional headline (for a total of 3) and an additional description line (for a total of 2) in all text ads, allowing the advertiser to take up more space on the Search Engine Results Page and achieve higher click-through rates.

GEO-TARGETING & GEO-FENCING Virtual perimeters for real-world geographic areas. These can be dynamically generated, as in a radius around a point location, or can be a predefined set of boundaries, enabling the software to trigger a response (a digital ad or search result) when a mobile device enters or leaves a particular area.

PAID SEARCH: Also referred to as Search Engine Marketing (SEM), Paid Placement, or Pay Per Click, paid search allows advertisers to pay to be listed within the Search Engine Results Pages for specific keywords or phrases.

QUALITY SCORE: A numerical score Google AdWords assigns to ads and campaigns based on ad quality, ad relevance, and landing page experience. Generally, the higher the quality score, the higher the ads can appear on a search engine results page.

REFERRAL MARKETING: The method of promoting products or services to new customers through referrals, usually word of mouth.

RETARGETING: Someone visits a website, and then after they exit and continue browsing, ads for the original website appear as a display ad on other websites or social media channels that accept ads from the ad network the advertiser uses for retargeting.

Email Marketing

A/B TESTING: An optimization technique that divides a list in two, then sends a different email version to each half to determine which variation converts best.

BOUNCE RATE: A percentage that measures how many emails have been returned by an email service. A bounce can happen because a subscriber's email address either no longer exists, their inbox was full, or because a server was unavailable.

CALL TO ACTION (CTA): A word or phrase used to inspire the end-user to take a specific action, often via a button or another stylized link.

DRIP MARKETING: A sequence of communication that is written in advance, and then sent to prospective or current customers at pre-determined intervals to advance them through the advertiser's sales funnel.

E-MAIL AUTOMATION: A feature that enables the advertiser to send out messages to their customers at designated times, such as: When a subscriber signs up for the advertiser's email list, when they perform an action on the advertiser's website (like download an e-book), or when they add an item to their shopping cart but don't complete the purchase (an "abandoned cart" email).

HARD BOUNCE: Hard bounces are emails that were not delivered.

LEAD MAGNET: lead magnet is a small giveaway, free eBook, guide, etc. that your business offers to customers in exchange for their email.

LEAD NURTURING: Lead nurturing is the practice of nurturing a lead into a customer. It can be in the form or sending emails, retargeting them on social media or actually calling.

OPEN RATE vs. TOTAL OPENS: The open rate report shows many users opened an email. Sometimes people will go back and open the same email two or three times, especially if there is a coupon or special offer associated with it. Total opens accounts for every time the email has been opened

SOFT BOUNCE: A soft bounce means that an email was delivered but bounced back because the user's inbox was full, their email server was down at the time of delivery, or maybe the email was too large.

SUBSCRIBER: A subscriber is a person who allows a company to them messages through email or other personal communication means. These subscribers are of high value to publishers and businesses alike.

Web Design & Development

APPLICATION PROGRAMMING INTERFACE (API): APIs allow applications to communicate with one another to access publicly available aggregate data. APIs are used to gather and share information on websites and user apps.

BELOW THE FOLD: In newspaper terms, "below the fold" refers to content on the bottom half of the page (below the physical fold in the paper). In web design terms, "below the fold" refers to the content that a user would generally have to scroll to view.

CSS: The acronym for Cascading Style Sheets, a style sheet language used for describing the presentation of a document written in a markup language like HTML, including colors, layout, and fonts.

CHECKOUT FLOW: The page-by-page experience a user has completing a purchase on an e-commerce website.

HTML: The acronym for Hypertext Markup Language, a standardized system for tagging text files to achieve font, color, graphic, and hyperlink effects on web pages.

JAVASCRIPT: An object-oriented scripting language commonly used to make HTML pages more dynamic and interactive.

LANDING PAGE: This is the page on a company's website that is optimized to act as the entry page to a site. When redirected from external links, this is where the visitors will arrive.

PIXEL: This is a snippet of code that is inserted onto A website for tracking purposes. It can gather analytics and data on customers and their movement across the website. Pixels are used for retargeting customers.

REALLY SIMPLE SYNDICATION (RSS): Really Simple Syndication is a technology that allows users to become subscribers of content and ultimately get automatic alerts if updates are made.

USER EXPERIENCE (UX): How a user feels when interfacing with a system such as a website, a web application, or desktop software. UX often determines how well a website converts or how much time users spend on a website or application.

Appendix G – Universal Buy/Sell Terms

AD-ID: Advertising Digital Identification is a new system developed by ANA and AAAA that provides the marketing and advertising industries with a new digital identification standard for their advertising assets. The assets can be any materials- radio spots, TV commercials, print ads, internet banners, out of home boards, and FSI's. The codes are 12 characters in length, replace the old ISCI codes, and link descriptive information about each ad to its code.

AFFIDAVIT: A signed or verified document from the affiliate that states that specific programs or commercials have been cleared as declared in their contract or with actual clearance times. Accurate and timely completion of the affidavit is a requirement of affiliation contracts between the station and the network or program syndicator. Completed affidavits can be returned to the networks or syndicator in printed form or by the Internet.

AFFILIATED STATION: A radio station that has a contract with a network or syndicator to clear national commercials in exchange for programs, services, or compensation.

AM DRIVE: Also known as morning drive, this is the morning broadcast time period for Radio, most often represented by Monday through Friday from 6 AM to 10 AM as defined and reported by Nielsen. An individual station's "daypart(s)" will not necessarily conform to this standard definition(s). Advertising contracts should include the specific hours that define the time period for each station's "daypart."

AVERAGE QUARTER-HOUR PERSONS (AQH): The average number of persons listening to a particular station for at least five consecutive minutes during a 15-minute period.

AVERAGE QUARTER-HOUR RATING: Average Quarter-Hour Persons estimate expressed as a percentage of the population being measured. This estimate is published for the MSA and DMA. It can also be computed for the TSA.

$$\frac{\text{AQH Persons}}{\text{Population}} \times 100 = \text{AQH Rating (\%)}$$

AUDIENCE COMPOSITION: The demographic or socioeconomic profile of a station's audience in terms of composition, usually including the percentages of the total audience that fall into each segment. These reports can express audience characteristics by age, gender, ethnicity, working persons, language preference, county, etc.

AUDIENCE DUPLICATION: The amount of one station's cume audience (see Cume Persons) that also listens to another station; also, the amount of the audience that is exposed to a commercial on more than one station. Duplication can be expressed either in terms of the actual number of exclusive listeners or as a percentage of the total cume.

AUDIENCE ESTIMATES: Approximations of the number of persons listening to or hearing a network radio commercial, network program, or syndicated program. The reliability of audience estimates are not precise mathematical values and are subject to statistical variations and other limitations. For radio networks reported in RADAR, audience estimates represent radio listening as reported by respondents in Nielsen diaries matched with commercial clearances as reported by affiliates in affidavits. For non-RADAR networks and syndicated programs, estimates are based solely on listening as reported in Nielsen diaries and do not take into consideration commercial clearances.

AUDIENCE TURNOVER: The ratio of a station's cumulative audience (see Cume Persons) compared to the average quarter-hour audience. Turnover equals cume persons divided by AQH persons. In theory, it is the number of times an audience is replaced by new listeners within a daypart.

AVAIL: The commercial position in a program or between programs on a given station or network available for purchase by an advertiser. It can also refer to the notification from a buyer to a seller that advertising dollars are up for discussion and negotiation.

AVERAGE AUDIENCE (AA): The average number of impressions per quarter-hour within a specified time period (e.g., a daypart) or to a network broadcast as reported in RADAR.

AVERAGE AUDIENCE RATING: The estimated average audience during a specified quarter-hour or a daypart expressed as a percentage of the population of the target audience. Usually, carried one place past the decimal point.

Formula: Average Audience / Population x 100 = Average Audience Rating (%)

AVERAGE DAILY CUME: The estimated average of cumulative audiences for each day of the week (e.g., Monday-Friday). This represents the average number of different persons reached per day.

BILLBOARD: In broadcast, sponsor mentions given to an advertiser in return for a significant commitment to a program, usually to one that purchases multiple commercials within a program (i.e., a "sponsor" of the program). In outdoor media, a billboard is an advertising structure.

BLACKOUT: A request by an advertiser for scheduled spots not to run on particular affiliates, usually in areas of the U.S. where the advertiser does not have product distribution. This is a valid reason for non-clearance on those affiliates.

BONUS: Additional commercials given to an advertiser, usually at no charge, in return for a paid schedule.

BROAD DAYPART: Dayparts with multiple component dayparts (e.g., 6AM-7PM, 6AM-12Midnight).

BROAD ROTATION: See "Run of Schedule."

BROADCAST CLOCK: The hourly schedule for networks or programs that breaks down the minutes of programming and the minutes of commercial inventory.

BROADCAST COVERAGE AREA: The geographic area within which a signal from an originating station can be received.

BEST TIME AVAILABLE (BTA): Commercials which are scheduled by the station to run at the best available time after all other sponsor commitments are met, usually at night or on weekends.

CANCELLATION POLICY: The terms under which an advertiser can cancel a schedule that has already been purchased and scheduled to be broadcast, including the required amount of time for advance notice and any applicable financial penalty or consequence to be applied for early termination of the schedule.

CLEARANCE: The broadcasting stations that carry or clear a network or syndicated program and/or its commercials. This list is usually accompanied by a coverage percentage indicating the percentage of the population in markets in which the program airs. Non-clearance refers to commercials that had been negotiated but could not be scheduled due to tight inventory. In such cases, the station will often try to offer a solution (i.e., opening up dayparts, making good within flight -- which moves the commercials from one week to another, etc.).

CLEARANCE LIST: Because not all affiliates broadcast programs at the same time, a "clearance list" provides the exact time that each affiliate has declared it will air that particular program. For example, some stations carry a program "live" when fed over satellite while other stations may tape the program and broadcast it later. A weekend syndicated program very often airs at different times - one affiliate may run a show on Saturday 1PM-3PM; another, on Saturday 3PM-5PM; and, another, on Sunday 10AM-12Noon.

CLUSTER: A cluster is a group of stations in the same market under common ownership or sales management. This usually refers to three or more AM and/or FM stations, or at least two stations on the same band, FM or AM. Groups of one AM and one FM are usually referred to as combos. A spot cluster refers to all commercials that run in the same commercial break.

CLOSE OF BUSINESS (COB): refers to any arrangement that is due or becomes valid or invalid at the end of the business day.

COMBO: Two Radio stations, usually operated by the same owner in the same market. A single station is frequently referred to as a standalone. Three or more commonly owned stations are commonly referred to as a cluster.

COMMERCIAL CLUTTER: commonly refers to an excessive amount of non-program content during the time period, including the number of commercials, public service announcements and/or promotional announcements that run in a commercial break, stop set or specified time period.

COMMERCIAL LOAD: The amount of commercial time or the number of units in a given period usually stated on an hourly basis.

COMMERCIAL POD: See "Pod."

CONFIRMATION: A written statement given to advertising agencies by a network, station, or publisher when accepting an order for a commercial or media schedule. This signifies that the order has been received and will clear.

CONFLICTS & CONFLICT CODES: A term used to define categories or codes for types of advertisers for spot placement and sales analysis purposes. (Examples: auto dealers, restaurants, banking institutions, etc.)

COUNTY SIZE DEFINITION: A system of categorizing U.S. counties by population into five categories (i.e., AA, A, B, C, and D). It was developed by Nielsen Media Research, except for the AA distinction, which is from Nielsen RADAR service.

COST PER POINT (CPP) The cost of reaching an Average Quarter-Hour Persons audience that's equivalent to one percent of the population in a given demographic group.

$$\frac{\text{Cost of Schedule}}{\text{GRPs}} = \text{Cost Per Rating Point}$$

COST PER THOUSAND (CPM) - The cost of delivering 1,000 gross impressions.

$$\frac{\text{Cost of Schedule}}{\text{GI}} \times 1,000 = \text{CPM}$$

$$\frac{\text{Spot Cost}}{\text{AQH Persons}} \times 1,000 = \text{CPM}$$

COVERAGE: The percentage of the total U.S. Persons 12+ population contained within all of the DMAs where an affiliate's signal can be received. Also called "DMA Coverage" or "Percent Coverage."

COVERED RATING POINTS: Delivered rating points.

CREDIT: A cash deduction for the loss of advertising time due to the station not airing or improperly scheduling a commercial announcement.

CUME PERSONS: The total number of different persons who listen to a Radio station during a daypart for at least five consecutive minutes.

CUME RATING: The CUME Persons audience expressed as a percentage of all persons estimated to be in the specified demographic group.

$$\frac{\text{CUME Persons}}{\text{Population}} \times 100 = \text{CUME Rating (\%)}$$

CUMULATIVE AUDIENCE: The total number of different persons who listen to a network or nationally syndicated program during a specified daypart for at least five consecutive minutes. Also, referred to as "cume."

DAYPART: The time segments into which a day is divided by Radio and television networks and stations to sell advertising time. In Radio, the primary dayparts are morning (or AM drive), midday, afternoon (or PM drive) and evening. An individual station's daypart(s) will not necessarily conform to standard definition(s). Advertising contracts should include the specific hours that define the time period for each station's daypart.

DAYPART DISTRIBUTION: Percentage of schedule across specific dayparts adding up to 100%.

DAYPART WEIGHT: The relative importance of one time period compared to another in a schedule that includes both, usually expressed as a percentage where the total of all dayparts equals 100%. Also refers to the relative distribution of commercials in one time period versus others in the schedule.

DAYTIME (MIDDAY): The late morning/early afternoon broadcast time period for Radio, most often represented by Monday through Friday from 10AM-3PM as defined and reported by Nielsen. Since an individual station's daypart(s) will not necessarily conform to standard definition(s), and since traffic departments use the term "daytime" to refer to a broader 6AM-7PM time period, all advertising contracts should include the specific hours that define the time period for each station's daypart.

DESIGNATED MARKET AREA (DMA): The area composed of sampling units (counties or geographically split counties) and is defined and updated annually by Nielsen Media Research, Inc., based on historical television viewing patterns. A county or split county is assigned exclusively to one DMA. Nielsen reports radio listening estimates for the Top 50 DMAs (ranked on TV households) in the Radio Market Reports of all standard radio markets whose Metros are located within the DMA and whose names are contained in the DMA name.

DIRECT RESPONSE ADVERTISING: refers to any advertising that has a built-in call to action to elicit a response within a defined period of time after exposure to the announcement. Phone calls, online orders, and visits to a location would be examples of direct response advertising.

DISCREPANCY: A situation where commercials do not run as ordered or do not run at all. A discrepancy may also refer to the difference between a purchased schedule and when the commercials actually were broadcast.

EFFECTIVE FREQUENCY: The concept that a certain amount of exposure (often three exposures) to an advertising message is necessary before it is effective.

EFFECTIVE REACH: The average number of people that will hear a commercial at least three times during a campaign.

ENDORSEMENT: Refers either to a situation where the station or personality "endorses" the advertiser's product or service, usually "live" on-air or the notification on the affidavit supplied by the station to the client that attests to the affidavit's accuracy as to how the spots were broadcast.

EQUAL DISTRIBUTION: Ensuring that commercials are scheduled to run in a broad time period or combination of time periods, getting distributed equally across each time period.

EQUAL ROTATION: While sometimes used interchangeably with "equal distribution," equal rotation is actually used by the agency and copy people, traffic directors, and continuity directors to indicate that all pieces of individual copy or pre-produced cuts are to be equally rotated. Equal distribution refers to ensuring that commercials are scheduled to run in a broad time period or combination of time periods and get evenly distributed across each time period (see Rotation).

EVENING: Also known as nights, this is the late evening broadcast time period for Radio, most often represented by Monday through Friday from 7PM-Midnight as defined and reported by Nielsen. An individual station's daypart(s) will not necessarily conform to this standard definition(s). Advertising contracts should include the specific hours that define the time period for each station's daypart.

EXCLUSIVE CUME: The number of different persons who listen to only one station during the daypart reported.

EXCLUSIVE REACH: An audience that can only be covered by a specific network or program.

EXPOSURE: A person's physical contact (visual and/or audio) with an advertising medium or message.

FIXED POSITION: A commercial scheduled to run at a precise time, or a commercial scheduled to run within specific programming content.

FIXED RATE: The rate charged for a fixed position commercial (see fixed position), usually a non-preemptible premium rate.

FIXED TIME: See fixed position.

FLIGHT: A scheduling tactic that alternates periods of advertising activity with periods of no activity.

FLIGHT DATES: The start and end dates of a schedule, including the weeks on and off-air.

FREQUENCY: The average number of times a person is exposed to a radio spot schedule.

$$\frac{GI}{Net\ Reach} = Frequency$$

FRONTLOAD: Refers to creating a schedule that tends to place more commercials on days of the week that have less demand, and fewer commercials on days with the heaviest demand. If a station is heavily sold on Thursday and Friday, but has fewer sales on Monday and Tuesday, a frontloaded order for Monday through Friday might place four (4) commercials per day on Monday and Tuesday, three (3) on Wednesday, and two (2) on Thursday and Friday.

FULL DAYPART NETWORKS: Networks whose broadcasts are found in all or virtually all component dayparts Monday-Sunday 6AM-12Midnight.

FULL INVENTORY NETWORKS: Networks with more than 100 minutes of commercial inventory.

GROSS IMPRESSIONS (GIs) The sum of the Average Quarter-Hour Persons (AQH) audience for all commercials in a given schedule. The total number of times a commercial will be heard over the course of a schedule.

AQH Persons   X   Number of ads in schedule   =   GIs

GROSS RATING POINTS (GRPs) sum of all rating points achieved for a particular spot schedule.

AQH Rating   X   Number of ads in schedule   =   GRPs

GUARANTEE: Usually refers to a station promise to honor a specific commercial rate for an agreed-upon period of time which is linked to certain criteria, such as schedules previously purchased, a minimum volume of business placed by the client or the rate charged by the station to other clients. May also refer to guarantees of spot placement or schedule clearance, frequently determined by the class of rate paid for the spot or schedule.

HOLD: A short period (usually several days) during which buyer and seller have agreed on what the schedule is to be booked while the agency gains final client approval.

HORIZONTAL ROTATION: Ensuring that commercial announcements purchased in a program or time period that includes multiple days (example: Monday-Friday) are placed across all days in order to increase advertising exposure to various prospects. Implies fair rotation across days of the week, so that spots not loaded into early week scheduling.

IDENTIFICATION (ID): A short on-air sponsor mention.

IN-PROGRAM CLEARANCE: When the network or program commercial is cleared by the affiliate within the program.

INDEX: A comparison between the market composition and the target composition. It is a measure of concentration or likelihood. It tells us whether a specific group is more or less likely to meet a given criterion.

ISCI CODE (INTERNATIONAL STANDARD CODING IDENTIFICATION): A code previously used to identify specific radio and television commercials. This coding system has been replaced by the Ad-ID system (see Ad-ID).

LEAD TIME: The minimum amount of time necessary for the station to be informed in advance of schedule placement, or changes that are requested by the client in a buy already scheduled to run. Can also refer to the amount of time between the announcement of a possible campaign and the actual dates it is expected to run.

LIMITED DAYPART NETWORKS: Networks whose broadcasts are found in only one component daypart (e.g., 6AM- 10 AM).

LIMITED INVENTORY NETWORKS: Networks with less than 100 minutes of commercial inventory.

LINE UP: A list of stations reflecting affiliates contractually obligated to clear the commercials associated with a network or national program. While the line-up is updated regularly, new affiliates can be added at any time, and some stations may disaffiliate. Every affiliate on the list is not necessarily obligated to clear 100% of all commercials scheduled. By contract, certain stations may clear a single commercial more than once or may not clear all of the commercials due to special circumstances.

LIVE FEED: When a network or syndicator feeds the program and/or commercials across the entire U.S. at one time. Thus, for example, it is heard at 9 AM in the Eastern Time Zone, 8 AM in the Central Time Zone, 7 AM in the Mountain Time Zone, and 6AM in the Pacific Time Zone.

LIVE READ: A specific commercial type where the announcement is read "live" on-air by the network or program personality. Also, called "Voice Read."

LOCAL MARKETING AGREEMENT (LMA): An arrangement where one station or owner takes sales responsibility for the commercial time on another station that it does not own.

LOCAL ADVERTISING: Advertising placed by companies within their home area, the limited geographic area where they do business. Also refers to advertising placed by agencies that is scheduled to run in the market where the agency is based.

LONG-FORM PROGRAMMING: See "Syndicated Programming."

LOWEST UNIT RATE: The lowest rate offered by the station to any regularly scheduled advertiser for a specific class and amount of advertising.

MAKEGOOD: Comparable commercial time or space is given to an advertiser at no additional cost when advertising is pre-empted, omitted, or airs in an unfit condition.

MEDIA PLAN: A plan developed with the sole purpose of determining media mix, dollar allocation, and weight levels that will result in a direct correlation to the media buy. It is the first stage of any media execution.

MERCHANDISING: While not a standard practice, on occasion, additional consideration is negotiated in advance as one of the terms of a schedule. There is no standard formula for determining merchandising amounts, and it is usually negotiated on a company-by-company, or station-by-station basis. Merchandising may be in the form of goods or services for the advertiser's discretionary use, or on-air promotional announcements, product giveaways or other promotional support.

METROPOLITAN STATISTICAL AREA (MSA): Includes a city (or cities) whose population is specified as that of the central city together with the county (or counties) in which it is located. The MSA also includes contiguous or additional counties when the economic and social relationships between the central and additional counties meet specific criteria. Nielsen MSA may correspond to the Metropolitan Statistical Areas defined by the U.S. Government's Office of Management and Budget, but they are subject to exceptions dictated by historical industry usage and other marketing considerations. MSA's are commonly referred to as Metros.

MIDDAY (SEE DAYTIME): The late morning/early afternoon broadcast time period for Radio, most often represented by Monday through Friday from 10AM-3PM as defined and reported by Nielsen. Since an individual station's daypart(s) will not necessarily conform to standard definition(s), and since traffic departments use the term "daytime" to refer to a broader 6AM-7PM time period, all advertising contracts should include the specific hours that define the time period for each station's daypart.

MONITORING: To check on the accuracy of the RADAR clearance information, Nielsen samples network affiliates on a continuous basis. Selected periods of times for the sample station are tape-recorded with broadcast programs and commercials transcribed. Affiliate affidavits are checked against the monitored record. Each network organization receives reports on their affiliates' accuracy that allows the networks the opportunity to address an affiliate that might not be completing its affidavit correctly.

MULTI-DAYPART NETWORKS: In RADAR, networks whose broadcasts can air across component dayparts (e.g., 6AM-7PM).

MULTIPLE CLEARANCES: Certain networks have affiliation agreements that allow certain stations to carry more than the full inventory offered by the network or the same inventory more than once.

NATIONAL ADVERTISING: Advertising placed by companies with national or regional distribution. The campaign runs in many markets outside their "home" area or region. Also refers to advertising placed by agencies that is scheduled to run in markets other than where the agency is based.

NET REACH: The number of different persons reached in a given schedule. Real net reach is available through Maximi$er® and Media Professional SM, for single station and multiple-station schedules.

NETWORK: A broadcast entity that provides programming and sells commercial time in programs aired nationally via affiliated and/or licensed local stations.

NO CHARGE: Commercials provided to the advertiser at no charge, usually in return for commercials purchased in other dayparts at higher rates.

NON-CLEARANCE: Commercials that had been negotiated but could not be scheduled due to a variety of reasons including tight inventory, offensive products, business conflicts, or the advertiser has requested that the commercial not be cleared in particular programs. In such cases, the station will often try to offer a solution (i.e., opening up dayparts, making commercials good within flight -- which moves the spots from one week to another, etc.).

OPTIMUM EFFECTIVE SCHEDULING (OES): OES represents a philosophy of buying and scheduling commercials that are designed to reach the majority of a Radio station's cume audience three or more times in a week by distributing commercials evenly Monday through Sunday from 6 AM to Midnight.

ONE-TIME-ONLY (OTO): Traditionally, OTO is an ad or spot that runs only one time.

OVERNIGHT: The overnight broadcast time period for Radio is most often represented by Monday through Sunday from Midnight-6AM as defined by Nielsen ratings. An individual station's daypart(s) will not necessarily conform to this standard definition(s). Advertising contracts should include the specific hours that define the time period for each station's daypart.

PACKAGE BILLING: A contract or order that charges a flat, fixed amount per invoice regardless of the number of commercials or other programs or features broadcast.

PIGGY-BACK: Two commercials scheduled to run back-to-back, purchased by the same advertiser. Examples include two individual commercials for two related products from the same client or one 60-second commercial where the first 30 seconds carries a message from a national advertiser and the second 30 seconds is provided to a local affiliate. Availability is determined by individual station policy.

PM DRIVE: Also known as afternoon drive, this is the late afternoon broadcast time period for Radio, most often represented by Monday through Friday from 3-7PM as defined and reported by Arbitron. An individual station's daypart(s) will not necessarily conform to this standard definition(s). Advertising contracts should include the specific hours that define the time period for each station's daypart.

POD: A pod is a TV term that refers to a grouping of commercials and non-program material in which (usually) more than one advertiser's commercials air. In Radio, a pod is more frequently referred to as a commercial cluster, commercial break, or stop set.

POLITICAL RATE: Stations are required to provide discounted rates for advertisements aired by candidates under certain circumstances during the prescribed "windows" before primary and general elections. (For additional information contact your company's communications counsel or the National Association of Broadcasters Legal Department.)

POST BUY OR POST ANALYSIS: A TV referring to the analysis of a media schedule after it runs -- generally based on physical evidence of its running (broadcast station affidavit of performance it generally incorporates a comparison of the TV station's projected ratings for specific programs ordered to what actually ran in terms of spot placement and actual audience delivery.

PRE-EMPTION AND PREEMPTIBLE: Pre-emption refers to the displacement of a scheduled commercial announcement by the station or network in favor of a higher-priced commercial or for some other reason. Pre-emptible refers to a class of commercial announcements that are usually purchased at a lower rate with the understanding that the placement may be changed by the station if other commercials are subsequently sold at higher prices.

PULSING: A technique that calls for either a continuous base of support augmented by intermittent bursts of heavy pressure or an on-off-on-off pattern (e.g., one week on, one week off).

QUINTILES: Quintiles is a five-scale measurement, in 20% increments, of an individual's media usage. The first quintile measures the heaviest use, and the fifth quintile measures the lightest use. For Radio, the number of quarter-hours listened to Radio determines quintile placement for a respondent.

RATE PROTECTION: Rate guaranteed for an agreed period of time.

RATING (AQH OR CUME) The audience expressed as a percentage of the total population.

$$\frac{\text{Listeners}}{\text{Population}} \times 100 = \text{Rating (\%)}$$

APPENDIX G – UNIVERSAL BUY/SELL TERMS

RELATIVE COST: The relationship between the price paid for advertising time or space and the size of the audience delivered. It is used to compare the prices of various media vehicles.

REP: Short for representative. Refers to either: A) A company (the "national rep") or the account executive who serves as the account executive on behalf of the station in markets outside of the station's home market or B) The station account executive who serves a local advertiser or agency.

RUN OF SCHEDULE (ROS): ROS commercials are scheduled to run across multiple dayparts within a broad daypart parameter.

ROTATION: While equal rotation means rotating various pieces of copy evenly to traffic departments, buyers and sellers use the term to refer to the distribution of commercials across a representative cross-section of days and hours within the purchased broad time period. Scheduling of advertising in the same program or time period on different days each week is referred to as horizontal distribution (or rotation), while distribution throughout the hours of a particular day is referred to as vertical distribution (or rotation).

SCATTER PLAN: Purchasing commercial time in broadcast media in many different programs.

SEASONALITY: The fluctuation around an audience estimate or an advertiser's target campaign that can result from changes in regional weather patterns during different times of the year, the lifestyle habits of audiences and/or the impact of sporting events, which can influence audience levels by season.

SEPARATION: A scheduling policy determined by individual stations that allows for a specified time or number of commercials between two competitive products of the same product type, either within the same commercial break or some other period of time.

SHARE: The percentage of those listening to Radio in the Metro who are listening to a particular radio station.

$$\frac{\text{AQH Persons to a Station}}{\text{AQH Persons Listening to Radio ("Total")}} \times 100 = \text{Share (\%)}$$

SIMULCAST: When two or more Radio stations broadcast the same programs and same commercials at ALL times, and use only one traffic system, they are said to be simulcast. If two or more stations broadcast only a portion of their day together, but are different at other times, they are considered to be "partially simulcast," but would require two-time order or traffic sections to schedule programs or announcements during the times when they have separate programming.

SPONSORSHIP: The purchase of more than one commercial within a program, usually at a premium rate. Can include bonus time via billboards, or exclusivity of advertising within the brand's product category, or all of the above. Can also refer to the purchase of all or part of a Radio program by one advertiser.

SUBSTITUTION: The policy concerning a station's right to provide the advertiser with alternate commercial placement from the positions purchased according to the original contract.

TOTAL AUDIENCE PLAN (TAP): TAP plans are usually a rotating schedule that places announcements in a pattern that utilizes all station dayparts for maximum station audience exposure. Actual plans vary from station to station.

TARGET DEMO: The age and characteristic make-up of the group deemed to be targeted to reach by the media campaign. The age group and make-up of the audience that you wish to receive your product or service message.

TILL FURTHER NOTICE (TF) OR (TFN): TFN are instructions by an advertiser to run a purchased schedule or advertisement(s) until notified to stop.

TIME SPENT LISTENING (TSL): An estimate of the amount of time the average listener spent with a station (or total radio) during a particular daypart. This estimate, expressed in hours and minutes, is reported for the Metro only.

$$\frac{\text{Hours in a Time Period X AQH Persons}}{\text{CUME Persons}} = \text{TSL in Hours}$$

TOTAL SURVEY AREA (TSA): A geographic area that encompasses the Metro Survey Area (MSA) and may include additional counties located outside the MSA which meet certain listening criteria to metro-licensed stations.

TURNOVER: The number of times the audience turns over within a given daypart.

$$\frac{\text{CUME Persons}}{\text{AQH Persons}} = \text{Turnover Factor}$$

UNIT: A unit is one commercial message regardless of length. Radio inventory is usually expressed in terms of units rather than minutes.

VERTICAL ROTATORS: Fair rotation across hours within a daypart.

WEEKEND: The Saturday and Sunday broadcast time period for Radio, most often represented by Sat/Sun 6AM-MID as defined by Nielsen ratings.

WEIGHT: The relative importance of one time period or demographic compared to another in a schedule usually expressed as a percentage where the total of all parts equals 100%. Also refers to the relative distribution of commercials in one time period compared to others in a schedule.

Index

INDEX

Printed in the USA
CPSIA information can be obtained
at www.ICGtesting.com
LVHW072121211123
764347LV00040B/1020